What music professionals are saying about
Hearing and Writing Music

"The best system for teaching ear training that I've ever seen. I've learned a great deal from this book and so will you."

RANDY NEWMAN, COMPOSER

"Invaluable! Written by one of the most talented men in our business today."

RICHARD CARPENTER, COMPOSER, RECORDING ARTIST

"A concise and wonderfully clear book on how to notate musical thoughts."

HERB ALPERT, RECORDING ARTIST, PRODUCER

"Learning to compose and orchestrate takes a great deal of time, discipline and effort. Anyone willing to apply those qualities to the exercises in Hearing and Writing Music will be greatly rewarded."

WILLIAM ROSS, COMPOSER

"Captures the essence of listening and music notation for professionals and students."

ROGER NICHOLS, SONGWRITER, COMPOSER, PRODUCER

"Hearing and Writing Music will help you instill confidence in yourself, no matter what your level."

RICK MAROTTA, COMPOSER, STUDIO MUSICIAN

"A standard reference for every serious musician or music educator. A wealth of practical information. A book that has needed to be written."

DR. THOM MASON, PROFESSOR OF JAZZ STUDIES, U.S.C.

"This book is forever on my desk."

DR. ANN RUCKERT, MUSIC EDUCATOR, PERFORMING MUSICIAN

"The 'new bible' for the musician who wants to know what it takes to make it in any facet of the music business. There is more precise and vital information in this book than you can imagine...should be required reading for all music students."

HAL ESPINOSA, PROFESSIONAL MUSICIANS, LOCAL 47 PRESIDENT

"Absolutely first rate. The book that really puts it all together. I wish that there had been something like this when I began studying music."

DENNIS DREATH, COMPOSER, RECORDING MUSICIANS ASSOCIATION PRESIDENT

"Heavy attention to ear training, the most overlooked aspect in the field of music education. Stresses the complete musician concept. One of the most valuable books any music student or educator could own."

BOBBY SHEW, TRUMPET ARTIST, EDUCATOR, CLINICIAN

"Extremely comprehensive, meticulously organized method.... Transcends styles.... Powerful for either a self study or classroom environment. A masterful and rich work."

ROGER STEINMAN, COMPOSER, MUSIC EDUCATOR, PERFORMING MUSICIAN

HEARING AND WRITING MUSIC

PROFESSIONAL TRAINING FOR TODAY'S MUSICIAN

RON GOROW

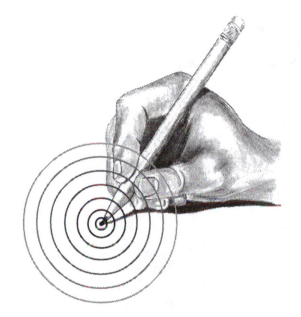

Hearing and Writing Music
Professional Training for Today's Musician

© 2000 Ron Gorow
www.rongorow.com

Published by:
September Publishing
Studio City, California

Distributed by:
SCB Distributors
15608 S. New Century Drive
Gardena, CA 90248-2129

Publisher's Cataloging in Publication
(Provided by Quality Books, Inc.)
Gorow, Ron
    Hearing and writing music : professional training for today's musician / Ron Gorow. — 1st ed.
        p. cm.
        Includes index
        LCCN: 99-60714
        ISBN: 0-9629496-3-9

        1. Ear training   2. Musical notation
I. Title.

MT35.G67 1999   781.4'24
                         QB199-1111

To my loving wife, Judy Kerr,
who is a constant source of inspiration
and whose book *Acting Is Everything*
taught me to write from the heart.

CREDITS

EDITOR: Morgan Ames

COVER: Thomas Cobb

ARTISTS:
Bob White (pages 7, 58, 83,143, 170, 286, 289)
David Miller (pages 34, 39)

MUSIC EXAMPLES:
Meg Maryatt (pages 256, 343, 349)
Rick Giovinazzo (pages 276-279)
Lloyd Luhman (page 343)
Scott Smalley (page 348)
Carl Rydlund (page 350)
Marlene Hajdu (page 352A)
Morgan Ames (page 352B)
All other music examples: Ron Gorow
        (Graphire *Music Press* software)

Thanks to my peer readers for their expertise and suggestions:
Michael Andreas, David Angel, Christina Bartmus, Russell Bartmus, Leland Bond,
Lars Clutterham, Susan Friedman, Harold Garrett, Rick Giovinazzo, Bob Harmon,
Jim Hoffman, Jim Honeyman, Erik Lundborg, William Motzing, Conrad Pope,
Carl Rydlund, Jeffrey Schindler, K.O. Skinsnes, Steven Smith, Roger Steinman,
Kerry Wikstrom.

Thanks to the students of the Grove School and Cal Poly Pomona.

Thanks to Robin Gee for inspiration and guidance.

CONTENTS

4. THE MATERIAL OF MUSIC

5. HEARING INTERVALS

6. HEARING PHRASES

7. TRANSCRIBING MUSIC

8. TRANSCRIPTION TECHNIQUE

9. PERCEPTION TO NOTATION

10. COMMUNICATING WITH MUSIC NOTATION

11. PREPARATION FOR PERFORMANCE AND PUBLISHING

12. REFERENCE AND RESOURCES

INDEX

INTRODUCTION

This book is designed to help you develop and refine your perception and communication of music—to know what you are hearing and to express your thoughts through music notation.

The goal is to help you notate without hesitation from an audio source or your own memory or imagination—without the aid of a keyboard or other instrument. The tools you develop will be woven into a seamless technique, a solid foundation for composition, orchestration, performance— any activity you encounter in your musical life.

You will find guidance, inspiration and information to help you clarify the abstract aspects of music, make the intangible tangible, and perhaps spark your interest to investigate further some of the vast areas of music.

The studies in this book require a fundamental knowledge of music: the ability to read notes on a staff and a familiarity with clefs, keys, and meters. This book does not attempt to duplicate the many existing sources of basic music skills. Rather, it will enhance and expand the knowledge and techniques that you have developed thus far.

> I had only my ear to help me; I heard and I wrote what I heard.
> I am the vessel through which Le Sacre passed.
>
> *Igor Stravinsky*

Many musicians, artists, actors have expressed the same thought with different words: "I am merely a channel/conduit/vessel/instrument; my art flows through me."

This work is concerned with that moment when music flows through you.

1

THE COMPLETE MUSICIAN

1

THE COMPLETE MUSICIAN

Your success as a musician—whether you are a performer, composer, arranger, orchestrator, conductor, recording engineer—depends on your ability to hear music, to know what you are hearing, to remember what you have heard, and then to communicate through music notation or performance.

The world's music, however diverse, shares common elements. The unique attributes of each culture/genre/style are merely variations of intervals, rhythms, temperament and timbre. We will concentrate on those elements with the goal of preparing you to work with any type of music and to master every step of the process of communication among musicians.

Today's working musician must be familiar with many styles, comfortable with both acoustic and electronic instruments, and prepared for any situation. Whether you are working one particular job in the music recording or publishing industries or entirely self-producing your music, the personal vision and set of tools presented here will help you prepare for the unknown and carry you through a lifetime of work and play in the sound environment.

You can reach a level of perception that will enable you to recognize and notate any musical sound, which in turn will allow you to develop unlimited compositional or improvisational abilities.

 # THE GOAL

This work is designed to help you perfect your musical skills, to advance your career, to communicate your musical thoughts so they are interpreted as you intend. Your job, like any artist or craftsman, is to know your materials intimately and to be aware of all the possibilities inherent in them.

The goal of this training is to provide you with the essential tools for hearing and writing music. With those tools, you will have the means to:

▶ Perceive and notate any style of music.

▶ Remove obstacles to composition or improvisation.

▶ Communicate accurately through music notation.

▶ Develop a fast sketch technique.

▶ Be able to jot down an idea anywhere, without using an instrument.

▶ Document and preserve your work.

▶ Consolidate your skills into an integrated, subconscious process.

PERCEPTION

A MENTAL IMPRESSION RECEIVED THROUGH THE SENSES;

COMPREHENSION OF THAT RECEIVED;

UNDERSTANDING;

AWARENESS;

INSIGHT.

 **THE METHOD**

We'll focus on the fundamental skills of creating music: hearing and writing. Developing these skills is essential to understanding each link in the music making process: composer to orchestrator to copyist to proofreader to conductor to performer to listener. This work will consolidate your hearing and writing techniques into a seamless, intuitive flow, as natural as breathing.

▶ *You inhale music*, whether listening externally (live performance, recorded media), internally (memory, imagination) or reading notation.

▶ *You process music*, whether memorizing, analyzing or just enjoying.

▶ *You exhale music*, whether performing (improvising, reading or playing from memory) or notating (composing, orchestrating, transcribing, copying).

Ultimately, your technique for hearing and writing music will reach a state of subconscious flow, as did your ability to read and write words. First, you learned each letter, then each word; now you read and write groups of words. When you have mastered each element, you'll perceive music as flowing seamlessly in time.

In this training, we will move from the simple to the complex, from the center outward, from melodic to harmonic to polyphonic, from diatonic to chromatic to microtonal, from the tradition of the world's music to the future.

In an ideal world, every composer has orchestrated for other composers; every orchestrator has been a music copyist; every copyist knows orchestration and has performed music and everyone has played every instrument! Since we cannot be all and do all, the best we can do is gather experience along the way—observing how others work, remembering the particular sound of a particular instrument, studying scores.

As you work with music, your decisions are guided by your instincts and experience, rather than by concrete rules. Always keep in mind the function of the music and your particular role. When composing, *be the listener;* when orchestrating, *be the composer;* when copying or conducting, *be the performer.*

The perception/notation process ties together all the disciplines in the music making process, from the inner world of feeling and thought to the outer world of performance and production.

In the following pages, you will find a progression of isolated exercises which are then combined to form a seamless technique. You are in control of the pace and extent of your training. Learning music is a very personal experience. Once you have it, you own it for life.

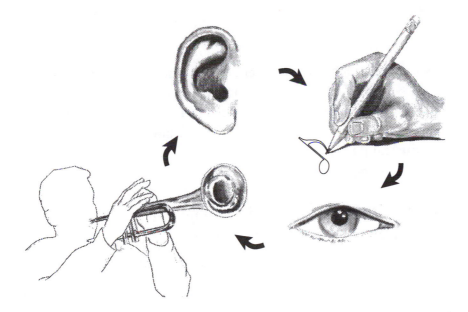

PARTS OF THE PROCESS

Your improved hearing and writing skills will contribute greatly toward mastering the following disciplines.

▶ COMPOSING   The ultimate art in the medium of sound. As a composer, you must be able to jot down ideas without hesitation and notate accurately what you hear; develop an ear for melodic lines and vertical sonorities; hear multiple voices and complex chords; extend ideas over time; control the elements of performance; organize and document your work.

Whether you use staff or sequencer, the art of composing music requires the careful selection of each element. Whether your music is innovative or reflects a familiar style, you must learn to trust your ear, proceeding without hesitation, confident that you are making the right choices.

▶ PERFORMING   Fine-tune your perception of intervals and rhythms, and your interpretation of music notation. Develop improvisation as well as interpretive skills. "Read with your ears."

▶ IMPROVISING   Composing in the moment of performance, the improviser needs "big ears"—the ability to respond immediately to the musical environment, to manipulate and transpose ideas and sequences. This work will help open your ears to instant comprehension and open your mind to a broader musical palette.

▶ TRANSCRIBING   Develop the aural/visual connection; coordinate the process of hearing/writing/reading/performing.

The transcription technique presented here is applicable to all styles of music. It refines the everyday, nuts and bolts activity of composing, orchestrating and arranging. Special applications include recreating scores from recordings or documenting an improvised solo performance. Eventually, you will develop a fast sketch technique and be able to jot down ideas anywhere. Transcribing from an audio source is a proven method for developing your hearing and writing skills.

▶ ARRANGING   Quickly notate themes and ideas. Be comfortable with transposition and key relationships. Apply editing techniques to produce concise scores.

▶ ORCHESTRATING   "Write what you hear," using appropriate notation for each instrument and the best notational choices for the style of music. Be able to transpose easily from one instrument to another.

▶ MUSIC PREPARATION   Understand conventions of transposing instruments and correct chord symbols. Integrate traditional notation with modern innovations. Configure your MIDI transcription/computer notation software to produce correct notation.

▶ EDITING AND PROOFREADING   Make quick decisions based on your ability to "hear what you see." Develop a *professional eye*—instantly detect errors in rhythm and transposition.

▶ MUSIC LIBRARIAN; MUSIC EDITOR (FILM); MUSIC CONTRACTOR; SCORE CONSULTANT; AUDIO ENGINEER   Those working in related jobs can benefit from *Hearing and Writing Music*. A Hollywood trade magazine lists 17 qualities of a good engineer. At the top of the list: "#1 GREAT EARS."

MUSIC TERMINOLOGY

While music is a pure medium, we depend on words while working with music, whether producing, performing or teaching. Verbal communication among musicians can be tenuous, as the words used to describe music are sometimes inexact and haphazard.

▶ A music term may have different definitions or shades of meaning according to style, period, locale and translation from other languages.

▶ Score terminology and performance indications may be in Italian, in the composer's native language, or in a mixture of several languages.

▶ Composers, theorists or authors have been known to invent a word when no other seems adequate.

We have tried to use words that will help you visualize and clarify the process as you develop your technique. A musician's training includes sorting out, accepting and rejecting concepts as well as the words that define them. Your goal in this work is to ultimately eliminate words from the process of perception. When you are actively hearing and writing music, the words will no longer be needed—music will flow through you to become symbols and sounds.

PERSONAL TRAINING

Music is a continuing process of discovery and development. Inspiration happens in an instant; the craft is developed over one's lifetime.

> Mozart, when asked how one would learn to compose:
> "Here, here and here (pointing to his ear, his head and his heart)
> is your school."

Every musician knows that music classes in theory, performance, history, etc., cannot provide all that is necessary to become a complete musician. Music, like all art, is ultimately self-taught. The fundamental connection you form with music is intimate and requires motivation, dedication, discipline, and action. The energy required can only be generated by your passion, curiosity and love for music.

This training will allow you to improve your ability to hear music and express yourself, starting at your present skill level. The text and exercises are designed to provide you with a well-rounded technique and to suggest paths that you may want to pursue toward areas of special interests.

Proceed at your own pace, propelled by your sense of discovery, pleasure and accomplishment. Through the understanding and mastery of the fundamentals of music making, you will be prepared for the unknown, the uncharted, the unexpected.

See pages 366 and 367 for study plans.

> Music has no boundaries. It is yours to discover,
> to enjoy, to draw from and to pass on to others.

2

DEVELOPING YOUR EAR

2

$$\text{DEVELOPING YOUR EAR}$$

PERCEPTION

> I listened more than I studied.
> Joseph Haydn

Music is the only art that is intangible. As musicians, we work with a very abstract medium; if you can't see or touch sound, how can you manipulate it to create music? By developing two skills:

▶ Active listening: knowing what you are hearing at any given moment.

▶ The ability to re-create what you are hearing or thinking—spontaneously, with an instrument, your voice, or with the symbols of music notation.

HEARING AND WRITING; input and output; perception and expression—the process is the essence of composing, arranging, orchestrating, transcribing and improvising music.

An important concept in this training is to make a distinct separation between the hearing process and the writing process. To help us clarify the distinction, we'll use the word *tone* only when we're referring to a *sound* and the word *note* only when we're referring to a *symbol*.

TONE ⟷ SOUND
NOTE ⟷ SYMBOL

Think of a *tone* as perceived through the sense of hearing and a *note* as perceived through the sense of sight. A *tone* lives in the air and defines a sense of musical space; a *note* lives on the music staff and serves to communicate musical thought. Musicians too often casually interchange the two terms.

We all have the same equipment for perception of sound—ears and brain— so music, traveling through the air, reaches everyone in the same manner. At the point of perception, sound assumes meaning or triggers emotions— becomes a personal experience. We evaluate what we hear through our own set of filters. Your filters include all the music you've ever heard, your cultural background, your understanding of music theory, your comprehension of acoustics, your knowledge of instruments and your emotional state and receptive awareness. When working with music, we try to listen with open, objective ears, yet call on our experience as we make musical decisions.

All musical activities are related and interconnected. When composing, your job is to get your thoughts into notation. If you are orchestrating or arranging someone else's music, you must be able to assess the musical situation. Sooner or later you will be required to make a transcription from an audio source. Your objective is to be able to perceive and notate any music, no matter how complex.

Separating the fundamental activities of hearing and writing music will allow you to give full concentration to each. When you are fluent and comfortable, they will be combined to produce a technique that is accurate, fast and efficient.

> Listening is the primary musical activity. The musician
> listens to his own idea before he plays, before he writes.
> Susanne K. Langer: *The Musical Matrix*

ACTIVE LISTENING

> There is an art of listening. To be able really to listen, one should abandon or put aside all prejudices, pre-formulations and daily activities. When you are in a receptive state of mind, things can be easily understood; you are listening when your real attention is given to something. To discover, there must be a state of mind in which there is a direct perception.
> J. Krishnamurti: *The First & Last Freedom*

Music is heard on many levels, through many parts of your body. You may feel emotions from music in your throat, heart or stomach; you may respond with hands or feet. You may listen very attentively, totally engrossed; you may listen casually to only the surface sound; you may listen passively, consigning music to the role of environmental mood enhancement; or you may tune out completely, choosing to listen to your thoughts instead.

The best training for all phases of music making is *active listening*. As musicians, we are obligated to listen attentively, constantly monitoring and evaluating what we are hearing. When performing, whether reading or improvising, you must adjust constantly to the music as it unfolds. If you are composing, orchestrating, arranging, or copying music, you need to listen internally to be accurate.

Most sounds that enter your ears are unconscious. You can develop a conscious awareness of external sounds and use those sounds to practice identifying intervals, rhythms and timbre. There is always something new to discover, for there are sounds happening all around you. Even non-musical sounds contain the essence of music, for music is just organized sound.

> All sounds are music; any sound can be a part of a piece of music. Enjoy sounds of your environment; you don't have to understand, simply experience.
> John Cage

EXERCISE 1

Improve your awareness and your ability to concentrate on a particular sound.

1   Find a spot where you can quietly sit or lie down. Relax. Listen to your breathing for a few minutes. Let any inner conversations play out; let that inner commentator settle down.

2   Now you've created space to allow all exterior sounds to enter your awareness. Listen to the sounds around you—near, far, high, low, intermittent, sustained. Notice that each sound occupies a certain portion of the total sound spectrum.

3   Concentrate on one sound for as long as you can.

4   Switch to another sound and focus for as long as you can.

5   Switch back to the first sound.

EXERCISE 2

1   Listen to a sound from nature and relate it to music. Birds are especially musical, usually maintaining the pitch as they repeat a phrase.

2   What register does the sound occupy?

3   What instruments are suggested?

4   How would you orchestrate it?

5   Visualize the notation you would use to describe the sound.

EXERCISE 3

1   Notice the acoustical properties of objects of various materials—woods, glass, plastics, metals—and how the shape, size and density cause differences in sound as the objects resonate. Who among us hasn't banged on everything in the kitchen?

2   Build an instrument with found objects. Choose the material for its acoustic properties. It may be as simple as suspending an object and finding the optimum striker to produce a resonant sound.

3   How can you alter the object to change the pitch, the timbre, the duration?

The active listening process may be practiced continually throughout the day with anything that you happen to hear.

Any two tones—successive or simultaneous—form an interval. Try to name the interval as soon as you hear it; your recognition will soon be spontaneous. Listen for intervals in car horns, doorbells, etc. This is active listening, productive learning. You may have a breakthrough in an idle moment!

You can constantly improve your technique and refine your ear. As a musician, you are in training all the time, every waking moment, all your life. Music is not an eight-hour job; nor is music training a series of class courses. It is a constant, lifetime pursuit, fueled by your creative spirit, love of sound and desire to make music.

Deep within us is the never-silent sound of our own vibrations...
which is the musical core of us all.
       Yehudi Menuhin and Curtis Davis: *The Music of Man*

Sound and light are energy, vibrating at various frequencies. Colors are a product of different frequencies of light waves, visible in a rainbow or prism.

Every object, including the earth and every cell in your body, vibrates at its natural frequency. An object's size, shape and composition determine its frequency.

RESONANCE   When a sound wave of a certain frequency encounters an object of the same frequency, the object resounds—responds by vibrating to the sound frequency. This sympathetic vibration is *resonance*. Musical instruments are built on this principle, amplifying each tone by physically resonating, even causing nearby instruments to resonate. The performance of music is dependent on the resonance of the room—from shower to concert hall.

Resonance is not only the basis of harmony, it provides us with one of the most important tools for hearing music.

TOOL KIT #1

The first set of tools will help you align the sounds of the outer world with your inner voice. These tools of perception are simple but powerful, the foundation of a technique that will allow you to perceive music independent of an instrument. Your tools will live in your subconscious, available whenever you need them.

MATCHING   When you sing or play an instrument in unison with another source, you are *creating resonance* or *matching* the pitch. The phenomenon of resonance assures us that we are indeed in-tune. Anyone who has played in an orchestra or sung in a choir has experienced the thrilling sensation of resonance. It is not only auditory; it is felt through the whole body. That same sensation may be put to use as a tool for hearing music.

When actively listening, you may verify the pitch of a tone by singing or humming in unison (or octave) with it, creating the sensation of resonance. Tones can be *matched* with your voice even while you are listening in head-phones. The sensation is much subtler than the orchestral or choir setting, but valid nevertheless. *Matching* is a tool that can be employed instantly to verify a pitch or the presence of a chord tone.

EXERCISE 4

Create resonance by matching.

1   Find a steady, single tone. The source may be the hum or buzz of an appliance or machine, or use a mallet, keyboard or string instrument.

2   Hum or sing "ah" in unison with the tone. When your voice is in tune with the source tone, you will feel resonance, a strong physical verification.

3   Shift your voice an octave up or down and match the tone, creating resonance.

4   Form the interval of a fifth with the tone and experience resonance to a lesser degree.

YOUR VOICE is by far the best instrument for training your ear, as your ear actually guides your voice without the influence of an external instrument. Unlike any other instrument, your ear has 100% control of your voice—there are no fingers, keys, frets, valves or other physical devices to influence the pitch. Your voice does not have to be trained; even if you "can't sing," your voice will serve you well as your personal, portable instrument—always available when you need it.

EXERCISE 5

Coordinate your voice with your ear.

Sing "ah" or hum, holding a steady tone (no vibrato) as long as possible. This is good practice, not only to train your voice to hold a tone without straying from the pitch, but also to train your ear to maintain a pitch.

✗ **INTERNALIZING** is listening to music with your inner voice. Think of a melody—say, "Take me out to the ball game." Listen. . . . That's it! You are listening to your inner voice. You may hear it being sung or played on a particular instrument, or no instrument.

Your internal voice is always available as a recorder/player for storing and retrieving melodic lines from memory. When you remember music, you are recreating a melodic line in your mind, silently singing or mentally playing an instrument. Internalizing is your primary tool as you transcribe, analyze or notate music—replaying through your silent inner voice.

When internalizing, the pitch or key is arbitrary; the perception of the line is not dependent on specific pitches. This concept—independence of pitch— is difficult for some musicians to comprehend. Make an effort to hear the line in the abstract, in the air, divorced from specific pitch or key. Later, when we go about setting music in notation, we will be able to easily notate it in any key.

EXERCISE 6

Internalize a line.

Internally play back a melodic line that you have just heard or remembered or imagined. Slowly focus on each interval and rhythm until you are sure of your perception. As you mentally play back the line, you have the opportunity to analyze the intervals and rhythms, slowing it down and repeating any part of the line as many times as necessary until you *have it*. It may be helpful to hum the line until you are able to internalize it silently.

Be aware of your inner voice—it is always there. Tune in to it at any time. Never read music mechanically or passively—always internalize. "Hear what you see."

TONAL MEMORY is the recollection of a previous tone of the same pitch that provides an aural verification. As you improve your hearing, your tonal memory will increase. You can consciously extend it by listening to a source, (striking anything nearby that has a pitch) waiting a short period then singing the tone before striking the source again to verify your tonal memory. Gradually increase the waiting time. As you proceed through phrases, tonal memory provides reassurances along the way, helps you stay on track.

EXERCISE 7

1 Create a **source-tone** by striking an object, anything that will provide a discernible pitch for a second or two.

2 **MATCH** the pitch with your voice, singing or humming in unison or an octave up or down.

3 **INTERNALIZE** Stop the source-tone and listen to the memory of the tone.

4 **TONAL MEMORY** Sing or hum the tone.

5 Strike the source-tone again to **verify** that you've maintained the pitch.

PHYSICAL CONNECTION If you are an instrumentalist, it is natural to mentally "play" your instrument while listening, fingering each interval (in an arbitrary key). Many musicians do this unconsciously; their physical connection to music maintained through the memory of playing a particular instrument.

REVIEW

1 Describe the difference between a tone and a note.

2 Describe the phenomenon of resonance.

3 Describe each tool and how you may use it to hear music.

    Matching

    Your voice

    Internalizing

    Tonal Memory

    Physical Connection

You've learned to focus your ear, to listen to your inner voice, to use your outer voice. You are on the path to hearing and writing music anywhere, anytime, without dependence on an instrument. Next, we'll look at sound and how it provides the substance of music.

3

FROM SOUND TO MUSIC

3

A music student sat in the audience, eager to hear his first composition. The piece opened with a single tone, a cello sustaining the low C string. The young composer was heard to utter, "Wow, did I write that?"

Music is truly magical and we all share some of that young composer's innocent wonder. However, with musical maturity comes the ability to predict with some degree the result of our labor. This book is directed toward that goal, the inspired quest for the mastery of your craft, whether it be composing or a related activity.

A musician's medium is sound and while we may take for granted the complex waves of energy that result and the physical and psychological reaction music has on us, a basic understanding of sound and the physical nature of music can only benefit our experience as musicians.

Here, we present an overview of the material of music and how the nature of sound influenced the evolution of music. Music is so deep, so broad, that to investigate every aspect would take several lifetimes. Perhaps your curiosity will be sparked and you'll be inspired to further pursue a particular aspect of music. An increased awareness of how sound becomes music will help you develop a visual image of music, a mental template that will enable you to perceive music without relying on the aid of an instrument.

MUSIC SPACE AND TIME

The investigation of the universe is advanced by studying the smallest things known as well as the largest. We'll discover that the essence of tonality and harmony, as well as the historical evolution of music, are contained in the basic building block of music—the **tone**.

While any sound is usable in the making of music, we'll limit our definition of tone as a sound with constant, discernible pitch. The simplest tone, a sine wave, is so pure it is uninteresting as a musical sound. As we'll discover, the tones we love to hear are complex, dynamic, energized, rich with content.

All objects and sounds that we are able to perceive with eyes and ears come to us in the form of waves of energy. Our eyes are capable of receiving waves of a certain frequency range which our brain interprets as sight. Our ears can receive another range of energy waves which we interpret as sound. A sound wave pulsates through the medium of air, disturbing the air but not carrying the air with it. Visualize a wave moving through water or a field of grain.

The difference between something we see and something we hear is merely a difference in frequency. Although our perception is limited to certain ranges of frequency by our senses, other forms of energy can be received, measured and utilized with the help of various scientific instruments.

The total range of energy that we humans are aware of is known as the electromagnetic spectrum, a continuous scale of frequency. The boundaries of each field are indistinct in the same manner that the ranges of musical instruments overlap. The following two pages will illustrate.

THE BIG PICTURE

The electromagnetic spectrum is a continuous range of energy waves which describe the interaction of all known things in our world. The spectrum spans about 70 octaves. The pulsations of atomic nuclei and galaxies lie at each end of the spectrum; what lies beyond is unknown at this time.

The scale of visual color and the scale of pitch are both part of the spectrum. The correlation between tones and colors, however, is proportional rather than direct, as visual frequencies are about a trillion times faster than audio frequencies. The range of music would have to extend more than 40 octaves to reach the frequencies of light.

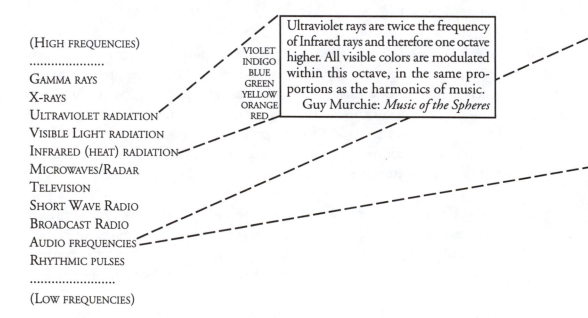

(HIGH FREQUENCIES)

....

GAMMA RAYS

X-RAYS

ULTRAVIOLET RADIATION

VISIBLE LIGHT RADIATION

INFRARED (HEAT) RADIATION

MICROWAVES/RADAR

TELEVISION

SHORT WAVE RADIO

BROADCAST RADIO

AUDIO FREQUENCIES

RHYTHMIC PULSES

....

(LOW FREQUENCIES)

VIOLET
INDIGO
BLUE
GREEN
YELLOW
ORANGE
RED

Ultraviolet rays are twice the frequency of Infrared rays and therefore one octave higher. All visible colors are modulated within this octave, in the same proportions as the harmonics of music.
Guy Murchie: *Music of the Spheres*

It wasn't until the beginning of the 20th century that instruments were developed to allow humankind to perceive beyond the limits of eye and ear, filling in the gaps to provide a continuous rendering of the electromagnetic spectrum. However, there has been speculation as to the continuity of all matter from the time of the Greek philosophers. Of course, the picture may never be complete, as the bounds of space/time are apparently limitless.

THE SOURCE OF TONES

Human perception of pitch spans from approximately 20 Hz (Hertz, or cycles per second) to 38,000 Hz, which translates into approximately 11 octaves. The palette of musically effective pitches is somewhat less, roughly 7 octaves. The human audible range varies with each person and decreases with age.

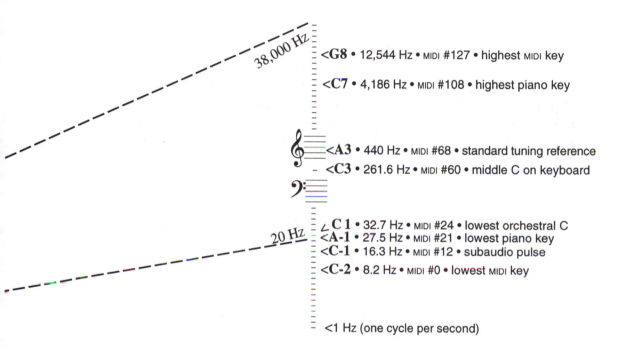

38,000 Hz

      <G8 • 12,544 Hz • MIDI #127 • highest MIDI key

      <C7 • 4,186 Hz • MIDI #108 • highest piano key

      <A3 • 440 Hz • MIDI #68 • standard tuning reference

      <C3 • 261.6 Hz • MIDI #60 • middle C on keyboard

      C 1 • 32.7 Hz • MIDI #24 • lowest orchestral C

20 Hz <A-1 • 27.5 Hz • MIDI #21 • lowest piano key

      <C-1 • 16.3 Hz • MIDI #12 • subaudio pulse

      <C-2 • 8.2 Hz • MIDI #0 • lowest MIDI key

      <1 Hz (one cycle per second)

Sound is at the low end of the frequency spectrum; it is where music space and music time intersect. When frequencies decrease, our perception of them changes from pitch to rhythm. Contrabass tones vibrate at frequencies so slow that pulses may be detected. The lowest orchestral C (approximately 32 Hz—just above the lowest A on a piano) is heard as a steady tone with fast but perceivable pulses. This is at the bottom range of orchestral instruments, obtainable only with the contrabassoon, extended Bb contrabass clarinet, tuba and extended string bass. The C an octave lower (approximately 16 Hz) lies at the threshold of pitch and rhythm—the pitch is difficult to discern and the pulses are slow enough to be heard distinctly.

LIFE TIME / MUSIC TIME

Music lives where space and time intersect. Below the range of human audibility, the earth vibrates at approximately 8 Hz (the Schumann resonance). Perhaps not coincidentally, the human body in a relaxed state resonates at the same frequency, as do alpha brain waves, characteristic of states of higher consciousness, inspiration and creativity.

Our most intimate measurement of rhythm, the human heart, may beat less than 1 Hz at rest to more than 3 Hz during intense exercise. Descending the scale, frequencies become cyclic events: minutes, hours, days, years, centuries—all periodic rhythms, the stuff sound is made of. The cyclical events of nature—biological, geological, stellar—may be measured against a time continuum. Rhythms of music occur in similar cycles and multilevel patterns.

Each species of life has its own sense of time, perhaps measured against its heartbeat rate or life span. We possess the natural rhythms of earth/human time as well as our unique consciousness of the passing of time and our own personal awareness of how time fluctuates.

> Life on earth is only as long as a dream.
> *Ancient Egyptian Inscription*

The musician has a unique view of time: subjective and objective, or music time and clock time. As musicians, we must be aware of both. When performing, we get in sync with the flow of the music. In the objective world of clock time, we anticipate and prepare so that we are never late to an event. A composer works simultaneously with subjective time—the beat of the music—and objective time—the pace, or tempo, of the beat, calculating the effect of the music on the listener. The performing musician hears internally, subjectively, anticipating, while simultaneously hearing externally, objectively, reacting.

ATTRIBUTES OF A TONE

While a note on a staff is two-dimensional, a tone is an event living in the four dimensions of space and time. A vibrating source (the impact of a struck object, the air column of a blown flute or the pulsation of a plucked string) causes sound waves to expand from the source in all directions.

A sound wave in its simplest form has three attributes: its period, amplitude and shape. The period, or frequency of undulations, corresponds to our perception of the tone's "highness" or "lowness"—its *pitch*. The amplitude, or pressure, corresponds to loudness in music. The shape of the wave is perceived as tone color, or timbre.

ENERGY WAVE	MUSIC	VISUAL ART
FREQUENCY	PITCH	HEIGHT, GRAVITY
AMPLITUDE	LOUDNESS	DEPTH, PERSPECTIVE
WAVESHAPE	TIMBRE	COLOR, TEXTURE

A rich musical tone is made up of a combination of waves—crossing, overlapping as ripples in water—blended into a complex shape. The characteristic tone color, or timbre, is determined by the tone's harmonic content—the relative intensity of each harmonic. The waveshapes below represent the timbre of various instruments. Timbre varies greatly with changes of frequency or amplitude.

SINE WAVE   FLUTE   CLARINET   VIOLIN

Timbre enables us to distinguish the sound of one instrument from another.

TONES OF NATURE

When a tone is sounded, it generates an array of supplemental tones (harmonics, or overtones.) We refer to this phenomenon as the harmonic series. Each harmonic is a multiple of the generating tone's frequency (the second harmonic is twice, the third harmonic is three times the frequency, etc.) When a frequency doubles, an octave results. A musical tone is rich with harmonics, although we are not usually aware of them. A tone with no harmonics (a sine wave) is flat and lifeless.

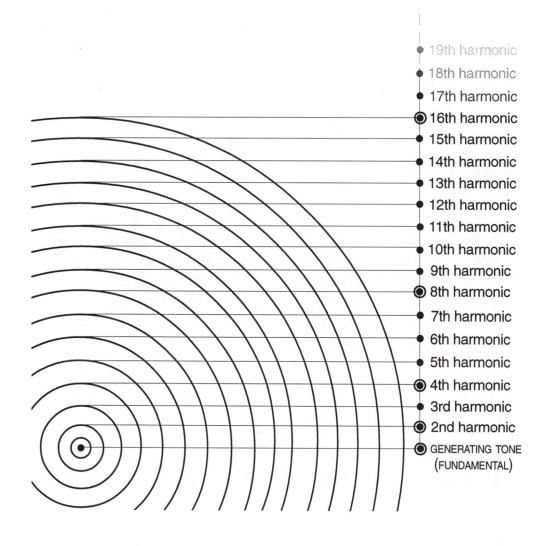

19th harmonic
18th harmonic
17th harmonic
16th harmonic
15th harmonic
14th harmonic
13th harmonic
12th harmonic
11th harmonic
10th harmonic
9th harmonic
8th harmonic
7th harmonic
6th harmonic
5th harmonic
4th harmonic
3rd harmonic
2nd harmonic
GENERATING TONE
(FUNDAMENTAL)

HARMONIC PROPORTION

On the opposite page, all harmonics are shown at an equal distance. Let's look at another view of the harmonic series, more familiar to musicians, where every octave is equidistant. Below, the harmonics are in a proportional relationship (logarithmic, rather than linear). It can be seen that each successive harmonic is slightly smaller (closer) while the octaves remain constant.

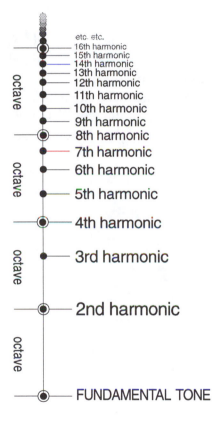

This proportion is known as *harmonic proportion, divine proportion,* the *golden section,* or the *golden mean.* A source of great beauty and mystery, it was known to Pythogoras, Leonardo da Vinci and other artists, architects and philosophers throughout history. It is found in nature as well as in art, architecture and music.

A proportion may be expressed with numbers as a ratio, such as 1/2 or .5 or 50% or 1:2. (To the ancient Greeks, "ratio" was synonymous with "harmony.") Harmonic proportion cannot be expressed by simple numbers, rather with the irrational number 1.6181818... It is symbolized in classical mathematics as *Phi.* (Ø) and can be approximated with the fraction 8/5 or 5/8.

Leon Alberti, the great Renaissance architect, philosopher and musician, wrote:
    The numbers by means of which the agreement
    of sounds affect our ears with delight, are the
    very same which please our eyes and our minds.

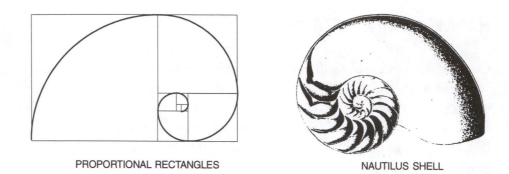

PROPORTIONAL RECTANGLES   NAUTILUS SHELL

The golden mean, as an ideal shape, rather than a mathematical formula, is found throughout nature—in the growth patterns of crystals, plants, animal life—in all living organisms. The natural harmonic curve is evident in shells and even the cochlea of the ear. It is a proportion of innate aesthetic beauty, present in many forms of art from antiquity to the present. It seems that early peoples had a sense of harmonic proportion, as evident in the monuments of the ancient world.

The scale of harmonic proportion is found in the forms
of nature as well as the intuitive designs of humankind.

Harmonic rhythm has been revealed in the periodic table of elements and intervals of electron shells within an atom—the very essence of matter and energy. All things in our physical world, from the subatomic to the cosmic, reflect or produce a rhythm of harmonic proportion. That includes every musical tone.

Every tone produced by a musical instrument generates a series of harmonics. Whether each harmonic is audible or not depends on the type of instrument, the intensity of the fundamental tone, the acoustical environment and the attention of the listener.

When a harmonic is twice the frequency of another (a ratio of 2:1) an octave is formed. Notice that each successive octave divides to produce twice the number of intervals and each interval is in the same harmonic proportion (Ø) to the preceding as well as the succeeding interval.

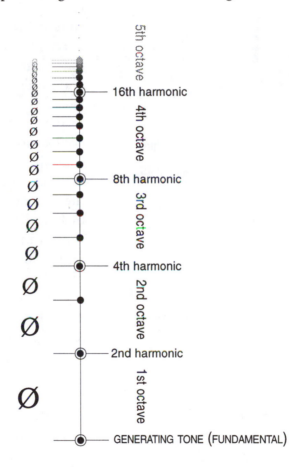

The harmonic series is nature's gift to us, the principle upon which instruments are built, the basis of resonance, tonality, and harmony—a capsule of the history of music.

The harmonic series provides the model for our palette of intervals.

The **first octave** gives us the purest of intervals, the **octave** itself: two tones so closely related (2:1) that they are often perceived as one tone.

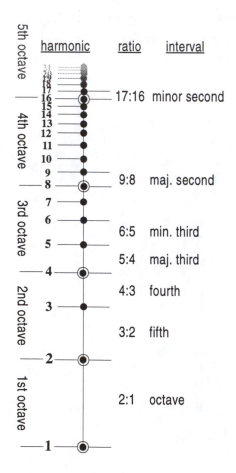

The **second octave** reveals the division of the octave in perfect proportion. The resulting interval (corresponding to the **fifth** scale degree) is so fundamental as to represent harmonic structure and stability. The complimentary **fourth** interval, while not as structurally significant, shares the primary interval status of the fifth.

In the **third octave**, another division occurs, producing four new intervals, a collection of intermediate size **thirds**. The major third and minor third echo the proportional relationship of the fifth and fourth. Notice that each succeeding interval is of the same proportion—the ratio of the aesthetically desirable golden mean.

The **fourth octave** further divides into 8 more intervals, providing a series of scale-step size intervals, the **seconds.**

The **fifth octave** provides 16 more intervals, from the minor second to those that we consider microtonal. Intervals found in the vicinity of the 32nd harmonic are approximately a **quarter-tone**.

It is the harmonics of proportion and relationship which give rise to beauty in every field of perception, for they mediate chaos with order.   Lawrence Blair: *Rhythms Of Vision*

The series continues (theoretically) to infinity, diminishing in intensity. Practically, harmonics are seldom audible above the 12th. Some of the higher intervals have been recognized by various cultures, such as the *Comma of Didymus* (81:80), "considered by the Greeks, Arabs and Hindus as the logical unit for any practical division of the scale." (Danielou: *Northern Indian Music)* Helmholtz lists 153 intervals within an octave and the historical significance of each. (Helmholtz: *On the Sensations of Tone)*

The "lower" tones of the harmonic series—those in simple numeric relation to the fundamental (3:2, 4:3, etc.)—provide the foundation of musical structure, the sense of stability and tonality. The "higher" or more distant tones provide the light and color of music—the sparkles, pastels, the subtleties of melodic inflection.

The order in which the intervals are produced in the harmonic series is the order in which they were discovered and accepted in the evolution of Western music: first the octave and fifth, then gradually smaller intervals.

Composers have always emulated the harmonic series when desiring to create ultimate resonance, i.e. the final chord of virtually every symphony. There are many instances where the harmonic series has been used to generate melodies symbolizing nature, grandeur or profundity. In John Williams' score for *Close Encounters of the Third Kind,* the first communication with the beings in the spaceship is signaled with a simple tune of harmonics, presumably understood anywhere in the universe.

EXERCISE 8

Find these **harmonics** on the opposite page and sing: #9, #10, #8, #4, #6. Notice that the drop from harmonic #8 to harmonic #4 is an octave. Sound familiar?

EXPERIENCE THE HARMONIC SERIES

Pythagoras (c. 530 BC) observed the harmonious relationship of tones in ratios of simple numbers. Although tangible evidence of the harmonic series is rather elusive, there are several means of producing audible results. The series is most evident on certain instruments.

Any stringed instrument (violin, guitar, etc.) will provide a visual tool for creating harmonics. Even if you have not played a stringed instrument, you will be able to produce harmonics within a few minutes by experimenting. Pluck an open string. Then place a finger midway between the nut and the bridge, lightly touching the string, then pluck or bow the string. If you've touched midway (at the node) you will have created the octave of the open string. Find the other nodes at one-third, one-fourth and one-fifth of the string and produce each consecutive natural harmonic.

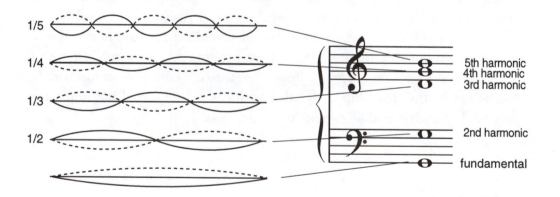

All brass instruments are essentially simple tubes. The bugle, representative of early horns and trumpets, can produce only the natural tones of the harmonic series. All bugle calls (*Taps, Reveille*, etc.) are played by simply running up and down the natural harmonics. The orchestrations of the 17th and early 18th centuries were similarly limited in the use of the horn and trumpet. Today's valve horn or trumpet is actually seven bugles, one for each valve combination, resulting in a complete chromatic instrument. The slide trombone is built on the same principle, although more visual. Each successive slide position provides a harmonic series a half-tone lower.

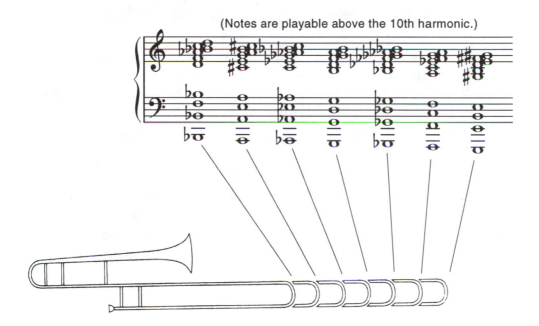

(Notes are playable above the 10th harmonic.)

EXERCISE 9

Produce the harmonic series, preferably with a brass or stringed instrument. If that is not practical, use a keyboard. Starting on any note, play from the fundamental up through the series to the 10th harmonic and down.

Some harmonics may be produced by "overblowing" woodwind instruments. The flute, especially, produces all the harmonics clearly. The clarinet produces a good twelfth, the other harmonics with difficulty. Each instrument produces harmonics in varying intensities. Helmholtz, who pioneered the relationship of sound to music, built glass and metal resonators to measure harmonics.

It is even possible to produce harmonics with the human voice, for it is the harmonic content that enables us to distinguish each vowel sound. You can hear the subtle shifting of harmonics in the traditional "om." You may want to practice this fundamental human sound in the spirit of harmony as others have for centuries. Or perhaps to acknowledge G. S. Ohm, who discovered that the ear analyzes the harmonic content of incoming sounds!

Try sustaining a low tone, forming an "Ah," then slowly changing to "Oh" by subtly altering the resonant cavity of your mouth. If you focus your ear, you will be able to discern the scale of harmonics, descending and ascending through the series as you slowly alternate "ah-oh-ah-oh" or "wow-wow." With practice, you can project harmonics that are quite audible.

Overtone singing, or toning, has been practiced throughout the world for centuries in spiritual, meditative or healing contexts. There are groups who practice overtone singing for no particular reason other than to achieve the experience of resonance. You may be able to locate people in your area with similar interests. See REFERENCE SECTION, page 383.

 THE OCTAVE

The octave and the beat are the universal measurements of music space and time, the common elements fundamental to all music.

When one tone vibrates at twice the frequency of another tone, they form the interval of an octave. The two tones are physically bonded, their mutual harmonics interacting, producing an acoustical blend that the ear often interprets as one tone. After the unison, the octave is the simplest possible relationship of two tones.

EXERCISE 10
Experience the unison (1:1) and octave (2:1)

You will need two pitch sources, one constant and one movable. Two similar tones will produce the most audible results. A stringed instrument is an excellent source, tuning one string against another. Or two synthesizer tones, one sustaining, one capable of bending the pitch. A simple but effective method is your voice against the steady hum of an electrical appliance or machine. Two musicians playing similar wind or stringed instruments can do this exercise.

Bring the two sources to a unison, then bend one tone slightly, sharp or flat, then slowly bend the other direction, returning to unison. When the two tones are perfectly *in tune*, the interval (unison) is free of beats, very clear and resonant; the two tones sound as one. When they are slightly *out of tune,* a harsh beat rate occurs, beating perhaps four times per second. As the two tones grow farther apart, you will hear the beat rate slow down, then eventually increase again as the two tones approach the interval of a half-tone. As you bring the two tones back to unison, the clarity and resonance returns.

Repeat this exercise at the interval of the octave. As you experience the tuning of these intervals, you are actually fine-tuning your ear.

NATURAL INTERVALS

The primary division of the octave produces the interval 3:2, known to us as the "fifth" because it happens to correspond to the fifth degree of the diatonic scale.

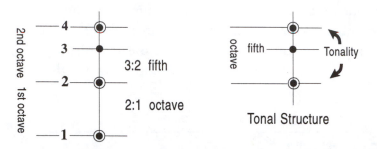

The fifth is fundamental to all music, the essence of tonality and the origin of Western harmony. Chinese musicians learned how to tune by natural fifths more than 5,000 years ago. Four consecutive fifths produce the tones of the pentatonic scale, a tonal relationship so fundamental that children everywhere instinctively improvise pentatonic melodies. Eventually, the Chinese added two more fifths to the pentatonic scale to produce the 7-tone diatonic scale, and still later extended more fifths to complete the full 12-tone cycle of fifths.

Other cultures independently invented tuning systems based on the fifth. There was no need to measure intervals mathematically; diverse peoples concluded that octaves and fifths sounded best. The collective ear of humanity was guided by the pleasing sound of natural intervals.

We'll refer to the octave and its fifth as the TONAL STRUCTURE, a reference with which to measure all other tones. This concept that will be of great value as our work develops.

EXERCISE 11

Experience the fifth.
Using the same method as EXERCISE 10, create the interval of the fifth and you will experience the same phenomenon of resonance.

 WHY 7?

When two fifths are combined, an interval is produced (the ninth) which is larger than an octave. The difference between a ninth and an octave is the ideal interval for melodic scale steps—the whole-tone.

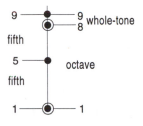

The octave, when filled in with whole-tones and half-tones, embraces the *tonal structure* which maintains the natural fifth and provides a variety of 7-tone (diatonic) modes.

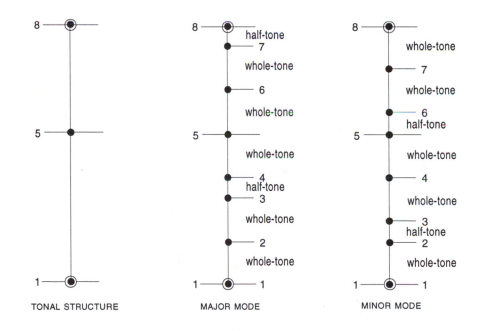

Several variations (modes) of the 7-tone diatonic scale may be constructed using only whole-tones and half-tones. (More about MODES in section 6.)

WHY 12?

Even in antiquity, both the Chinese and the Greeks realized that the 7-tone diatonic scale and its various modes could be constructed with 12 half-tones.

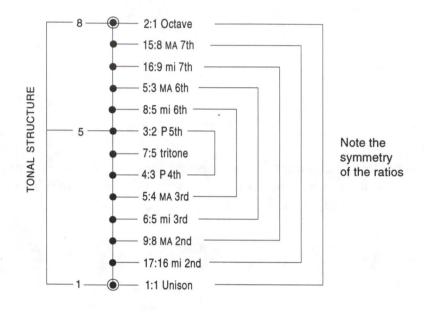

The 12-tone scale, when composed of the proportional intervals of the harmonic series, guarantees pleasing, harmonious sounds. The intervals, however, are not precisely equal-spaced.

For more than 2000 years, musicians, philosophers and mathematicians tried to derive a 12-tone scale that would provide the natural intervals of the harmonic series. Pythagoras constructed a scale from a series of natural (3:2) fifths, known as the Pythagorean scale. About 300 years later, the scale was improved by Aristoxenus, who formed a scale with two tetrachords, known as the Greek scale. Zarlino, around 1560 in Venice, refined the scale so that the thirds and sixths reflected the true intervals of the harmonic series. Zarlino's scale is known as the natural scale.

EQUAL TEMPERAMENT

The natural scale is ideal for music that stays on one tonality (Eastern-type music). However, the beautiful proportional curve of the harmonic series refused to fit into the linear system of 12 keys. When a fundamental (root) tone is transposed, the same 12 tones will not produce the exact harmonic intervals in another key. Pythagoras knew that the system was not mathematically perfect: 12 fifths are slightly larger (sharper) than 7 octaves.

During the Baroque era, the inclination to modulate was hampered by an imperfect system of 12 tones. This was especially true for keyboard instruments; once tuned, the chromatic scale was set and could only be utilized for a limited number of keys. Stringed and wind instrument players were (and still are) capable of producing natural intervals simply by bending tones, the player adjusting the pitch by ear. However, all musicians must adjust to a fixed temperament when playing with a keyboard instrument.

Several solutions were implemented to provide melodic scale-tones built on the pleasing intervals of the natural harmonics. Most notable were *just intonation*, which used natural fifths (3:2) and natural major thirds (5:4) and *mean-tone temperament*, which compromised the fifths and thirds in order to accommodate keys of one or two flats or sharps. These systems of tuning served only keys close to home; modulation to remote keys resulted in intervals that were so unlike their harmonic models that they were intolerable to the ear.

It was inevitable that the *just* and *mean-tone* systems with their problems of transposition would be replaced by a system of equal intervals. The question, then, was how to divide the octave equally and still produce pleasing intervals that would approximate the harmonic series. How many equal portions would provide the desirable intervals of the harmonic series?

Several systems of equal temperament have been implemented and many more proposed. Equal interval cycles of 31 and 53 produce near-perfect fifths and thirds. Other systems divide the octave into equal parts of 19, 29, 43, 50, 55, 301 and even 3,010.

After much resistance and controversy, the 12-equal system survived. 12 tones proved to be the clear winner for economy, efficiency and maneuverability. The elegance of the equal-tempered system, however, did not come without a price. When equalized, every interval lost, to some degree, its perfect harmonic proportion.

Most of today's musicians accept equal temperament without question. While the 12-equal system provides near-perfect fifths and ninths, the remaining intervals are tolerable at best. The rich benefits of 12-equal intervals—the cycles of modulation, the manageable number of tones and the symmetrical division of the octave into 2, 3, 4 and 6 parts—are traded for imperfect thirds, sixths and sevenths.

EXERCISE 12

Using the chart on the opposite page, compare the natural intervals of the harmonic series with the artificial intervals of 12-equal temperament. The circled numbers are the natural harmonics and the ruled lines are the equal-tempered intervals. Notice that each octave produces twice the number of harmonics and that each successive harmonic is proportionally smaller. Which tempered intervals are close to being acoustically perfect?

Cents are units of proportional (logarithmic) measurement used for the comparison of intervals. A cent is 1/100 of a half-tone, therefore an octave contains 1200 cents. The cent is attributed to A.J. Ellis, the English translator of Helmholtz: *On the Sensations of Tone.*

THE RELATIONSHIP OF THE NATURAL HARMONIC SERIES TO THE 12-TONE EQUAL TEMPERED SCALE

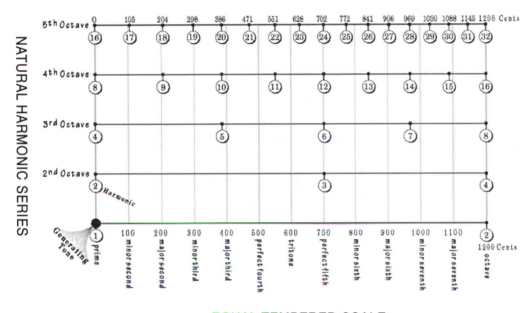

EQUAL TEMPERED SCALE

At the bottom of the chart, the equal-tempered intervals are labeled in increments of 100 cents. At the top of the chart, the size of each natural harmonic is measured in cents. Using cents, you may compare equal-tempered with natural intervals.

Everyone, musician or not, appreciates a good, *in-tune* acoustic fifth. In 12-equal temperament, the fifth is only 2 cents smaller (flatter) than the natural harmonic (702 cents). The tempered ninth is also a very good replication of the natural ninth (9th harmonic). As the ninth is a projection of two fifths, the out-of-tuneness is twice the error of a fifth, an interval of only 4 cents.

Below, all the harmonics that are closest to equal-tempered intervals have been collapsed to one octave. Remember that one equal-tempered half-tone equals 100 cents. Considering that the lower harmonics are more prominent, which tempered intervals are close to being acoustically perfect?

NATURAL INTERVALS (cents)   (cents) TEMPERED INTERVALS

	1200	1200 OCTAVE
15th harmonic	1088	1100 MAJOR 7th
7th harmonic	969	1000 MINOR 7th
27th harmonic	906	900 MAJOR 6th
13th harmonic	841	800 MINOR 6th
3rd harmonic	702	700 PERFECT 5th
		600 TRITONE
11th harmonic	551	500 PERFECT 4th
21st harmonic	471	
5th harmonic	386	400 MAJOR 3rd
19th harmonic	298	300 MINOR 3rd
9th harmonic	204	200 MAJOR 2nd
17th harmonic	105	100 MINOR 2nd
	0	FUNDAMENTAL

Keep in mind that equal-temperament is an idealized system. Musicians constantly adjust to produce the natural intervals unless they are playing instruments of fixed pitches (keyboard and mallets). Vocalists, string and wind instrumentalists instinctively gravitate toward the natural intervals.

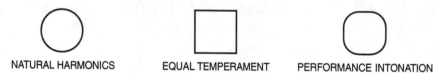

NATURAL HARMONICS   EQUAL TEMPERAMENT   PERFORMANCE INTONATION

Performing musicians everywhere exhibit the tendency to adjust tempered intervals toward the natural intervals.

> The West's creation of the 'tempered' scale, to which Bach contributed so much, is one of those instances where man's artistic will is manifest, adjusting nature to meet aesthetic and practical needs.
> Yehudi Menuhin and Curtis Davis: *The Music of Man*

BEYOND 12

The evolution of music produced an increasing number of usable intervals within the octave, from the initial tuning in fifths through the development of 5- and 7-tone scales to 12-tone chromaticism. It is but a step from chromatic music to the world of microtonal intervals.

For our purposes, microtonal refers not only to intervals less than a half-tone, but an interval of any size which is obtained through a system other than the 12-equal interval system. Eastern music emphasizes melodic nuance using various size intervals, many derived from a quarter-tone temperament. (The Arabic ¾ interval is one-half of a minor third.)

> What is the smallest interval admissible in a scale is a question which different nations have answered differently according to the different direction of their taste, and perhaps also according to the different delicacy of their ear.
> Helmholtz: *On the Sensations of Tone*

Western musicians can best understand other tuning systems in terms of what we already know. If you have a good grasp of the 12-equal intervals, it is a matter of adjusting a familiar interval in order to perceive an infinite variety of intervals. (Indian scales of 22 and 53 tones per octave are derived as alterations of the 7 diatonic tones, rather than equal intervals.)

Just intonation tuning systems have survived and are, in fact, championed by some. If you are interested in pursuing the world of alternate tuning, see page 392.

EXERCISE 13
Experience microtones.

Using a stringed instrument, divide a half-tone into quarter-tone intervals. Divide a whole-tone into ⅓-tone and ⅔-tone intervals. After listening to microtones for a few minutes, a half-tone will sound quite large!

 RELATIVITY

Our work is to define sound in terms of the elements of music. An examination and clarification of each element will help to consolidate the hearing and the writing of music.

A single tone, a single word, a single brush stroke does not convey much in the communication of emotion or thought. We find meaning, not in the elements of music, but in their relationships. If you learn to hear and think relatively, you will be able to hear anything at any time without being dependent on an instrument. You can achieve such a state of receptivity if you think in terms of intervals, rather than notes. Let's look at the relativity of each element.

Pitch is arbitrary. Selected tones have been assigned note-names for convenience, but the pitches they represent are approximate. The "standard" pitch of instruments and orchestras has varied throughout history and across regions. When musicians agree to tune up, there remain differences of pitch perception among them, discrepancies of temperament peculiar to each instrument, as well as a rising pitch as instruments warm up.

Dynamics are relative, placed on the score by the composer, who can only estimate what the appropriate level should be. The actual dynamic level is a result of the performer's interpretation, the interaction of the surrounding musicians, the influence of the conductor, and the acoustics of the environment.

Tempo is relative, especially apparent in the different interpretations of a work by various conductors or performers. We can think in broad terms of slow, medium and fast or equate tempo to walking, dancing, running. We have traditional tempo indications that may be adequate for performance. Music need not be locked to a particular tempo unless it is synchronized with other media. When we need to be precise, we have digital metronomes, MIDI time code and SMPTE time code.

Key is arbitrary. One of the endless and unresolved discussions among musicians is that of the preference and significance of keys, a residual of pre-equal temperaments. Any work may be transposed and retain its identity; the intervals maintain the integrity of the music. When music is transposed to another key, differences in sound, other than the obvious higher or lower pitches, result from the combined characteristics of all instruments performing. Each tone would be produced by a different harmonic of a string or wind column, resulting in a collective difference of timbre, perhaps brighter, perhaps darker. A composer considers instrumental technique, timbre and the placement of a particular phrase relative to an instrument's register when choosing a key, rather than non-musical attributes associated with keys.

Temperament is relative. The intonation of an instrument's scale varies from one instrument to another and varies among cultures. Some instruments have a fixed temperament, inherent in their sound while others are built with the capability of producing variable temperaments. There are many instances of idiomatic temperaments performed in equal temperament— baroque music played on modern instruments, orchestral settings of folk music, etc.

Timbre is relative. A composer notates a clarinet line but the actual *sound* of that line is dependent upon the sound of that particular clarinet as well as the musician's interpretation of that notation during a certain performance.

The interval is the only constant in music—all other elements are relative. Fortunately, any given interval is consistent because it is, by definition, a fixed ratio. A fifth sounds the same now as 5,000 years ago and presumably will sound the same anywhere in the universe. Since intervals are proportions, retaining their shape under any type of manipulation, identification by ear is absolutely reliable.

What is melody but a series of intervals? When you notate a melody, you actually superimpose an interval template of that melody over the scale/mode matrix at a selected pitch or key. The choice of pitch/key is orchestrational, rather than compositional—determined by considerations of vocal or instrumental register. A melody may be sung or played at any pitch, in any key, and it retains its melodic shape, its identity.

A familiar scenario: someone starts to sing "Happy Birthday To You." Others join in. Most people gravitate toward the pitch and sing in unison or octaves; others may sing in parallel fifths—or any other interval! Those with no sense of pitch are still able to sing a recognizable contour of the melody. Everyone can hear and sing the intervals, yet no one knows or cares what key the song happens to be in. The pitch level or note names have no significance; the song sounds the same in any key. A song in an unaccompanied setting may drift to another tonality (key) before it is finished. Nevertheless, the intervals maintain the integrity of the melody. We recognize a particular phrase/tune/song as a pattern of fixed intervals with associated rhythmic patterns. Intervals of tone and rhythm define music.

Tones are sounds in the air; notes are symbols on a staff. Once you have accepted the concept of divorcing tones from notes, you'll be able to perceive music in the abstract, unencumbered by keys or note names. The relationship of tones is measured by the ear in terms of intervals with no information required as to particular pitches. When your perception is certain, you'll be free to notate or perform what you are hearing in the key of your choice.

> Whether a painter, a chef or a musician, the refinement of the senses is fundamental to the craft. Your primary sense is hearing; your primary tools are intervals of tone and rhythm.

SIGHT AND SOUND

Since we cannot see sound, we use visual symbols to represent the elements of music. Music notation was created to convey and preserve musical thought.

Music has a correlation to visual art: the two-dimensional spatial field corresponds to the vertical image of the audio range plus the horizontal *stereo image*. Drawing is much like the composition of melodic lines, while painting is very much like orchestration, concerned with contrasts of color, texture and the subtleties of light and shade. Depth and perspective are created in music with the use of dynamics and octave doubling.

Harmonics grow out of a tone, as trees grow out of the earth. That they grow "upward" is our human perception, our orientation with gravity. We hold the image of pitch as high and low, rather than fast and slow vibrations. Music staff notation promotes that image, as do composers who write high notes to represent things that are small, quick, feminine, cheerful, innocent, dream-like or floating; and low notes for things that are large, slow, masculine, somber, threatening, powerful or ominous.

Even the dimension of time has a correlation to visual art: If a viewer is absorbed in the perception of art, the sensation of time passing may be suspended. Music has the same effect: 15 minutes of music may seem like a moment or an eternity. Music time is very subjective; a composer listens internally in real time to gauge accurately the effect of the music.

Tones that become music are related in space and time. All music is created with these basic building blocks: various size intervals of pitch and rhythm that are combined to form larger structures of scales and modes, chords and clusters, phrases and sections.

ABSOLUTE PITCH VS. RELATIVE PITCH

Absolute pitch is the ability to identify tones;
relative pitch is the ability to identify intervals.

Since the perception of music has relevance only in the abstract, in terms of intervals, musicians possessing absolute ("perfect") pitch have only one advantage: a built-in pitch reference. If you don't have absolute pitch, have confidence that you are not handicapped; a 1 oz. tuning fork is your "absolute" pitch. (See ESTABLISHING PITCH AND KEY, pages 191-193.)

Nearly all musicians with absolute pitch have studied a keyboard instrument from an early age and have developed the ability to compare an audible impression with an acoustic archetype stored in memory. Studies of musicians claiming to have absolute pitch revealed that only a small percentage were able to name the correct pitch infallibly. Some musicians possessing absolute pitch have stated that they can "turn it on and off at will" while others say that it is always there. One pianist remembered having absolute pitch from age three, yet he lost the ability for a period of several years while learning wind (transposing) instruments, then regained it as he returned to the piano. You've probably heard horror stories of musicians with absolute pitch having to play gigs on acoustic pianos a half-tone flat. In these situations, absolute pitch is more of a detriment than an advantage.

Those with absolute pitch must also hear in terms of relative pitch in order to comprehend music. Since pitch itself is variable, having absolute pitch is not entirely reliable. If you have developed absolute pitch, practice listening to music in a free-form state, concentrating on interval relationships rather than note names as you pursue these studies. Keyboard players who have undergone this training returned to the keyboard with "open ears."

There are claims that "Anyone can develop perfect pitch." We maintain that "Almost anyone can develop pitch memory." If you have been playing music all your life, you probably have a good sense of pitch due to habitual repetition and you can probably identify pitches more accurately if they are played on the same instrument you have studied. You may be able to improve your ability to name pitches in the air but, as we have seen, pitch is an arbitrary element of music. Your time is better spent concentrating on intervals.

A definite advantage in listening with relative pitch is that we are comfortable with tones sounding at any pitch in the sound spectrum, not just those related to a=440. If we are not conditioned to hearing "absolute" pitches, music may be perceived in its organic state, in terms of intervals. The essence of music is not dependent on the mechanical apparatus of pitch and key with which we can become so preoccupied.

When recorded music is transferred from one machine or media to another, there is the possibility of a change of pitch. You may receive recorded music that is a half-tone sharp or flat or "in the cracks," perhaps a quarter-tone sharp or flat. Yet the intervals have not changed; the intervals preserve the identity of music at any pitch level.

Using relative pitch, you can easily listen in one key and notate in another key, a great time-saver in situations that require transposition. The goal is to hear intervals and be able to instantly relate them to any key/tonality.

A refined sense of relative pitch—interval recognition—is invaluable in all aspects of working with music. Hearing intervals is essential when composing, orchestrating and copying parts for transposing instruments. If you have absolute pitch, develop the ability to turn it on and off at will. Free yourself to be able to hear music in its organic state.

STANDARD PITCH

The selection of pitches or frequencies represented by note-names is arbitrary. Temperament aside, the actual pitch when music is being played is determined by the conditions of the moment. When singing to accompaniment, we immediately adjust to the prevailing pitch without questioning its frequency. Musicians tune to a reference pitch from a designated instrument, listen to each other and constantly adjust to play *in tune,* to produce acoustically pleasing intervals. A tuning, or reference, pitch may be set at *any* frequency according to local, regional or national custom. Large ensembles, bands or orchestras, tune to a "standard" pitch, provided by the pianist or principal oboist. See Helmholtz: *On the Sensations of Tone* appendices (History of Musical Pitch in Europe) and you will find that the reference tone *a* has represented pitches ranging from 370 Hz to 567.3 Hz, a difference of over a fifth!

Orchestras from Handel to Beethoven generally tuned to *a*=422 or 423. Gradually, pitch began to rise although there was no standard until the London Philharmonic Society adapted *a*=433 in 1820 and a French commission established *a*=435 in 1859. Finally, in 1939, an International Conference representing major European countries and America adopted *a*=440, which was again standardized and dubbed *International Concert Pitch* in 1960. Today, performances of early music may be transposed a half-tone or whole-tone lower to simulate the pitch of the original key.

Standard pitch is certainly not mandatory; an orchestra or ensemble may tune to any pitch. Musicians performing with a keyboard or mallet instrument must necessarily tune up to it. Once a tuning pitch is established there will surely be variation due to the rise and fall of the temperature of each instrument. Musicians must respond to the prevailing pitch; it is the intonation of the moment that produces beautiful music.

In recent history, pitch was finally liberated from a physical source with the introduction of synthesized musical tones. 1984 is significant to us not for George Orwell, but for the introduction of MIDI, providing the means to assign any pitch to any key of a keyboard or other triggering device. Modular keyboards emphasize the historical fact: a note-name may be assigned any pitch; there is no *absolute pitch*.

YOU ARE THE INSTRUMENT

The goal of this training is to write music—transcribe, arrange, orchestrate, even compose—without using an instrument. Some students have more than doubled their transcribing speed once they liberated themselves from a keyboard or other instrument. You may already have developed the ability to hear and write without an instrument. If not, the suggestion may be enough to liberate you. Or it may take all your will power to break the habit. Hard cases must take extreme measures, such as working in a room where there are no instruments. Like any habit, once it is broken, you will have gained more than you lost. You can certainly use an instrument to check your work until you feel confident enough to trust your ear.

> Schubert did not need a piano. It made him lose his train of thought.
> Harold Schonberg: *The Lives of the Great Composers*

The process of composing is uniquely personal to each composer, even though we may use the same intervals, sonorities, rhythm, structural forms, etc. At some point, ideas are usually sketched (notated or sequenced). The idea must be assigned an arbitrary key or tonality when captured in symbols or sound. When the idea is formalized—arranged or orchestrated—a final pitch level or key must be determined, depending on the purpose of the music. Orchestration and arranging decisions ascertain the best key for a particular piece of music. Careful consideration is required as to the range and abilities of vocalists and instrumentalists.

When you are listening to music casually, choose an arbitrary key and practice your perception, mentally playing or writing lines you hear, or just naming the notes as they occur.

As you rely more on your ear, your compositions or improvisations will include more of your personality, rather than formulas or devices.

We've looked at the raw material of music and how we perceive it, the phenomenon of natural harmonics, and how humankind has fashioned sound into systems of tonal resources.

Perhaps next time you place a note on a staff, you'll think of it as a seed, an egg, an atom—a potential tone. The shape, color, intensity and ultimate destiny of that tone are guided by your artistic choices.

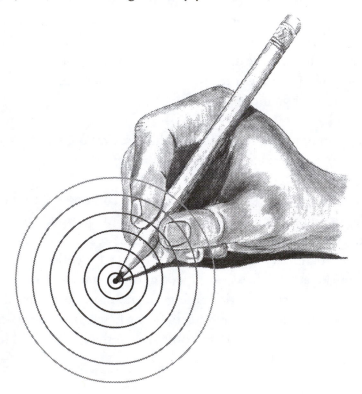

The remainder of the book is devoted to developing your personal relationship with the materials of music, with the goal of hearing and writing virtually any sound.

REVIEW

1 What is sound?

2 What is the basic building block of music and how is it defined?

3 Why is a melody recognizable at any pitch, in any key?

4 Are all sounds material for music?

5 What are the attributes of a tone?

6 How has nature contributed to the shape of music?

7 Which of the elements of music are natural and which are artificial?

8 Which intervals are common to all tunable music systems?

9 What are the advantages and disadvantages of equal temperament?

10 Describe the TONAL STRUCTURE.

4

THE MATERIAL OF MUSIC

4

When tones are combined (vertically or melodically) the space between them is perceived as an interval. Think of any melody: it is defined by intervals of space and time. It may be transposed to any pitch or key, set in any meter, performed at any tempo; its identity is retained because the intervals are constant. A melodic line is merely a succession of tones but the character, the significance of the line is determined by the intervals separating those tones.

In section 3, we've observed that intervals have different properties due to the influence of the harmonic series. In this section, we'll examine further the characteristics of the primary components of music—the intervals.

In every stage of music making, the same elements are used over and over and over. Rhythm, timbre and articulation are relatively easy to work with and are discussed later. Our immediate purpose is to differentiate and become familiar with each interval.

The importance of intervals in music perception cannot be overemphasized; your success in all musical endeavors depends considerably on accurate interval recognition. This section discusses the essence and function of intervals.

IDEALIZED INTERVALS

There are an infinite number of intervals within an octave, yet we confine our palette to 12, a grid of manageable units.

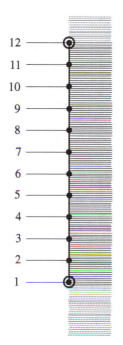

The 12 intervals are *idealized* intervals, conceptual models for the sake of simplicity and convenience in notation. The color red, for example, is idealized; we know there are infinite varieties of red, yet we agree on the concept of red. A major third in music notation symbolizes a variety of possibilities: an equal tempered major third (if played by a keyboard or sequencer); a natural, or *just*, major third (if played by a wind or stringed instrument or sung); or perhaps a detuned major third in an alternate tuning system.

Limiting our selection of intervals to 12 within an octave makes composition and notation accessible. However, we acknowledge and benefit from the musician's spontaneous adjustments that produce natural intervals. The concept of idealized intervals affords the convenience of music notation and recognizes the reality of music performance.

We may use words, symbols (such as arrows) or numeric values (such as fractions of a tone or cents) to indicate fluctuation from the nearest idealized interval. The method of notation depends on the degree of accuracy required which in turn depends on the purpose of your work. There are conventions of notation for bends, falls, etc. which suffice for jazz and pop arrangements. More accurate performance deviations require symbols with instructions. Exotic tuning systems may be represented with conventional notation simply by indicating deviations from the 12-equal grid. Some MIDI devices allow for microtonal intervals. Music created by a primitive carved flute in which the holes accommodate the fingers rather than a measured scale may be replicated accurately.

The ear will identify a particular interval as the idealized interval while perhaps observing that it is sharp or flat—as the eye recognizes red, then concludes that it is a purple-red or an orange-red. If an interval happened to be midway between a minor third and a major third, the Eastern-trained ear would accept the interval as such, whereas the Western ear would decide it was either minor or major, depending on the musical context.

Fortunately, the tempered fifth and ninth (second) are very accurate harmonic intervals. The tempered thirds, however, are so out of alignment with the natural series that we have grown to accept wide variations of both major and minor thirds. There is a tradition of singing and playing 3rds and 7ths with a great deal of inflection. These variations (*expressive intonation*) exist in many styles of music.

Perhaps the most powerful attribute of 12-equal tempered music is that the structural intervals (octave and fifth) are "perfect" acoustic intervals and the remaining intervals are malleable, subject to expressive flexibility.

We approach intervals in both forms:
vertical (simultaneous tones) and
melodic (consecutive tones).

VERTICAL INTERVALS

A vertical interval generates a certain amount of resonance which helps us to identify it. An octave and fifth are virtually transparent, whereas seconds and sevenths generate a "buzz." Thirds combine qualities of both, producing a rich mixture of purity and distortion. (We avoid the terms "consonance" and "dissonance" as their traditional connotations are rather stylized and subjective.)

▶ You can internalize or sing a *vertical interval* simply by alternating tones.

▶ You can internalize or sing a *chord* by scanning the tones, as a keyboard or harp arpeggiates.

MELODIC INTERVALS

When we hear a melodic interval, we don't have the benefit of its vertical resonance but we do have the memory of it. If you are familiar with the sound of a vertical fifth, you will have no problem recognizing a melodic fifth. Sing the two tones alternately until the interval feels secure. Then internalize the interval, listening to the memory of your voice.

Melodic and vertical intervals possess similar attributes;
learn both simultaneously.

INTERVAL IDENTIFICATION

There are several methods of designating intervals: numbered scale degrees, solfege syllables, or pitch-class numbers. In each method, a scale-tone is designated by name or number according to its diatonic or chromatic scale position above the root or tonic. It is not important which system you have learned or prefer; ultimately the label can be eliminated. When you acquire instant recognition of each interval, you will be able to notate smoothly, without pausing to recall the name of the interval.

SCALE DEGREES, most common among musicians for verbal communication, are diatonic scale tones, numbered from the root (1) and altered chromatically with words such as "minor," "major," "diminished," "augmented," "flat," "sharp," or "raised." Numbered scale degrees are commonly used to describe chord elements as well as intervals.

SOLFEGE (solfeggio; sol-fa) was devised by Guido d'Arezzo in the 11th century and is still in use throughout the world. It can be confusing as there are two methods: The *Fixed Do* method employs syllables for actual note-names ("Fa" is a particular note **F**) whereas the *Movable Do* method uses the same syllables to represent scale-degrees ("Fa" is the fourth degree of the scale in any key).

PITCH-CLASS   Chromatic numbering from 0 to 11 is a convention of the 20th century. Not particularly intuitive for tonal music, it lends itself to 12-tone composition and mechanical manipulations such as MIDI transposition. This method may be applied to equal-interval systems other than 12.

ASSOCIATION   Some musicians think of the first interval of a familiar song to remember the sound of a particular interval. This method is not recommended, as it detracts from the immediate music at hand.

Use the interval names or numbers that are familiar to you. As you develop your technique, the path from hearing to writing will be a direct one, without the need for words.

SCALE DEGREE	FUNCTIONALITY (DIATONIC)	PITCH CLASS	SOLFEGE (Italian)	(phonetic)
OCTAVE	TONIC	12	DO	DOH
MAJOR SEVENTH	LEADING TONE	11	TI or SI	TEE or SEE
MINOR SEVENTH		10	LI/TE	LEE/TAY
MAJOR SIXTH	SUBMEDIANT	9	LA	LAH
MINOR SIXTH		8	SI/LE	SEE/LAY
FIFTH	DOMINANT	7	SO or SOL	SOH or SOL
TRITONE		6	FI/SE	FEE/SAY
FOURTH	SUBDOMINANT	5	FA	FAH
MAJOR THIRD	MEDIANT	4	MI	MEE
MINOR THIRD		3	RI/ME	REE/MAY
MAJOR SECOND	SUPERTONIC	2	RE	RAY
MINOR SECOND		1	DI/RAH	DEE/RAH
PRIME	TONIC	0	DO	DOH

Each method of identifying intervals has its particular benefits and limitations. Use any method that suits you. Whether you think of the interval 3:2 as "a perfect fifth," "a natural fifth," "sol," "so," "7," or any other name, the distinct *sound* of the interval is unique and constant. The ultimate goal of this work is to establish a direct connection between sound, perception and notation without the association of words.

 TOOL KIT #2

Each interval has its distinct sound, due to its unique characteristics—relative size, tension and tonality. As we isolate each interval in section 5, we'll focus on its uniqueness by comparing the following attributes: *tonality, span,* and *resonance.* These tools will eventually be stored in your subconscious tool box, ready to help if you cannot immediately recognize an interval.

☓ TONALITY

Inherent in our perception of music, tonal reference—in a word, tonality—enables us to "make sense" of melodic phrases and vertical sonorities. Tonality can be compared to gravity—fundamental to human perception. The ear tends to group tones and establish tonal relationships just as the eye organizes elements of a painting.

Tonality is subjective; each of us may perceive a different tonality within the same phrase. The mind recognizes tonality in music even when the composer did not intend tonality. When two or more tones are sounding, your mind creates an ordered relationship; you perceive one of the tones as the tonal center.

The concept of tonality is provided by the harmonic series. If two tones delineate one of the harmonic intervals, such as 3:2, the tonality is profound and we perceive the lower tone as the root. As we will see in the next section, some intervals possess a definite tonality while others are more ambiguous.

Tonality is a valuable tool and may be used most efficiently if applied in a natural and spontaneous manner.

✗ SPAN

The size of an interval, relative to the octave, is measured in ascending or descending scale-steps. Performance technique depends on the subtle physical measurement of each interval.

The production of an interval requires a certain amount of energy—velocity (wind instruments) or stretch (stringed and keyboard instruments). When singing, the relative size of intervals is very apparent in the amount of energy expelled. Melodic intervals contain the dynamic energy of their span.

✗ RESONANCE

We've learned that resonance is a physical phenomenon, a sound wave reinforcement caused by two or more tones that share a harmonic relationship.

Each interval generates a different degree of resonance, a different amount of vibrancy. Composers and theorists have never agreed as to an order of resonance (or consonance/dissonance). Nevertheless, the variation of resonance allows us to discern intervals, just as we are able to visually recognize colors. Resonance is generated only by vertical intervals but the effect is transferred to the melodic form of each interval.

OWNING THE INTERVALS

> Whereas most of us can name—and therefore distinguish—
> perhaps twelve or fifteen colors, there are professional dyers and
> painters who have a color vocabulary of several thousand shades.
>   Lawrence Blair: *Rhythms of Vision*

Each interval possesses unique character traits and personality. Your awareness of these factors will contribute to accurate perception. Fortunately, we
only have to distinguish a few intervals.

The tools (tonality, span and resonance) will help us distinguish each interval
until we can recognize any interval instantly. When you are hearing phrases,
the tools will work in combination to hold you on course. If you miscalcu-
lated the span of an interval, and continued listening only to interval spans,
your notation would be erroneous from that point. However, your sense of
tonality would immediately tell you that an error had occurred.

The combination of tools assures accuracy of perception.

In the next section, we will look at each interval as an independent entity,
removed from the influence of surrounding tonalities and harmonies, and
concentrate on the uniqueness of that interval until it becomes as familiar as
an old friend. Later, we'll examine each interval in the company of other
intervals, in the context of real music.

The time you invest learning to distinguish each interval will
pay off every day, in all aspects of creating and producing music.

REVIEW

1 Name three methods of identifying intervals.

2 What is an idealized interval and why is it practical?

3 What attribute does a vertical interval possess that is missing in a melodic interval?

4 Describe how these tools help us distinguish each interval:

TONALITY:

SPAN:

RESONANCE:

The following section focuses on each interval as a distinct entity.

5

HEARING INTERVALS

5

HEARING INTERVALS

Interval recognition is vital to hearing and writing music. Fortunately, our music is made up of comparatively few intervals. We use those same intervals in infinite combinations every day to create music, so it is imperative that we are able to distinguish one from another.

If you are familiar with each interval, you may move ahead to the next section or just review. If you have not become intimate with each interval, devote enough time to each so that you will never confuse one with another. Your time invested now will pay off every day for the rest of your life.

In this section, each interval is investigated in its isolated state. In section 6, we'll see how they interact in combinations, in musical context. The uniqueness of each will become apparent as you apply the tools—comparing the attributes of *tonality, span* and *resonance.*

We approach the intervals in pairs, those sharing similarities of sound and function. We'll note the similarities, then learn to discern the differences in each pair. Most errors in perception are a result of interchanging a pair of intervals, a fifth for a fourth or a major second for a minor second. Accurate interval identification is essential for the correct perception of music.

In the discussion and exercises in this chapter, music notation is purposely avoided, as we are concentrating on hearing—tones, rather than notes. The exercises are configured with diatonic scale-tone numbers, using ♯ or ♭ for chromatic alterations. Start each exercise at any pitch that is comfortable for your voice.

TIPS FOR LEARNING INTERVALS

⬧ Commit yourself to learning each interval intimately: the sound, the structure, the personality.

⬧ Concentrate on one interval at a time until it feels very solid and secure, until you *own* it.

⬧ VISUALIZE intervals as large, even huge, so the contrast of similar intervals is exaggerated.

⬧ Create each interval with your voice, singing with another person or instrument, or against a constant pitch, such as a buzz or hum from a machine, motor or electronic device.

⬧ Produce each interval accurately. An interval retains its characteristic sound as it moves up and down the pitch spectrum. Sing or play the intervals at different pitches; experience each interval in different registers.

⬧ Active listening: Using a string instrument, create each interval by plucking one string while tuning an adjacent string.

⬧ Develop a physical connection with the interval, fingering an instrument. You don't need the actual instrument. The physical memory of playing an interval will help you produce it mentally.

⬧ Listen for intervals as they come to you throughout the day *out of the blue,* as you listen to music casually.

⬧ Take time to INTERNALIZE an interval until you have identified it. MATCH your internal voice with the external source.

⬧ Spend as much time as necessary with each interval; the goal is immediate recognition of all intervals.

⬧ If you have a problem with a particular interval, study its characteristics again and devote more attention to it.

SOURCE OF THE PRIMARY INTERVALS

LEFT SIDE: THE NATURAL INTERVALS OF THE SCALE OF HARMONICS.
RIGHT SIDE: THE CORRESPONDING 12-EQUAL INTERVALS.

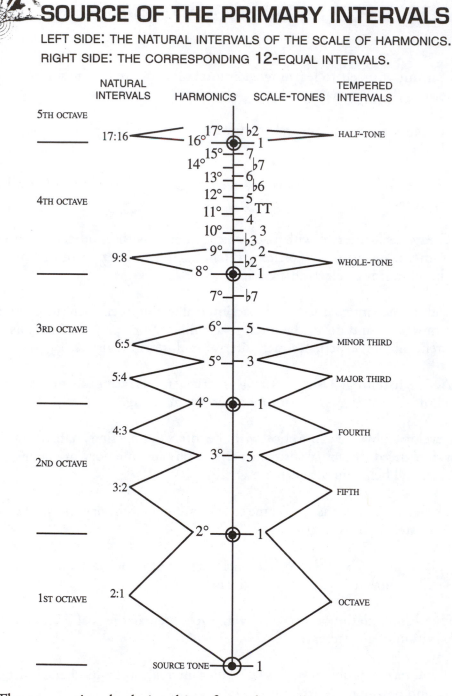

The proportional relationship of simple numbers as the source of ear-pleasing intervals is as true now as it was for Pythagoras (c.500 B.C.)

THE OCTAVE: NATURE'S FOUNDATION

◗ OCTAVE

The prime interval. Its component tones are harmonically linked, blending into what is often perceived as one voice. The octave is often felt, rather than heard. A composer or orchestrator who adds a voice at the octave is merely reinforcing what is already there in the natural harmonic.

TONALITY   The octave is the embodiment of tonality. Two tones forming an octave—even when produced by unlike instruments—may blend into what we perceive as one tone.

SPAN   The pitch difference of an octave is twice the frequency. The simple ratio bonds the two tones (harmonically) by only one generation. Vertically, the span of an octave is the path of least resistance, as natural and effortless as the flow of water or electric current. Melodically, the opposite— the difference of frequency results in a tremendous leap requiring great energy. An octave is quite dramatic in a melody.

RESONANCE   Purest of intervals, the octave is free of resistance (interference beats). The transparency of the octave allows us to perceive subtle differences of timbre, attack and vibrato of the participating instruments.

◗ UNISON

Unison (1:1) is the phenomena of two or more voices sounding at the same pitch. The discernment of unison or octave is one of the most challenging decisions in the perception of music.

Unison doubling of similar instruments adds weight or authority to a melodic line. Doubling of unlike instruments produces a timbre of their combined colors. Orchestral blending can result in unique, rich and interesting unisons.

FIFTH & FOURTH: ESSENCE OF TONALITY

The second octave of the harmonic series divides to produce the 3rd harmonic. This natural division creates the intervals 3:2 and 4:3, the fifth and fourth respectively.

Each of these second generation intervals suggests their derivation from the generating tone that produced them; each contains the essence of tonality within their sound. The fifth "points" to its lower tone as its fundamental or root, whereas the fourth "points" to its upper tone as its root. These intervals contain an inherent resolution, reflecting their respective positions in the harmonic series. Thus the concept of tonality is born: the fundamental relationship of all musical sounds. This relationship with the harmonic source is inescapable, even in abstract or "atonal" music.

Tonality, like gravity, is an aspect of nature that influences art. All humans seem to respond to the mathematical relationships of the primary intervals. Pythagoras discovered the eloquence of simple ratios that form the primary intervals: the fifth, fourth and major third. In each of these intervals, the non-root tone (odd-numbered harmonic) seems to "point" to the root tone (even-numbered harmonic). As you listen to each interval, do you hear the fundamental tone as the root? The primary intervals have strong tonal references, as each reflects its position in the harmonic series. Throughout history, acoustic instruments have been constructed on the principles of tonality.

Review page 36 as needed when studying the intervals on the following pages.

Visualize the *tonal structure* of music—the octave and its primary division, resulting in the fifth and fourth. This is the framework of tonality, the embodiment of a variety of scales and temperaments that characterize the music of the world.

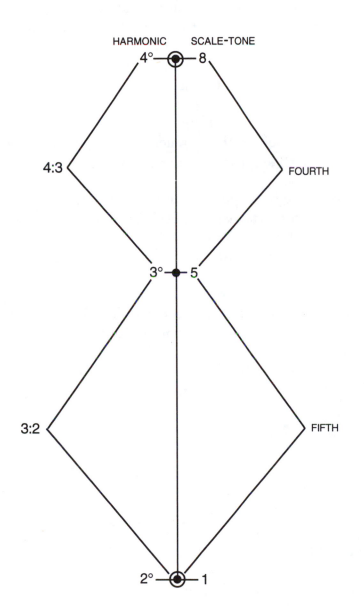

▶ FIFTH

The tonic/fifth relationship is the essence of tonality. Two tones a fifth apart create a natural blend, as they are emulating the 2nd and 3rd harmonics. They are so closely linked that they often sound like one tone. Since every tone produces or implies a strong 3rd harmonic, the same tone played by another instrument reinforces what is already there and validates the fundamental tone. The presence of the 3rd harmonic (the interval of the 5th or 12th) is subtle in most instruments, but most obvious in the amplified feedback of the *power chord*.

TONALITY Associate the tonic/fifth relationship with the concept of tonality. A clear visualization of the fifth's position within the octave provides a secure framework in which to perceive all other intervals.

SPAN Experience by singing up and down from the root to the fifth, starting at any comfortable pitch. Feel the amount of energy required to produce a melodic fifth. You must be able to sing a solid fifth before proceeding to the other intervals.

RESONANCE The characteristic sound of the fifth is stable, open, free of interference beats. In the appendices of Helmholtz: *On the Sensations of Tone,* there are tables of temperaments gathered from music of the world (Greek, Arabic, Persian, Indian, Chinese, Japanese) reflecting ancient, medieval and modern eras. A survey of tunings reveals a universal preference for the natural (*just* or Pythagorean) fifth.

EXERCISE 14

Sing an ascending fifth until comfortable and stable. Be able to produce a fifth at any time. Notice how the presence of a fifth solidifies the fundamental tone.

EXERCISE 15

Sing a descending fifth. A fifth below the tonic coincides with the 4th scale degree. This symmetry is the source of much confusion so it is imperative that you have a clear visualization of the fifth/fourth relationship.

◆ FOURTH

The fourth is the complement of the fifth: In the harmonic series, the fifth occupies the lower half of the octave and the fourth the upper half. The fourth is part of the *tonal structure,* the initial division of the octave.

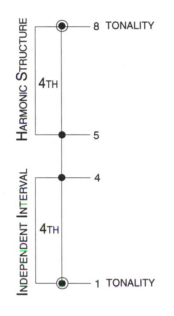

TONALITY Everyone hears the lower tone of a fifth as the root. However, a fourth may be perceived with the root above, as it appears in the harmonic series, or with the root on the bottom, independent of harmonic context. This ambiguity has caused theorists to disagree for centuries over the function of the fourth. However, we need not be concerned with the role of the fourth. Our goal is to recognize the sound of the interval in any situation.

EXERCISE 16

Independent context: sing 1-4-1.
Harmonic context: sing 5-8-5.

SPAN Learn to hear the fourth as an independent entity as well as in the context of harmonic structures.

RÉSONANCE The fourth shares the openness and clarity of the fifth.

♦ FINE TUNING

The fifth and fourth share the closest relationship of all intervals. Similar in span and resonance, they are often confused. The tonality of the fifth is definite while the tonality of the fourth is ambiguous. The difference in tonality helps us to distinguish between the fifth and fourth.

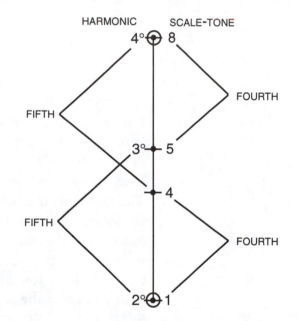

EXERCISE 17

Sing up and down the scale tones: tonic, fourth, fifth, octave, watching the diagram. Become very familiar with the 1, 4, 5, 8 structure.

TONALITY   The fifth and fourth are complementary; together they span an octave. Both intervals contain a strong sense of tonality due to their prominence and their shared function of dividing the octave. The inherent tonality of the fifth and fourth is a characteristic feature of these intervals.

RESONANCE   Both intervals produce an open, tension-free sound. The difference in vertical resonance (3:2 and 4:3) is subtle, but the fifth is decisively more transparent, closer to the octave sound.

SPAN   There is a definite distinction between the fifth and fourth in melodic span.

EXERCISE 18
Vocalize an ascending fourth; then experience the extra energy required to span an ascending fifth. Visualize each interval's relation to the octave "larger than life" so you can appreciate the difference.

Measure the span of each interval before you sing or play, as an athlete sizes up each event.

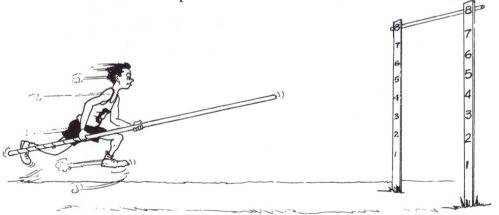

EXERCISE 19

Sing (ascending) 1—5, feeling the span of a fifth; then 5—8, feeling the span of a fourth.

EXERCISE 20

Sing (descending) 8—5 feeling a fourth; then 5—1, feeling a fifth.

EXERCISE 21

Sing the fourth/fifth structure, alternately:
1—5—4—5—1.
1—4—5—4—1.
1—4—1—5—8—4—5—1 etc., ascending and descending until the structure feels secure.

EXERCISE 22

Name the 5th scale degree in every key. Name the 4th scale degree in every key.

EXERCISE 23

Listen for the 5th (or 12th) scale degree in the harmonics of various instruments.

EXERCISE 24

Sing two ascending fifths. Did you end on the 9th? Then start a whole-tone lower (the tonic) and sing two descending 5ths. Did you end a whole-tone below the original tone?

EXERCISE 25

Sing three ascending fourths. Which scale-tone did you end on?

EXERCISE 26

Sing three descending fourths. Which scale-tone did you end on?

THIRDS: ESSENCE OF MODALITY

In the 3rd octave of the harmonic series, the fifth is divided proportionally, creating a large (major) third and a small (minor) third. Refer to page 47.

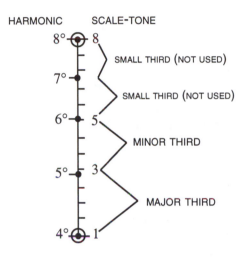

Again, the harmonic series has provided a pair of intervals that are essential for everyday music making. The configuration of large and small thirds defines the shape of each mode.

While 12-equal temperament has provided a near perfect fifth, the major and minor thirds are only crude replicas of their harmonic counterparts 5:4 and 6:5. The equal-tempered major third (400 cents) is larger (sharper) than its harmonic counterpart (5:4) which is 386 cents. Its complement, the minor third, is similarly imperfect: the equal-tempered version is 300 cents whereas the harmonic (6:5) interval is 316 cents. Consequently, our ears will tolerate a wide range of intervals identified as thirds. In your casual listening, notice how performers are able to deviate the pitch of a minor or major third.

The remaining two intervals (7:6 and 8:7) are inappropriate for 12-equal tempered music, as the 7th harmonic is too far from the tempered interval grid.

◆ MAJOR THIRD

TONALITY In the major third (5:4), the 5 "points" to the 4 (multiple of the fundamental) as the root. (Refer to the diagram on the previous page.) When listening to an isolated major third, we would naturally identify the lower tone as the root.

SPAN The major third in root position is all too familiar. Become aware of major thirds as they appear in other positions of scales and chords, i.e. in the major mode: 4th/6th and 5th/7th degrees; in the Phrygian mode: 2nd/4th, 3rd/5th, and 6th/tonic scale degrees.

RESONANCE Bright, vibrant.

EXERCISE 27

Sing: 1—3—1. 8—♭6—8.

◆ MINOR THIRD

TONALITY In the minor third interval as found in the harmonic series (6:5), the 6th and 5th harmonic seem to "point" to the fundamental (4). You may also perceive the lower tone of an isolated minor third as the tonality. Musical context ultimately determines the perceived tonality.

EXERCISE 28

Listen internally to a major triad (alternating the three tones). Now alternate only the upper two tones, a minor third which "points" to its silent root. Still listening to the minor third interval, start to hear the lower tone as the root. The ambiguous tonality is dependent on musical context.

SPAN The minor third is easier to sing than the major third and is therefore more common in melodies. Find minor thirds in various scales and chords.

RESONANCE Dark, mellow.

EXERCISE 29

Sing: 1—♭3—1. 8—6—8.

♦ FINE TUNING

RESONANCE   Both thirds share a rich, vibrant resonance. In the scheme of all the intervals, they are intermediate, possessing the tonal qualities of the fifth and fourth as well as the melodic functions of the seconds. The major third is distinctly brighter than the minor third.

SPAN   The relationship of the major and minor third mimics the relationship of the fifth and fourth; they are of the same proportions. Visualize the interval of the fifth as it is divided to produce the two sizes of thirds.

It is helpful to realize that two major thirds equal an augmented fifth, two minor thirds equal a diminished fifth, and a mixed pair of thirds results in a perfect fifth. The pattern of alternating mixed thirds is the foundation of chord structures. (See page 223)

MODALITY   The two types of thirds are often mistakenly interchanged, as they are similar in all qualities: tonality, resonance and span. The obvious difference is modal context—we never confuse major with minor. In scale passages, the choice of third is often a modal concern. Hearing thirds in the context of the prevailing mode or scale will guarantee accuracy.

In modal context, the differentiation of the two thirds is obvious, even definitive. In melodic context, the distinction is subtle. The modes will be explored as valuable tools of perception in section 6.

EXERCISE 30

Sing a major scale, alternating thirds, i.e. 1-3-2-4-3-5, etc. noting which thirds are major and which are minor. Repeat, singing a minor scale.

SECONDS: ESSENCE OF MELODY

The whole-tone (major second) and half-tone (minor second) are the building blocks of melody. Various configurations of the major and minor seconds define the characteristics of each mode.

In the fourth and fifth octaves of the harmonic series, we find major and minor seconds that are near perfect for the 12-equal tempered interval set (9:8 and 17:16).

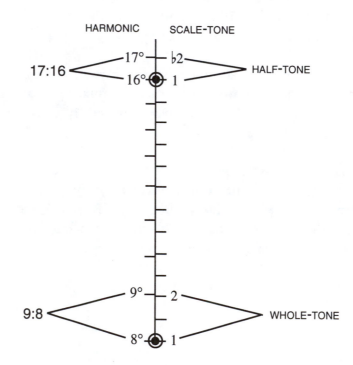

♦ WHOLE-TONE

The whole-tone is an important structural element, as well as a primary component of melody and scales.

In the 4th octave, again, there is a proportional division which produces more intervals. The first interval in this octave (9:8) is a whole-tone that is ideal for 12-equal temperament. The 9th harmonic—being a multiple of the 3rd harmonic—shares the structural (near perfect) acoustic properties of the fifth. (Review page 43.)

TONALITY   The whole-tone is ambiguous because it appears in the harmonic series in both positions—the root on top (8:7) and the root on the bottom (9:8). (Refer to the diagram on page 76.) The tonality of a whole-tone usually mimics the harmonic series, whether the interval is a 2nd, 7th or 9th.

SPAN   The whole-tone has great melodic potential—it is probably the most natural interval to sing. The span is critical, as a whole-tone is sometimes perceived as a half-tone.

RESONANCE   The ninth contains the tonal and structural characteristics of the fifth, as it is a projection of two fifths. When collapsed to a whole-tone, those qualities are combined with the compressed vibrancy of a second.

▶ HALF-TONE

Continuing to the 5th octave of the harmonic series, the 9:8 whole-tone is harmonically divided to produce 17:16, a very accurate equal-tempered half-tone. (Refer to page 47.)

TONALITY   Because the half-tone is the smallest unit used in equal temperament, it contains no index of tonality; either tone could be a root.

SPAN   Melodically, a half-tone is conspicuous. Even when not functioning as the traditional leading tone, half-tone movement is perceptible, as one tone is usually harmonic (a chord tone) and the other tone non-harmonic. Concentrate on singing and hearing a half-tone until the movement is definite.

RESONANCE   There is little doubt when hearing a half-tone, as the vibrant "buzz" is apparent in any type of vertical. A half-tone, added to an established vertical tonality, lends a sense of sadness, drama or emotional depth.

♦ FINE TUNING

The basic materials of melody are whole-tones and half-tones. Various combinations of major and minor seconds define the scale configuration of each mode.

Interchanging major and minor seconds is a common error in perception. The goal here is to never confuse the two intervals—each has a distinct, characteristic sound. The whole-tone is a powerful interval; it is stable, harmonic, and independent. On the other hand, the half-tone is fluid, melodic; it begs to move, to resolve. While the vertical whole-tone creates a rich, prominent drone, the half-tone creates a "buzz," suggesting activity, anxiety or turmoil.

Since music space is virtual space, you can imagine intervals to be any size. Exaggerate to clarify and distinguish between a whole-tone and half-tone: Imagine a whole-tone to be a two-story building. Mentally sing a whole-tone as you look from the ground up to the roof of the second story. Next to it is a single story building. Sing a half-tone as you look at it. If you can keep the whole-tone and half-tone in perspective, the difference between them will always be distinct.

Sing the following combinations of whole-tones and half-tones.

EXERCISE 31
1—2—8—9—8—♭7—8—2—1.

EXERCISE 32
1—♭2—8—♭9—8—♮7—1—♭2—1.

EXERCISE 33
(slowly) 1—♭2—♮2—♭2—1.

EXERCISE 34
(slowly) 8—♮7—♭7—♮7—8.

THE TRITONE

It is curious that while the fifth divides the octave harmonically, the tritone divides the octave linearly. It has the ambiguity to be a flat fifth or sharp fourth and the symmetry of containing six half-tones, three whole-tones and two minor thirds.

RESONANCE   The tritone has its own distinct sound. It contains the brightness of the whole-tone and major third, yet the mellowness of the minor thirds that it encompasses. The tritone is the determining factor in the dominant seventh chord and its extensions; its presence or absence is felt immediately. Identify the tritone in dominant chords, not only the 3rd/7th, but altered tones such as ROOT/#11, 5/b9, 9/b13 and #9/13.

Traditional harmony treats the tritone as the restless interval, yearning for resolution either up or down a half-tone. In the late nineteenth century, composers such as Satie and Debussy used the tritone to emphasize tone color, rather than formal progression. During the 1940s and 1950s, jazz innovator Thelonious Monk incorporated the tritone as an integral part of his style, allowing it to sustain unresolved in melody and occasionally to replace the fifth as a resolved vertical structure.

SPAN   How we perceive a tritone depends on its function: if there is melodic movement, the tension/resolution will be felt. It may be helpful to slide up or down a half-tone to find the proximity of a fifth or fourth. The tritone is the essential ingredient of dominant seventh-type verticals and the bridge to chromatic music.

EXERCISE 35

Sing, ascending and descending, until comfortable:
1—5—TT; 1—TT. 1—4—TT; 1—TT. 1—TT—8—TT—1.

TONALITY   A truly symmetrical interval; either tone may be the root. The choice depends on the context of the moment. While an isolated tritone is singular, it has dual, contrasting roles as either a flat fifth or a sharp fourth. In terms of hearing, we need only acknowledge the interval as a tritone. When committing to notation, it is necessary to decide if we're hearing a flat fifth or a sharp fourth.

The tritone as flat fifth is related to the minor third—heavy, dark, a "blue" tone, resolving to the fourth if at all. Conversely, the tritone as sharp fourth is perceived as Lydian—light and bright, related to the major third. If it resolves, it will resolve upward to the fifth. Note that the lydian tone (♯4) coexists with the natural fifth and the ♭5 coexists with the natural fourth. The flat fifth and sharp fourth define the opposite ends of the modal spectrum—Locrian and Lydian.

The tritone is as important as the half-tone in determining tonality and modality. Because a diatonic scale contains only one tritone, its unique position within each mode is definitive. (Modality is discussed in section 6.)

EXERCISE 36

Sing: Tritone as sharp four (lydian): 1—♯4—5. 8—♯4—5.
Tritone as a flat five: 1—♭5—4. 8—♭5—4.

EXERCISE 37

Learn to name—immediately—the tritone relationship of any given note. (What is the tritone of A♭? etc.)

The tritone is unique among all intervals. Its sound is distinct and its presence—melodically or vertically—is conspicuous. Listen for tritones in all musical contexts.

> You've completed the basic interval set. If you are familiar and comfortable with the fifth, fourth, thirds, seconds and tritone, you are ready to expand your interval palette.

COMPLEMENTARY INTERVALS

When dividing the octave at any point, the resulting intervals are complementary. The traditional term "inversion" may be confusing when applied to intervals. In the interest of clarity, we'll use "complement" when referring to intervals and "inversion" when referring to chords.

Complementary intervals have their own distinct identities, yet share some of the qualities of their harmonic counterparts. Completing the span of an octave are the sevenths and sixths.

♭ MAJOR SEVENTH

TONALITY   Unlike its complement, the minor second, the major seventh has gained a strong presence as an independent interval and exhibits a definite sense of tonality with the lower tone as the root. We may hear the implied chord-tones, filling in a complete major seventh chord. The interval itself is a stark outline of that chord and may be perceived as biting, lonely or dramatic.

SPAN   Just short of an octave, the major seventh may have a tendency to resolve by expanding or contracting by a half-tone. However, as the perimeter of a major seventh chord, the interval stands resolved.

RESONANCE   may vary with context. A complete major seventh chord may be mellow and dignified while the stark, isolated interval emits the buzz of a minor second, although somewhat softened by the open span.

EXERCISE 38

1—7—8—7—1. 8—♭2—1—♭2—8.

EXERCISE 39

Name the note a major seventh above and below any given note.

♦ MINOR SEVENTH

TONALITY   The harmonic series provides a minor seventh (7:4). Unusable as a 12-equal interval, it nevertheless retains its harmonic identity; therefore the lower tone is usually perceived as the root. The interval itself can function as a 7th chord without the inner chord-tones sounding.

SPAN   The minor seventh is a common jazz keyboard voicing for the left hand—a combination of comfortable hand position, economy of voicing and rich sound. The interval has the same function in lower brass, wood-wind and string voicings. When necessary, mentally fill in the implied chord-tones, completing the familiar dominant 7th chord.

RESONANCE   It possesses the strength of its complement, the major second: rich and vibrant in the lower registers and ringing in the upper registers.

EXERCISE 40

1—♭7—8—♭7—1. 8—2—1—2—8.

EXERCISE 41

Name the note a minor seventh above and below various notes.

♦ FINE TUNING
Although the spans of the major and minor sevenths are similar, there is little danger of confusing them if the qualities of tonality and resonance are observed.

EXERCISE 42

Proceed up a major scale: 1—7—2—8—3—9, etc., deciding whether each seventh is major or minor.

▶ MAJOR SIXTH

TONALITY Like its complement, the minor third, the tonality of the major sixth is ambiguous; you may hear the lower or upper tone as the root depending on musical context.

SPAN The closeness of the minor third produces a unified sound, whereas the open voicing of the major sixth allows us to hear each tone independently.

RESONANCE The richness and mellowness of the minor third is contained in the major sixth.

EXERCISE 43

Sing a major sixth above the root, then below. Recognizing the complementary minor third may help establish the major sixth.

EXERCISE 44

1—5—6. 1—6.
8—6—1.
1—6—8—6—1.

EXERCISE 45

8—♭3—1—♭3—8.

▶ MINOR SIXTH

TONALITY　Ambiguous: the root may be the upper or lower tone. The minor sixth may in fact be an augmented fifth; musical context determines spelling.

SPAN　If you hear the lower tone as the root, you may sing up a fifth, then a half-tone to arrive at the minor sixth. If the upper tone seems to be the root, the interval is easily perceived as the compliment of a major third.

EXERCISE 46

Listen to an isolated minor sixth. Concentrate on hearing the upper tone as the root then the lower tone as the root.

EXERCISE 47

1—5—♭6. 1—♭6.

EXERCISE 48

1—♭6—8—♭6—1.
8—♭6—1—♭6—8.

EXERCISE 49

8—5—3. 8—3.

RESONANCE　The minor sixth possesses the brightness of the major third. Its proximity just above the fifth adds a certain amount of unresolved tension, an edge.

▶ FINE TUNING

Like the thirds, the sixths are often used in parallel voicing, interchanging major and minor according to the prevailing mode. In diatonic music, the incidence of major or minor sixths are determined by the mode and any exception (altered scale-tone) will be obvious to the ear. In non-diatonic music, great care is required to determine if a sixth is major or minor. Use tonality, span, and resonance to perceive accurately.

EXTENDED INTERVALS

We usually perceive music in segments of two-octave spans: Most melodies occur within a two-octave range and our system of chord structure spans two octaves. Intervals which exceed an octave, both melodically and vertically, are distinct entities.

The larger intervals may be perceived either as transpositions of their corresponding primary intervals or as components of extended chords, depending on musical context. When an extended interval is not immediately recognized, you may transpose either tone one octave, collapsing the interval to within an octave.

▶ NINTHS

The MAJOR NINTH has a stronger tonality than the major second due to its position in the harmonic series. Its resonance is more fifth-like, open, as it does not possess the compressed "buzz" of the second.

The MINOR NINTH is the most biting of intervals. In a traditional setting, it would scream for resolution; in modern usage, it is reserved for moments of extreme intensity. Both the major and minor ninth should be discernible without collapsing to seconds.

▶ TENTHS

The MAJOR TENTH, like the ninth, is in a powerful tonal position, a natural harmonic. Once you have experienced this interval, it will always be recognized instantly.

The MINOR TENTH is simply a minor third in melodic context. As a vertical structure, it functions as a ♯9. (See CHORDS, section 9.)

▶ ELEVENTHS

Sometimes referred to as the NATURAL ELEVENTH, this interval functions melodically as a fourth and vertically as the perimeter of the dominant eleventh chord.

The AUGMENTED ELEVENTH, when an isolated interval, may function as a tritone (♯4 or ♭5) but does not possess the resonance of a tritone; the octave-plus span decreases the characteristic tritone sound. When it is the perimeter of a vertical structure, the augmented eleventh encompasses a rich sonority.

▶ TWELFTH

The TWELFTH appears in the harmonic series as a transposed fifth and has all the characteristics of a fifth. There is no extended vertical equivalent; a fifth is a fifth in any octave.

▶ THIRTEENTHS

Melodically, a transposed sixth. Vertically, a quite different sound, as the THIRTEENTH interval usually embodies a dominant-type chord. The sixth is quite passive, whereas a dominant thirteenth chord contains the bite of a major seventh span (7th/13th) as well as a tritone (3rd/7th).

Likewise, a melodic MINOR THIRTEENTH is merely a transposed minor sixth, while a FLAT THIRTEENTH implies dominant qualities in a vertical context.

Sixths and thirteenths are quite different in sound and function. The sixth is a tone added to a triad while the thirteenth normally implies the presence of a dominant 7th. (See CHORDS, section 9.)

EXERCISE 50

Sing the extended intervals using intermediate patterns such as:
1—8—9;   1—5—9;   1—3—5—♭7—9;   1—9—1.

THE INTERVAL PALETTE

This completes the study of the 12-equal intervals and their extensions. We've looked at the harmonic implications and the unique traits of each.

The first four octaves of the harmonic series have provided the basic interval set that defines our music. Each pair of intervals has a particular function. The fifth and fourth are structural and possess a strong sense of tonality. The seconds are the components of melody. The thirds combine elements of both. Complementary and extended intervals contain some traits of the basic interval set.

EXERCISE 51

Create each interval using a steady tone source and a movable tone or your voice, as you did in section 3.

REVIEW

1   Sharpen your perception of the interval set so that you recognize any interval as instantly as you recognize a color.

2   Sing each interval with comfort and confidence. Be able to reproduce immediately any interval, whether sightreading, improvising or writing.

3   Review the interval pairs and continue to work on those distinctions until you are confident you will never confuse them.

6

HEARING PHRASES

6

HEARING PHRASES

In this section, all previous work is utilized to develop your perception of the line, which leads to the perception of counterpoint and vertical sonorities in later sections.

When intervals are combined into melodic lines or vertical sonorities, they interact to produce meaningful musical statements in which some intervals predominate and others play secondary roles. While each interval retains its unique characteristics, the interaction creates dynamic relationships of tonality, contour and harmonic context.

 MODULES OF MUSIC

All structures of nature and art are composed of a few basic shapes.

Music, like all art, is constructed of simple elements that have little or no significance until they are composed or arranged into relationships. A musical tone contains very little information or aesthetic value. Two tones form an interval that delineates a portion of musical space, defines a harmonic ratio, infers tonality, contains perhaps a reference of some personal significance. Add another tone and musical meaning increases exponentially. Ancient unison melodies of the Jewish temple and Eastern Christian churches were created by combining short melodic motives.

You are now ready to increase your speed and accuracy, to move past the tedious stage of hearing one interval at a time, to perceive music in phrases. Nothing you encounter will be new because every line is merely

a combination of familiar intervals. Eventually, you will gain the capacity to perceive increasingly longer phrases and quickly notate them. Hearing lines is the means to hearing and notating *all* music, even complex
scores.

A musical *phrase* is a statement, the equivalent of a sentence, often the length
of one breath. In jazz terminology, a *lick* is the smallest group of notes that
constitute a meaningful statement, perhaps 3 to 10 notes. In traditional
terminology, a *motive (Fr. motif)* is "The briefest intelligible and self-existent
melodic or rhythmic unit, consisting of two notes or more." (Oxford
Dictionary of Music.) Whatever term you prefer—phrase, lick or motive—
it is the building block of music and *its intrinsic or implied meaning is
contained in the intervals.*

For our purpose, a phrase is any portion of a melodic line, as short or as
long as is comfortable to work with. Starting with short phrases, then
gradually increasing your perception, you'll eventually be able to internalize
and reproduce—vocally, instrumentally, or in notation—any line that
you encounter.

When listening to a phrase, take a step back and try to absorb the whole
phrase or a segment of it as a unit. Some phrases may be as familiar as
common words and instantly perceived. Rather than thinking, "That's
an ascending fifth followed by a descending major second, followed by
a descending minor second, followed by a descending major second,"
your mind will conclude, "Oh, that's one of those." Instant recognition
of a phrase or segment is possible if we are aware of common patterns of
tonal organization. Often a complex phrase is merely a familiar phrase
with one or two tones altered chromatically.

When you encounter difficulty with an interval, use your inner voice,
slowing down the tempo so you can focus on the problem. Employ one or
more of the tools—tonality, span or resonance. In this section, you'll acquire tools for the perception of a phrase. Your subconscious will provide
the applicable tools for the musical context of the moment. Eventually, you
will gain confidence and speed; your ears and mind will be open and
prepared for any musical endeavor.

TETRACHORD MODES

> The division of the scale into octaves, and the octave into two
> analogous tetrachords, occurs everywhere, almost without exception.
> Helmholtz: *On the Sensations of Tone*

A tetrachord spans the interval of a fourth and contains scale tones which may be arranged to produce various diatonic configurations, or modes. As early as 1000 B.C., the Greeks used tetrachords as a system of tuning as well as a source of vocal and instrumental melody.

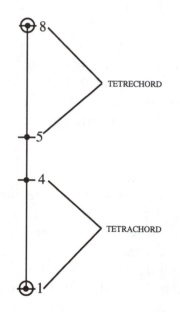

In order to perceive a phrase intelligibly, we must hear each interval accurately. Melodic lines, counter lines and inner parts are constructed mostly of small intervals with an occasional leap of a fifth or larger interval. We can sharpen our perception of the line by concentrating first on combinations of the smaller intervals. The tetrachord provides an accessible means to those intervals.

Each mode embodies a characteristic sound which may be identified aurally. Since all configurations of seconds and thirds are addressed, the study of tetrachords leads to flawless perception.

▸ DIATONIC TETRACHORDS

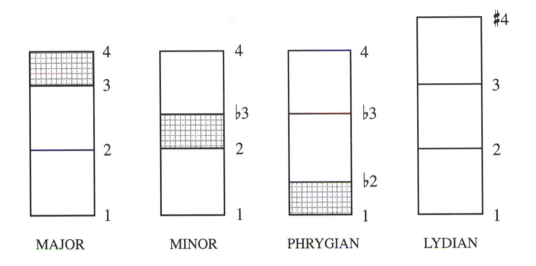

MAJOR   MINOR   PHRYGIAN   LYDIAN

The location (or absence) of a half-tone within the tetrachord provides an index to the unique combination of intervals that describes the sound of the mode.

EXERCISE 52

Sing up and down each tetrachord mode, carefully forming each whole-tone or half-tone. Associate the name of each tetrachord with its characteristic configuration (visualize) and its distinct sound (internalize).

EXERCISE 53

Sing and identify the mode of the following phrases.

1—4—♭3—1—2.

1—♭2—4—♭3—1.

1—3—2—♯4—3.

1—3—4—2—1.

▸ EXOTIC TETRACHORDS

Combining two modal traits produces tetrachord modes containing an augmented second, more characteristic of Eastern music than Western. We'll label exotic tetrachords according to their characteristic tones. Since Phrygian normally implies a minor third, we'll specify only when Phrygian and major exist in the same tetrachord. Likewise, Lydian and the minor third.

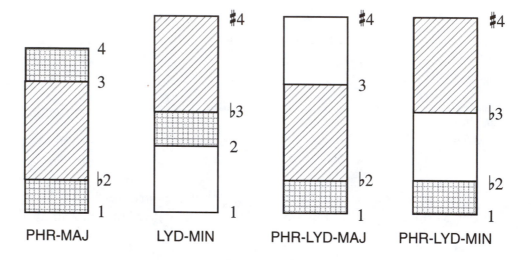

PHR-MAJ   LYD-MIN   PHR-LYD-MAJ   PHR-LYD-MIN

It is important to differentiate the augmented second from the minor third. As isolated intervals, they are the same but in the context of a scale or line, they are products of particular scale-tones. An augmented second is formed by two adjacent scale-tones (such as ♭3, ♯4), whereas a minor third encompasses a middle scale-tone (such as ♭3, ♭5).

EXERCISE 54

Sing up and down each exotic tetrachord mode, carefully forming each interval.

1—♭2—3—4—3—♭2—1.

1—♭3—2—♯4—♭3—♯4—♭3.

1—♭2—♭3—♯4—♭3—♭2—1.

EXERCISE 55

Sing and identify the mode of the following phrases.

1—4—3—♭2—1.

1—2—♭3—♯4—♭3—2—1.

1—♯4—♭3—♭2—1.

1—♭2—3—♯4—3—♭2—1.

The tetrachord has proven to be most valuable in the perception of a phrase. Even a phrase of three tones has a particular character which we can identify as characteristic of a mode. When you are familiar with the tetrachord modes, you will have mastered the most frequent interval combinations, the substance of every phrase.

In the diatonic modes on the following page, observe the evolving pattern of upper and lower tetrachords and their influence on the sound of each mode.

DIATONIC MODES

A diatonic scale is generally understood to possess seven tones within an octave, each tone occupying only one scale position, such as a minor third or major third, but not both. The particular arrangement of intervals provides the diatonic scale with a tonal identity and functional economy that is the foundation of much of the world's music. People can easily identify and sing any melody that is diatonic.

The diatonic scale may be configured in seven modes, simply by establishing tonality on any one of the seven tones. The seven diatonic modes share the same interval content: six 5ths, five major 2nds, four minor 3rds, three major 3rds, two minor 2nds and one tritone.

Each diatonic mode—like each tetrachord—is unique, aurally recognizable by its interval pattern. Each tetrachord contributes its respective sound to the diatonic mode. Since you are now familiar with the tetrachord modes, all configurations of the diatonic scale are immediately accessible.

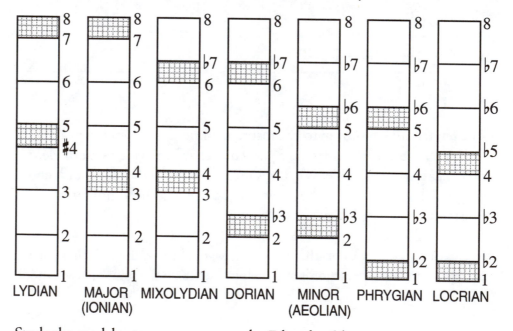

LYDIAN   MAJOR   MIXOLYDIAN DORIAN   MINOR   PHRYGIAN LOCRIAN
           (IONIAN)   (AEOLIAN)

Study the modal patterns—compare the 7ths, the 6ths, etc.

◗ Diatonic Modes as related to a single tonic:

Mode	C Tonality
LYDIAN	1 sharp
MAJOR	natural
MIXOLYDIAN	1 flat
DORIAN	2 flats
MINOR	3 flats
PHRYGIAN	4 flats
LOCRIAN	5 flats

◗ Diatonic Modes as related to a single key signature:

Mode	C Modality (white keys)
LYDIAN	F LYDIAN scale
MAJOR	C MAJOR scale
MIXOLYDIAN	G MIXOLYDIAN scale
DORIAN	D DORIAN scale
MINOR	A MINOR scale
PHRYGIAN	E PHRYGIAN scale
LOCRIAN	B LOCRIAN scale

Become familiar with these relationships. Notice that the (5th-related) pattern of diatonic modes corresponds to the cycle of key signatures.

‣ HEARING MODES

We are able to recognize modes aurally because of their unique pattern of intervals. Each mode provides a characteristic sound which may be identified aurally, due to the location of its half-tones and the tritone.

All orchestral instruments are configured in the key of C (except the trombone, in which the first position is B♭). The "natural" key of C sounds at various pitches according to the instrument's size and its transposition. (An E♭ instrument sounds an E♭ scale while playing a C scale.) Because the diatonic scale is asymmetrical, we are able to perceive the relationship of each scale tone at any pitch.

If you heard someone running up or down the white keys of a keyboard, the interval pattern would allow you to identify tones as actual notes. Only one diatonic scale has a half-tone immediately below and another half-tone between the third and fourth scale-tones above. Those audible clues (leading tones) "point" to **C** as the root of the major mode on the white keys.

Once tonality is applied—simply by starting or ending on a particular note—a mode becomes apparent to the ear. If you start on **E** and run up and down the white keys, you are hearing the Phrygian mode on E. Similarly, you could identify the **D** as the root of the Dorian mode or the **A** as the root of the minor mode or any other note according to its place in the diatonic pattern.

The modes are transposable; each of the 12 notes is a potential root of each of the seven modes. The result is a complete system of 12 diatonic/modal scales, all accessible by ear.

EXERCISE 56

Sing up and down the scale of each mode, visualizing the pattern of whole-tones and half-tones. Notice the unique position of the tritone in each mode. If you need a visual guide, refer to page 108.

EXERCISE 57

Continue singing freely in one mode until you feel comfortable with the intervals and familiar with the sound. Repeat in each mode.

EXERCISE 58

Indicate the corresponding key signature (number of sharps or flats) to designate the following modes:

F MINOR

G LYDIAN

Eb DORIAN

Db MIXOLYDIAN

F# MAJOR

Ab MINOR

E LYDIAN

A PHRYGIAN

B DORIAN

C LOCRIAN

D MIXOLYDIAN

Bb PHRYGIAN

MODALITY AS A TOOL

While the 5th and 4th provide structure and tonal stability within the octave, the remaining scale-tones provide variety and color. The 2nd, 3rd, 6th and 7th—in either major or minor configuration—complete the diatonic scale. Combinations of these four color tones produce the modal variations.

The ear's preference for perfect 5ths, rather than tritones, created altered scales, or modes. The simple altering of a scale-tone by a half-tone *(musica ficta)* to avoid a tritone led to the formalization of the modes. The modes changed names several times as they evolved from the ancient Greeks to the Ecclesiastical modes of the early Christian Church and again before the present day nomenclature was established. As harmony became structured, the Lydian and Mixolydian modes merged into the major (Ionian) mode and the Phrygian and Dorian modes merged into the minor (Aeolian) mode.

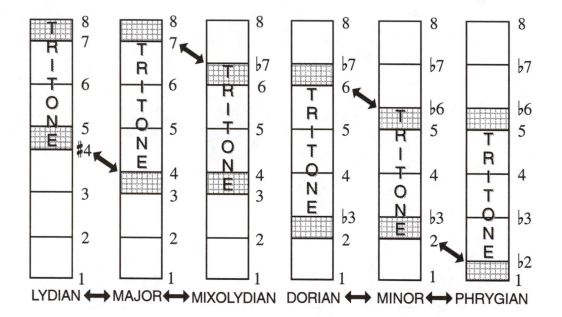

LYDIAN ⟷ MAJOR ⟷ MIXOLYDIAN   DORIAN ⟷ MINOR ⟷ PHRYGIAN

In modern practice, we normally indicate key signatures for major and minor modes and use accidentals to express the other modes.

♦ MODAL EFFECTS

What is useful to us today is the *effect* of each mode, its unique intervallic configuration, immediately apparent to the ear. Surviving modal effects are:

LYDIAN—augmented 4th scale degree
MIXOLYDIAN—minor 7th in the major mode
DORIAN—major 6th in the minor mode
PHRYGIAN—minor 2nd scale degree

A modal effect is evident to the ear due to the alteration of a particular scale-tone, a departure from the usual major or minor scale configuration. Notice that the altered tone is always a component of the tritone. (See opposite page.) The tritone plays an integral role in producing the modal effect.

A mode may govern an entire piece of music but more often a momentary modal effect is utilized to give a unique quality to a melody or harmonic progression.

LYDIAN (Prokofiev: *Lt. Kije Suite*)

DORIAN (Traditional: *Scarborough Fair*)

▶ MODAL SHIFTING

Changing the mode creates subtle differences in a melodic line. Scale-degrees may be altered by a half-tone while preserving the melodic contour.

EXERCISE 59

Sing the following phrase, altering scale-tones accordingly to place the phrase in the specified mode:

  1—5—6—4—5—2—3—7—8.

  1) MAJOR
  2) MINOR
  3) LYDIAN
  4) DORIAN
  5) MIXOLYDIAN
  6) PHRYGIAN

EXERCISE 60

Repeat, applying each diatonic mode to the following phrase:
  1—3—5—4—6—7—5—2—1.

EXERCISE 61

Repeat, applying each diatonic mode to the following phrase:
  4—7—3—5—2—3—6—2—7—6—4—3—8.

Each mode possesses a characteristic identity, a unique interval pattern. Take the time to learn the sound of each mode so that you will be aware of modal effects whenever you encounter them.

▶ COMBINED MODES

Other combinations of tetrachords produce intriguing modes. Notice that these modes contain two tritones.

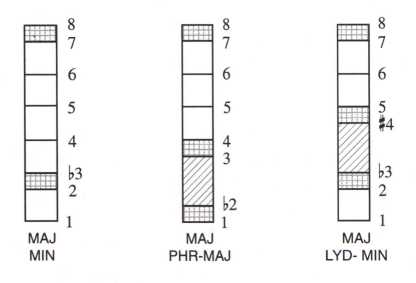

▶ COMBINED EXOTIC MODES

The exotic tetrachords, combined with the Phrygian/major upper tetrachord, produce 7-tone exotic modes. Notice the four half-tones.

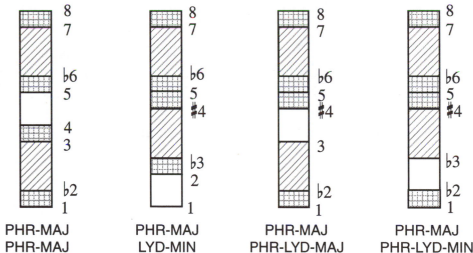

♦ PENTATONIC MODES

The superimposition of four fifths generates the 5-tone pentatonic scale, which may be configured in five modes. Since there are no half-tones in the pentatonic scale, each mode may be identified by its particular arrangement of three whole-tones and two minor thirds. The pentatonic modes are less distinguishable from each other because of the absence of half-tones and tritones

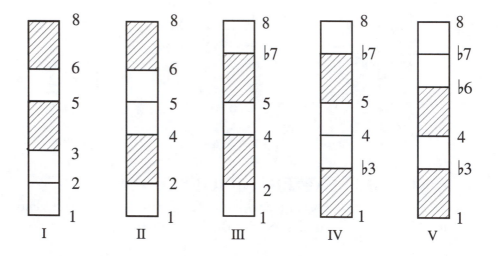

The study of modes is an important tool of perception; the goal is to hear and think groups of tones rather than one at a time. Familiarity with the diatonic modes is essential for the perception of both Eastern and Western music.

You now have the ability to easily perceive any melodic line because you've experienced every combination of intervals; **you've heard it all.**

▶ SYMMETRICAL STRUCTURES

A chord or scale containing equal intervals is not modal because the symmetry offers no unique pattern of identification, no index of tonality. Symmetrical structures retain their interval patterns when inverted.

Symmetrical scales or chords do not contain intrinsic tonality. Any tonality associated with a symmetrical structure is the result of musical context—one of the tones may be prominent or placed in the bass. Composers have used symmetrical structures to represent the absence of gravity (floating in the sky or in the sea) and disorientation (dreams, drunkenness, drug trips, neurosis, fear).

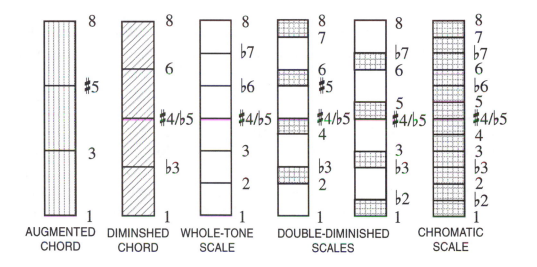

| AUGMENTED CHORD | DIMINISHED CHORD | WHOLE-TONE SCALE | DOUBLE-DIMINISHED SCALES | CHROMATIC SCALE |

EXERCISE 62

Sing up and down each symmetrical structure (chord or scale) until you feel comfortable. Be sure that when you reach an octave your tonal memory verifies the pitch against the initial tone. The double-diminished scale is reversible (start with either a whole-tone or half-tone).

TONALITY AS A TOOL

Sing a tone—"ah." You've established tonality,
simply by sounding a pitch that dominates your perception.

Tonality is perhaps our greatest tool for hearing music. Without it, we would hear unrelated tones without meaning. The perception of music, like that of the solar system, requires a point of reference. Tonality provides such a reference.

When we look at abstract art, the mind creates relationships of shapes and colors, and a sense of orientation with the earth, with gravity. When we hear tones, even random tones, the mind perceives tonal relationships. Even when music is deliberately atonal, we will try to form tonal relationships.

Our goal is to be able to perceive and notate any music, regardless of its style or structure. To that end, we need not be analytical; we simply use tonality as a tool of perception when it is evident. For our purpose, tonality is temporary and fluid, having little relevance to previous or subsequent phrases.

If we use the TONAL STRUCTURE (refer to pages 42 and 79) as a mental template, the relationship of each tone within a phrase will be apparent. As a melody progresses up and down the diatonic/chromatic palette, each tone occupies a place in the tonal structure. When the tonality shifts, the tonal structure shifts accordingly. This shifting of tonality (modulation) is the essence of Western harmony.

The TONAL STRUCTURE provides a template, a map of tonality, which may be utilized in the perception of a phrase.

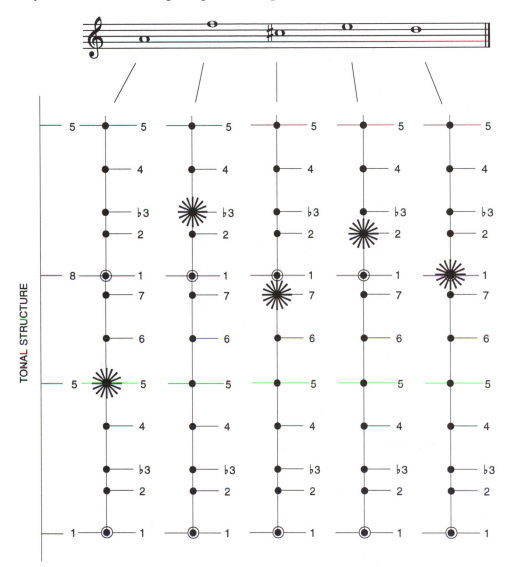

Tonality is implied in the intervallic relationship of **A** to **D** (5 to 8 or 5 to 1), this being the only fifth/root relationship found in the phrase.

The minor 3rd and major 7th indicate the minor/major mode (minor lower tetrachord/major upper tetrachord).

▶ DIATONIC PHRASES

The tonality intrinsic in each interval contributes to our perception of a phrase. However, each person may interpret the influence of tonality a little differently. *Tonality is a subjective tool.*

In the following diatonic phrase, the tonality may shift as we progress. Here are four possibilities of applying tonality.

EXERCISE 63
TONAL SHIFTING
Sing the following diatonic phrase.

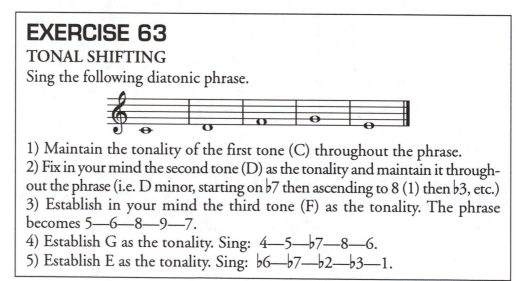

1) Maintain the tonality of the first tone (C) throughout the phrase.
2) Fix in your mind the second tone (D) as the tonality and maintain it throughout the phrase (i.e. D minor, starting on ♭7 then ascending to 8 (1) then ♭3, etc.)
3) Establish in your mind the third tone (F) as the tonality. The phrase becomes 5—6—8—9—7.
4) Establish G as the tonality. Sing: 4—5—♭7—8—6.
5) Establish E as the tonality. Sing: ♭6—♭7—♭2—♭3—1.

♦ CHROMATIC PHRASES

After the dust has cleared from the musical revolution of the 20th century, we are left with 12 tones which we may use freely or methodically, with various degrees of tonality.

The term chromatic refers to the use of altered diatonic intervals, or a non-diatonic 12-tone music which we may prefer to label non-tonal, atonal or abstract. We use all that we have learned about diatonic music, with its seven modes and altered tones, to aid in the perception of non-diatonic music.

Even when there is no apparent tonality, we are not prevented from making our way through any melodic line. Each tone, however remote, maintains an intervallic relationship with preceding tones. We may identify several consecutive tones as a tonal group, then proceed to the next perceived tonal group.

When you're grounded firmly in tonality,
you're free to move through chromatic space.

EXERCISE 64

Sing the following phrase. Use any available tone as a pitch source. For this exercise, pretend that the source tone is an F♯. After singing, check your pitch source. Does it match your last note?

When you encounter abstract lines, where the tonality is not apparent, let your ear guide you in perceiving tonality where you find it. In Thelonious Monk's *Ruby, My Dear,* there are three sequential phrases followed by two sequential phrases. Once we find the tonal center of each 4-note phrase, a familiar shape is revealed. Then it is a matter of finding the relationship of one phrase to the next. Of course, harmonic accompaniment (chord structure) solidifies the tonality of each phrase, but we can benefit from singing this tune a cappella. If you have never heard this tune, you may hear different tonal centers—that's okay: remember that tonality is a subjective tool.

Ruby, My Dear by Thelonious Monk © 1945 (renewed) by Embassy Music Corporation (BMI)
Int'l. Copyright Secured   All Rights Reserved   Reprinted by Permission

EXERCISE 65

Sing the following 12-tone rows, using a reference pitch for the first tone (any tone will do). After singing the last tone, repeat the first tone and check it against the reference tone. Employ tools as necessary: tonality of segments, modality, familiar contours.

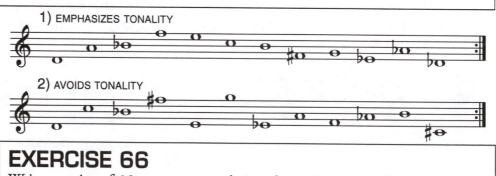

EXERCISE 66

Write a series of 12-tone rows and sing them. Be aware of when you are emphasizing or avoiding tonality.

♦ SEQUENCES

Sequences are patterns of modulation which are usually governed by diatonic, chromatic or symmetrical organization. If the intervals of a sequence are altered to accommodate the prevailing scale, mode or harmony, we refer to it as *diatonic*. If the intervals are absolute, the sequence is *chromatic*. Sequences are an effective compositional device; everyone recognizes them, even if subconsciously.

♦ Diatonic sequence: Haydn: *Symphony #95:* IV @ c. :53

♦ Chromatic sequence: Hindemith: *Concert Music for Strings and Brass* @ c. 2:34

♦ Symmetrical sequences: John Coltrane: *Bass Blues* @3:10

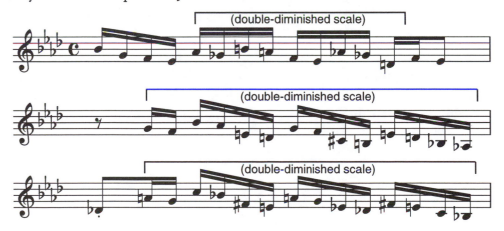

PERCEPTION OF A PHRASE

At this time, we are still not concerned with actual pitch or the key of a phrase. We want to continue perceiving lines "in the air" so that when it is time to commit to the music staff, we can easily notate at any pitch or in any key.

TIPS: TO PERCEIVE AND REMEMBER A PHRASE:

▶ Sing or internalize the phrase, slowing down if necessary.

▶ Visualize and identify each interval by name.

▶ Determine the nature of the phrase—modal or chromatic. Identify the tonal center(s).

▶ Visualize the general shape of the phrase as an accumulative span of intervals.

▶ As you scan the melodic horizon, look for points of interest—high and low tones, chromatic tones, large leaps, unusual intervals.

▶ Notice rhythmic shape—the relative duration of each tone.

▶ Is there harmonic implication? Do some tones outline a chord?

▶ Assign an arbitrary note-name to the first note and determine the name of each successive note.

Eventually, you will be able to perceive any phrase without consciously thinking of notes or intervals. This leads to the ultimate technique of playing or notating any phrase in any key—spontaneously.

TOOL KIT #3

SYMBOLS BECOME SHAPES
When intervals are joined together, meaningful phrases result. Following
are tools to help guide you through any type of line that you might encounter.

TONALITY

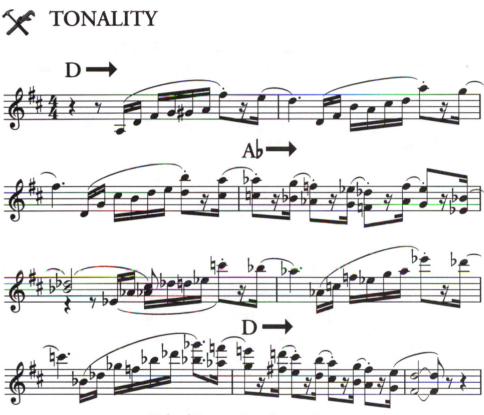

Richard Strauss: *Don Quixote* @ :13

This passage, depicting the noble, yet bewildered Quixote, is constructed
entirely of diatonic scale tones, governed by the tonalities D major, A♭ major,
and the return to D major.

⚒ MODALITY

Your familiarity with modes in tetrachord or scale form will aid greatly in the perception of phrases.

Dizzy Gillespie solo: *Africana* @ 3:36 (album: *Gillespiana;* composer: Lalo Schifrin)

Diz used the open (chordless) tonality of the first four bars as an opportunity to explore some exotic modes.

The first part of *Greensleeves* is in the Dorian mode (E minor with major 6th and minor 7th scale-tones.) Another version of the song uses C♮ instead of C♯, the minor, rather than the Dorian mode. The major 7th scale-tone is found at the half-cadence (bars 6 and 7) and the full cadence (bar 14), implying the minor/major mode.

Greensleeves (Traditional)

⚒ CONTOUR

The shape, or contour, of a melodic line describes its general nature. The intervals characterize its essence. Points of interest (high and low tones, large leaps, chromatic tones, unusual intervals) contribute to the uniqueness of a phrase and serve as aids when memorizing.

Your experience with intervals, modality and the tonal structure provide you with a sense of musical space, so that any phrase you encounter will have a certain amount of familiarity.

J. S. Bach: *The Well Tempered Clavier, Vol. I: Fugue #10*

Charlie Parker: *Laird Baird* @ :12 (album: *Now's The Time*)

⚒ CHORDAL HARMONY

The prevailing harmony, when applicable, contributes greatly to tonal identification.

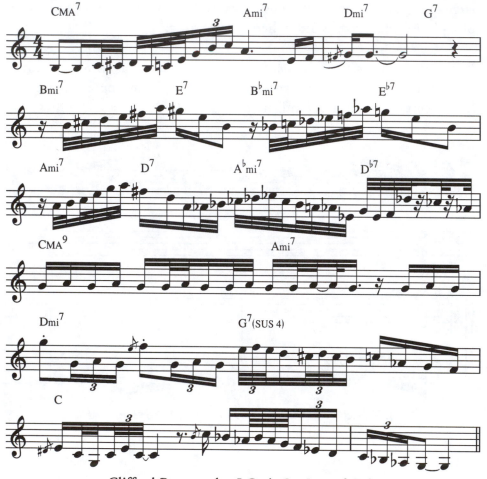

Clifford Brown solo: *I Can't Get Started* @:43
(album: *Max Roach and Clifford Brown in Concert*)

Listen to the complete improvisation to hear how Clifford incorporates sequences and variations each time he plays the chromatic progression (bars 3 and 4). Chords are explored in section 9.

The tools presented in this section—tonality, modality, contour and chordal harmony—will remain in your subconscious toolbox until you need them.

TONAL ORGANIZATION

The radiant beauty of a star may hold our attention for a while. Its position in the ever-evolving pattern of stellar bodies provides us with a means of recognizing and identifying the star. Similarly, the perception of a single tone gains identity and significance when surrounded by other tones.

The tones of music are usually organized in some manner which may or may not be immediately apparent. Awareness of tonal organization— the recognition of familiar patterns or motives—helps us to discern a phrase. Whether or not the music was consciously organized in a specific manner by the composer is unimportant; we are only concerned with immediate perception.

Tonal organization, if consistent throughout a song, movement or an extended work, helps to establish and maintain the style of the piece. In our pursuit of knowing what we hear, an awareness of different types of tonal organization can only be helpful. Determining the type of tonal organization is not an exercise in analysis. Rather, it is an instant, intuitive distinction that is obvious to the ear, another tool to aid in the perception of music.

TYPES OF TONAL ORGANIZATION—TONALITY

Perhaps the broadest category of tonal organization is the way in which tonality encompasses the music.

▶ MONOTONAL   Sustained, unchanging tonality; a single line over a drone. The basis of Eastern music.

▶ MODULATORY   Changing tonalities; modulating chord progressions. The basis of Western music.

▶ ABSTRACT   Abstract music, like abstract art, may contain no apparent order, no sense of gravity, no stylistic reference. Tonal relationships may be momentary or vague. However, with tools of conventional music, you may be able to reduce complex elements to familiar interval patterns.

▶ RANDOM   A collection of tones, tuned or untuned, sounding in a random order, such as wind-chimes. It is important to recognize randomness and not waste time trying to establish order when there is none.

Music of the world exists in two great traditions, Eastern and Western. We must generalize in order to include all music.

Eastern-type music refers to all music of the world from antiquity and continuing today in many traditions. It includes every culture on earth, music of every village on every continent, from primitive peoples who had music before speech was developed, to the refined styles of many great civilizations.

Western-type music, on the other hand, refers only to the polyphony that gradually developed during the middle ages, culminated in the Baroque, Classical and Romantic eras and continues today in orchestral music for concert and film as well as many styles of jazz, pop and rock music. The fundamental element that is unique to Western-type music is harmonic modulation, or chord progression.

In terms of music perception, we can distinguish the two basic types of music according to the manner in which it is organized and performed. Eastern-type music maintains one tonality while Western-type music tends to modulate, to change tonality, as typified by the movement of chords. While Eastern-type music is normally improvised on melodic patterns, Western-type music is either improvised on harmonic patterns or set in notation to enable the composition and performance of ensemble music. Eastern-type music achieves various degrees of complexity through fluid melodic and rhythmic development while Western-type music is vertically structured, developed on stylistic principles or formalized processing.

Present day music may blend these traditions, perhaps contrasting a chord progression with a "vamp" section based on one tonality. Music at any given moment is either monotonal or modulatory. A well-known example of combining monotonal and modulatory structure may be found in the tune *So What* on Miles Davis' *Kind of Blue* album.

TYPES OF TONAL ORGANIZATION—SCALE FORMS

A scale is the consecutive ordering of a number of tones, usually confined to within one octave. A "major scale" is the major mode in scale form. If you can maintain the distinction between scale and mode, it will help your perception.

Diatonic music is very accessible to the untrained ear, constructed of phrases that contain a certain amount of familiarity. Songs are usually limited to diatonic scale-tones, whereas instrumental music is more apt to include chromatically altered tones.

Chromatic music requires more scrutiny; the organization of tones may not be obvious. However, even a seemingly random tone-row contains segments of tonality that may be easily perceived.

Beyond chromatic lies microtonal music, which may be the result of an alternate temperament system, Just Intonation or simply a detuning of 12-equal intervals. See MICROTONAL INTERVALS, page 49.

TYPES OF TONAL MOVEMENT—TEXTURE

The way in which voices move is another consideration in our perception of music.

▶ MONOPHONIC   Single line melody without harmony or counterpoint.

▶ POLYPHONIC   Several lines moving independently, contrapuntally.

▶ HOMOPHONIC   Several lines moving together in parallel, as block chords.

▶ CHORDAL   Single line (melody) with accompaniment, governed by harmonic progression.

These broad categories trace the history of Western music from the development of chant—influenced by Eastern melodies—through the era of counterpoint to the formation of a system of chordal harmony. The labels are not important; the awareness of what you are hearing is important.

While traditional music is very stylistic, maintaining a single method of tonal organization, contemporary music may shift abruptly from one type to another. Today, you may encounter several types of movement integrated in one piece of music.

The many styles of the world's music were developed locally, spreading slowly from one region to another by traveling musicians until music printing enabled the publishing of music and further distribution. It was not until the 20th century that recorded music, air transportation and electronic media provided access to the world's music. Whether we choose to work within a traditional style or blend various styles, familiarity with music of the past will prepare us for any music that we may encounter.

EXERCISE 67

Choose a recording of a short orchestral piece or movement and determine how it is organized in terms of tonality, scale forms, and texture.

NUTS AND BOLTS

While your right brain is composing, improvising, interpreting, your left brain is busy with the nuts and bolts of music—intervallic relationships which are transformed into notes. This transformation—the process of hearing and writing (or performing) depends on your ability to manipulate music.

When the 12 tonalities (pitch names) are combined with the seven modalities (interval patterns), we are confronted with a matrix of multiple configurations, the diatonic system. If we are to be fluid in music, we must be familiar with every mode in every key.

This may seem overwhelming but it is really very simple—the solution is in your mind. Your eyes and ears are wonderful receptors, gathering huge amounts of information each second. However, your mind focuses on only one element at a time; your awareness is limited to one visual object or sound. The mind processes music as a computer functions: one step at a time although very fast.

Your training, then, is to attain familiarity with each mode in each key. When you have experienced all the intervallic relationships of a particular mode in a particular key center, it is yours for life. It just has to be dusted off once in a while to refresh your memory. When you are familiar with the 12 major and 12 minor modes (the diatonic key system), each remaining mode is merely a half-tone away. (Refer to page 112.) When you apply the modal variations to any key, you have reached complete chromatic freedom, you have access to all 12 tones through tonality. When you are grounded in tonality, you can always find your way home.

The memory of physically playing an instrument transfers much of the work of remembering to the fingers. Each time you experience an intervallic relationship while performing, it is reaffirmed, and you are a little more confident in your perception. You can use the same "muscle memory" when writing or listening to music, solidifying each interval within a key or tonality.

These nuts and bolts are the mechanics of music—your basic tools.

Your technique becomes fluid as you develop the ability to change gears; to "be" in one modality/tonality and instantly change to another. These are the dynamic relationships of Western-type music, to be continually developed throughout one's lifetime.

Much of the groundwork of making music is becoming familiar with these relationships. To gain command of the tonal/modal matrix, slow down, focus, become intimate with each interval in the context of each key center. Your tools of the trade are knowing all the interval relationships. What is the fifth of the key of B? What is a major third below F? etc. Practice these relationships mentally at any time, all the time, until they are second nature. Your familiarity with the nuts and bolts of intervals and key centers will set you free to modulate effortlessly.

EXERCISE 68

Mentally sing or play a short phrase in the key of your choice. When you are internalizing a phrase, make a mental *loop,* repeating the phrase until you are familiar with it. Examine the characteristic intervals until you are able to reproduce it in any tonality.

EXERCISE 69

Transpose the same phrase to another key. Work in the keys that are most awkward until you are equally at ease in all keys.

Each key is a personality. Your experience of each key depends on the instrument you play, the music that you have learned in that key, etc. It is best to learn one key at a time—think in that key, hear in that key, *live* in that key for a few hours or a few days until you know each interval within that key and are able to play or notate any phrase in that key. The matrix of interval/key relationships is so extensive that you cannot learn all combinations immediately; your experience of them will deepen continually as you work with music. Your familiarity with each key will grow throughout your lifetime but concentrated effort now will bring you closer to your goals.

EXERCISE 70

Find a diatonic score, music with a key signature. It may be a simple orchestral piece, a concert band, marching band or swing band arrangement. Sing each part as a melody; *be the performer.* Of course, when you are working alone, the actual pitch is of no importance as long as you maintain the tonality. If you have a problem with a phrase, perhaps with chromatically altered tones, look for the harmonic implications in the score.

TRANSPOSITION

Transposition is a fact of life due to the many transposing instruments, as well as the necessity of shifting music up or down to accommodate vocal or instrumental registers. It is essential to be able to transpose quickly and accurately when arranging, orchestrating, copying or proofreading. Since any phrase or composition may be set in any key or tonality, the sound of the intervals must be retained even though the resulting notation will have a different "look" in each key.

You will always transpose correctly if you transpose aurally, rather than visually. Simply read the phrase, internalize, then repeat it (from memory) as you notate it in the new tonality or key. When you repeat it (singing or internalizing) keep it at the original pitch. Your pitch memory will verify that the repetition is the same as the original. You are hearing it at the same pitch both times but mentally changing the key. This *transposing on the fly,* thinking in two keys at once, is common among jazz players and classically trained brass and woodwind players. If you are not experienced at transposition, it will be worth your time to practice this technique. If you have your tools working, this method is fail-safe at any interval of transposition.

TRUST YOUR EAR!

SEE—HEAR

Read music with your ears; always singing internally as you read. Notes on a staff can be deceiving. If you merely look at notation, your perception is passive. If you *hear* what you are reading, each interval will be precise, your perception will always be accurate. While composing, orchestrating, copying, proofreading, scorereading: *perform* the music as you read or write.

INNER SKETCH PAD

How many times have you had a musical thought but forgot it before you could write it? Of course, you should have pencil and staff paper stashed in your bedroom, bathroom, car, etc. Following are tips to help you remember a phrase until you are able to capture it in notation.

Remember the phrase in terms of diatonic scale numbers, using **1** as the tonal center. You can place your phrase in any mode, indicating modality without thinking actual notes or key. You can also use this method to quickly sketch a phrase without staff paper. Simply write the numbers (scale-degrees) and assign rhythmic values by sketching eighth, quarter stems, etc. over or under.

TIPS: REMEMBERING A PHRASE

▶ Focus on melodic contour, characteristic intervals or suggestion of chord or chord progression.

▶ Repeat the phrase until familiar.

▶ Choose an arbitrary key and play the phrase on an imaginary instrument, establishing a physical connection through your fingers.

Hopefully, one of these tips will trigger your memory when you are able to notate.

THINK MUSIC

Use the experience of casual listening to refine your perception. Whatever music you happen to hear, follow along as if it were in the key of your choice, mentally naming notes or fingering an instrument. Always listen actively. It's an ongoing process of refinement that will pay off every day for the rest of your life.

As you sing, play or write a phrase, the procedure (perception/cognition/ execution) will become more cohesive until seamless. Ultimately, you will *know the sound* of every phrase.

TRAIN YOURSELF

The perception and creation of music is a personal experience and the process of learning music should be just as personal. Although there are many eartraining methods available in classes, audio media and software, it is strongly recommended that you create your own exercises, design your own program of eartraining. If you choose your own materials, your involvement will stimulate interest and action. Not only will you focus on your particular needs, you will have the opportunity to expand your knowledge of the music that attracts you.

Seek the guidance of other musicians. There is always help available when you need it. Most musicians are flattered when asked for advice and are willing to share their experience and expertise.

Your nut and bolt skills—all left brain activities—will free your right brain to explore and develop your musical frontiers. Those who are not efficient with the basic materials of music are severely limited in their ability to function in the world of performance and production. Your cognizance of the mechanics of music will provide a solid foundation for the intuitive, creative musician that is within you.

Take charge of your own training. Investigate. Be curious about your own perception, and how music is communicated through you.

YOUR OWN LANGUAGE

We all share the same materials of music. The way in which you organize and develop them becomes your own personal language of self-expression.

The smallest bit of phrase—two intervals (in four possible contours)—can generate over 500 combinations of notes within an octave. You may think of these minimal phrases as words. Adding more intervals increases the possibilities incrementally, resulting in countless potential melodic lines. Two and three-interval "words" grow into phrases—the stuff music is made of.

It is beneficial to invent interval combinations, creating phrases of particular interest to you. The great jazz improvisers have always done this. During the 1940s and 50s, there were no jazz methods. Each musician developed a personal technique based on favorite interval patterns. Merely reading printed exercises can be a passive, mechanical experience, whereas if you actually invent the exercise, your training will be immediately personal and meaningful. With each choice of interval, your personality will emerge.

- Create your own exercises.
- Design your own practice method.
- Build your own library of licks.
- Sketch phrases for later development.
- Develop your personal language of composition/improvisation.

We've pursued the materials of music from raw sound to meaningful phrases. You now own the tools of perception—the ability to hear any sound and to know what you're hearing. From this point, we apply the tools, developing a technique that melds hearing and writing music.

REVIEW

1 Name the four diatonic tetrachords and describe in terms of scale degrees, that is, 3 or ♭3, etc.

2 What is the characteristic interval of an exotic tetrachord?

3 Name the seven diatonic modes in descending or ascending order of key signatures.

4 Describe the characteristics of the four modal effects.

5 Which intervals are not contained in the pentatonic modes?

6 Name and describe the interval content of each of the symmetrical structures.

7 How does tonality enable us to perceive melodic lines?

8 Describe four types of tonal organization in terms of tonality.

9 Describe four types of tonal movement.

10 Group the diatonic modes that are closely related to the major mode and those that are closely related to the minor mode.

7

TRANSCRIBING MUSIC

7

TRANSCRIBING MUSIC

The technique of transcription—also known as *take down*—is the surest way toward the goal of *knowing what you are hearing* and being able to recreate it in notation or performance. The development of your transcription technique will increase your competence as a writer and performer, open your ears and broaden your experience.

Successful musicians have varying abilities to transcribe music. Some are able to sketch basic, minimal ideas. Others seem to be able to capture anything they hear with ease. Still others have never even tried. The point is, we all have the potential and even the most accomplished musician has had to make that first attempt—awkward, laborious, frustrating, but ultimately so rewarding.

Many students take a rather passive approach to pre-designed ear training dictation exercises. However, if you use real music of your own choosing to train your ear, your personal involvement will motivate you. In this section, you'll be encouraged to choose recorded music for your training materials. You will go far beyond the dictation/repetition of traditional ear training as you make notational choices of the composer and orchestrator.

Transcribing has proven to be the most direct method of connecting perception with notation.

Transcription is an indispensable tool for all phases of music production:

▶ Communicating through notation among those involved in the preparation of music for performance, recording or publication.

▶ Notating previously recorded music to be rearranged or transposed.

▶ Preserving an improvised solo for study or practice material.

▶ Documenting new music for copyright.

▶ Preparing music comparison reports for sampling licenses and copyright infringement cases.

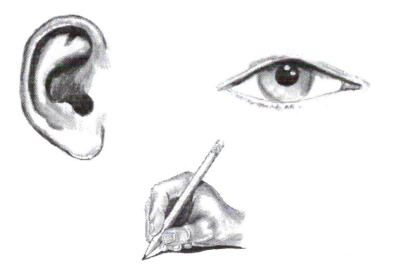

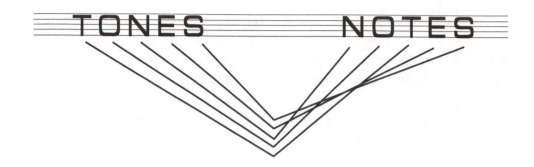

Transcribing music is essentially converting TONES into NOTES—relative intervals of space and time into specific pitches and rhythms. The development of your technique will include music from the following sources, each with slightly different requirements and emphasis:

◗ TRANSCRIBING FROM MEMORY Be able to notate a familiar tune in any key. This simple procedure allows you to evaluate your transcription ability—whether to review or advance to:

◗ TRANSCRIBING FROM RECORDED MEDIA (TAPE OR DISC) offers a world of music to choose from. This is where you refine your technique—adding all necessary elements of notation to recreate a recorded performance. You'll sharpen your perception as you make specific choices.

◗ TRANSCRIBING "LIVE" If you work as an orchestrator, you may be required occasionally to transcribe from a "live" source: someone playing an instrument, singing, humming, whistling, even over the telephone. You may be working with a collaborator, quickly jotting down ideas. You'll be prepared to notate anything at any time.

◗ TRANSCRIBING FROM YOUR IMAGINATION In a word, composing. Training with the above techniques will prepare you to express any musical idea in notation.

Whether transcribing from memory, media, live or your imagination, sounds are translated into visual symbols—the reverse process of reading music. When transcribing, you have the luxury of slowing down the music in your mind, so that you may comprehend each tone, each interval, each rhythm. The act of committing sounds to notation compels you to be specific; it requires constant editorial decisions. Your experience and knowledge of music will guide you in making correct choices. All of the tools you have developed thus far will be employed in a check-and-balance system that guarantees accuracy.

The goal of this technique is to develop your capability of notating anything you hear—externally or internally, perceived or conceived.

BENEFITS

Anyone who has mastered transcription will tell you of the benefits. Not only will your ears open up but you'll discover another level of appreciation for music—examining the leaves, branches and bark of a tree rather than the forest. Once you get past the initial awkwardness and achieve a flow, you'll not only increase your competence as a writer and performer, you'll gain a greater understanding and insight into the process of creativity, whether it be composition, orchestration or improvisation.

You will learn to **trust your ear**, rather than relying on an instrument for each note. The transcription technique will not only open your ears, but physically set you free to hear and notate music anywhere, anytime. You are the instrument!

If you've been using a musical instrument for transcribing, now is the time to wean yourself, to start transcribing directly from ear to notation. Students who have eliminated dependence on an instrument have more than doubled their transcription speed.

Whether you're jotting down a melody or composing an elaborate orchestral work, it's the same process: externalizing your musical thought. If you can hear and notate recorded music, you can hear and notate your own thoughts.

You'll be encouraged to choose your own materials for transcription—music that you love, that intrigues you. Your passion and curiosity will propel you to develop your technique from one-step-at-a-time to a smooth flow.

Each transcription will be a new and unique challenge. You'll know a piece of music intimately; you'll hear details that would escape you with a hundred passive listenings. You'll gain insight into the conception of the masters of composition and improvisation. You'll discover (again and again) that music looks simpler in notation than it sounds. If you already have some transcribing experience, you'll increase your speed and accuracy and be able to accept more challenging music.

MIDI sequencing has changed the way in which many composers work. Seasoned composers have adapted the technology to their procedures, while MIDI has enabled a new breed of "composers who don't write." Ironically, the new technology has created a greater demand for transcribers. Editing computer notation printouts for live performance or publishing requires transcribing and orchestration skills.

If your experience has been limited to MIDI sequencing, this training will prepare you to write for live musicians. The occasion can arise at any time and nothing compares to the thrill of hearing your music in live performance.

Your time and energy invested in transcribing will give you the skill and confidence of knowing what you are hearing and how to notate it—connecting sound with the visual language of notation.

FOCUSING YOUR EAR

Passive listening is experiencing the pleasure of letting the music float in and out, your attention shifting from one element of the music to another or perhaps to other thoughts. Listening for pleasure is much the same as looking at a picture; we casually perceive one element then another then another. There is no mandate to view every element or the entire picture.

Active listening, however, is work: concentrating on one element within the sound spectrum. When transcribing, we proceed by following a single *voice*—one or more instruments moving in unison or octaves. Focusing, or isolating a voice, is achieved through concentration on that voice to the point of ignoring the other sounds. A particular voice, a face in a crowd, becomes a personality once that voice is singled out.

The unique characteristics of a voice will help you visualize it. Timbre, register, intensity and articulation all help to define its personality and set it apart from the surrounding sounds. Whether a melodic line is played by a single instrument, a unison choir of similar instruments or a combination of diverse instruments, the line possesses the timbral qualities of those instruments. If a line is particularly obscure, close your eyes and visualize the musician(s) playing that line as you listen to the recording. When you have isolated a single line, internalize it until you have it memorized or notated. (Refer to HEARING AND WRITING: ORCHESTRATION, pages 260-263)

Clarity is a result of contrast, allowing each element its own space in the sound mix. The composer, orchestrator, conductor, recording engineer and mixer combine their respective skills to achieve clarity in the production of music. The listener is thus encouraged to hear each line as a separate voice. The resulting clarity aids the transcriber in focusing on a particular voice.

Chords or abstract verticals that are not immediately recognizable may be perceived using the same technique. When listening to a vertical, isolate each tone until you hear all the component tones and can recreate it in your mind. *Matching* each tone confirms its presence or absence in a vertical. More about HEARING AND WRITING CHORDS AND VERTICALS in section 9.

We don't have ear lids, but the mind acts like a filter, allowing sounds to enter our consciousness as we need them and repelling unwanted sounds. Notice how you are unaware of a constant sound, such as a machine, but your attention is immediately drawn to the sound when it starts or stops. Similarly, orchestral voices, like stage actors, are most conspicuous when entering or exiting.

EXERCISE 71
Develop your focus

Repeat the *active listening* exercises #1 and #2 on page 17. Notice any change in your perception. Are you more aware of what you are hearing? As you focus on one sound, imagine how you would recreate that sound—or the effect of that sound—orchestrally. What is the instrument or combination of instruments most capable of producing the effect—register, articulation, etc. How would you notate the effect?

 **EAR CARE**

Transcribing music requires mental concentration with no physical activity for relief so frequent breaks are necessary to rest the ears and eyes. When you are tired, your ears and brain tend to shut down. Take a break periodically—get up, move around, breathe, let the blood circulate, look at something distant. If you tend to get involved with your work and forget about time, set a timer. Five minutes of transcribing may be enough at first. Gradually increase your work sessions.

High volume causes distortion and obscures detail. When transcribing with headphones or listening to room speakers, find the optimum volume to clarify each element of the music. Sometimes just turning the volume down slightly will bring a particular voice into focus. Form the habit of periodically lowering the volume.

The process of hearing depends on a wonderfully elegant mechanical-electrical-chemical reaction. The ear is constructed of a remarkably complex set of bones, membranes and fibers, designed to transmit constantly changing waves of air pressure into what we perceive as sound. Each ear contains approximately 24,000 tiny fibers, configured like the strings of a piano. Each fiber transforms a particular frequency into an electrical current which reaches the brain via a network of chemical transmitting nerves.

It's a sad fact that the upper limit of our hearing declines as we age. The process is called *presbyacusis*. The fundamental tones are not affected so much as the range of harmonics above them. The net effect is a diminishing sense of tonal color, and eventually the inability to distinguish pitch. By the age of forty, you will have lost 90% sensitivity to the highest frequencies. By age sixty, discrimination at all frequencies is less than half as that of a young person.

> Over a lifetime, you lose about one-half cycle per second per day from the roughly 20,000-cycle-per-second range you were born with.
> Robert Jourdain: *Music, the Brain, and Ecstasy*

Intense levels of sound can cause stress, high blood pressure and fatigue as well as permanent damage to hearing. Protect your ears—avoid loud music. Musicians who work in an environment with amplified music at high levels should wear protective ear plugs. The unit of loudness, or sound level, is the decibel (dB). A sound's intensity—its physical pressure, not the brain's perception—is measured at a particular distance from its source. Typical levels are a whisper. 30 dB; normal conversation, 60 dB; the sound of a heavy truck, 90 dB. A siren, jet takeoff, or rock concert can register 120 dB. An orchestra in a concert hall produces a range of about 40 dB to 100 dB.

Musicians, as well as engineers, may be exposed to constant noise in the studio, sound stage or concert hall. You cannot build resistance to noise; constant exposure to loud noise—explosions, crashes, very loud special effects or amplified music can only deteriorate your hearing. Even consumers attending a two-hour movie or concert experience are at risk. Films, especially trailers, seem to be getting louder. At this writing, there is no regulation governing sound levels in theaters.

> After exposing the ear to sound above 110 dB or so for a few minutes, audiometry will show a temporary hearing loss, and after sufficient exposure time this temporary loss becomes permanent. It is certain that hearing loss is produced by noise. Noise induced hearing loss is an irreversible nerve type loss. No known therapy will reverse the process. It is a tragedy that nearly all [this type of hearing loss] could be prevented.
>
> House Ear Institute

The ear, like the eye, is an amazing, intricate receiver of information. However, unlike the eye, damage to the cochlea or the auditory nerve is irreparable. The body cannot spawn new nerve cells as it does cells of bone or muscle or skin. The entire tuning of the cochlea can be thrown off.

> The ill effects of noise are cumulative... Strong vibrations from excessive noise actually wear out the sensory cells of the ear until they can no longer respond... If you are exposed to sounds in the upper-decibel range for long periods of time, sooner or later your hearing may be harmed.
>
> Steven Halpern: *Sound Health*

Despite this gloomy forecast, there is much you can do to protect your ears. Consult an audiologist. Have wax buildup removed from your ears, have your ears tested at various frequencies (an audiogram) and determine the optimal earplug for your perceptive requirements as well as your performance situation.

> Ear plugs with filters can provide protection without inhibiting your work. They are custom-molded to your ear and can be acquired from most hearing aid dispensers. They offer 15 dB or 25 dB of noise reduction across all frequencies and usually cost about $100 for one pair of plugs with one pair of filters. Many engineers and artists are using the plugs with great success. They report that there is a short adjustment period, but beyond that, the plugs are so helpful that they no longer work without them.
>
> House Ear Institute

"Using the wrong ear protection can [result in] an unfortunate loss of the beauty of music [as well as] loudness perception." AFM Theater Musician's Association.

"Other hearing protectors may involve the use of acoustic shields...and even the slight effect of thick hair worn over the ears."

Marshall Chasin: *Musicians and the Prevention of Hearing Loss*

Here's more good advice from the House Ear Institute:

> Cut down on cigarette smoking, caffeine and drug and alcohol consumption. All of these elements can distort your perception of sound. If you have a concern about your hearing, if you have ringing in your ears, or if you feel you are not hearing sound the way you used to, please see an otologist and an audiologist. These hearing professionals can give you an accurate evaluation of your condition. Your symptoms may be an indication of a problem totally unrelated to your work, or they may be easily corrected so that you can do your work better. At worst, you will know exactly what you are dealing with and what you can expect so that you can make appropriate decisions for your future.

# WORK ENVIRONMENT

Transcribing requires constant focused concentration. You can learn faster, work longer and hear with more clarity if you minimize distractions and maximize comfort and convenience.

Most important is a quiet environment where you can listen internally and externally without distraction. If that is not possible, you will have to develop super concentration. Headphones are highly recommended.

In order to build your perception muscles, set up your transcribing space away from your keyboard or other instruments. If you have to get up and walk to an instrument to check your accuracy, you'll be more inclined to wean yourself from relying on an instrument. Soon, you will trust your ear completely!

You must be comfortable in order to endure long periods of work. Try different combinations of desk and chair heights. Arrange equipment and materials efficiently, your tools and supplies within reach but not in your work space. Place your music source (tape or disc player) opposite your writing hand and learn to manipulate it with one hand and no eyes.

Good lighting with a minimum of reflection is important; you are using your eyes as well as your ears.

Finally, work at a time of day when you are receptive, alert and relaxed. Transcribing can be tedious work. Set time limits so you don't reach the point of exhaustion.

Make it easy on yourself. Don't let poor conditions or inadequate equipment drain your energy and enthusiasm. Provide an environment that will allow you to be relaxed and receptive.

 **SKETCHING**

The process of transcribing requires two steps: sketching and copying. Your transcriptions should always be sketched, then re-copied for performance or other use. Sketching is quick and rough, not intended for a musician to read. The final copy is communication from you to the world. Never try to transcribe the final copy! Here are some of many reasons for the two-step process:

◗ Concentrate on listening while sketching; concentrate on notation while re-copying.

◗ Sketching emphasizes accuracy; copying emphasizes clarity.

◗ Develop a fast technique. While sketching, you need not be concerned about neatness, spacing or proper notation. Ultimately, your sketch technique may approach real time, a pace equal to the tempo of the music.

◗ Transcribe only intervals and rhythm; add refinements of expression later.

◗ Develop a language of shortcuts and symbols—a personal shorthand— to be notated properly when re-copied. Only you (or your copyist) need to see or understand the shortcuts. (See SKETCH SHORTCUTS, page 156.)

◗ Establish the key signature (if applicable) which may not be apparent until you've transcribed several phrases.

◗ Establish the meter signature. You may transcribe several phrases before the meter reveals itself. You may have to decide on the "best" meter, which may include odd-metered measures. These decisions can only be determined in retrospect. (See pages 208-209.)

◗ Establish range and registration. Only when the transcription is complete can you determine the best clef and placement on the staff.

◗ Compare similar phrases for continuity; difficult or awkward passages may seem simple or obvious when repeated in a later section.

♦ Observe harmonic patterns (when applicable) and check melodic notes against harmonies.

♦ Some adjustments may be necessary to achieve consistency of intervals, rhythms and harmonic texture as sections of the music repeat. These decisions are best postponed until you've completed the sketch and viewed the total picture.

♦ Determine the form. After sketching, you have the opportunity to "step back" and determine which sections are capable of repeating, where a D.S. or D.C. or coda is appropriate. The entire form influences the layout of the final copy.

♦ Calculate the best layout for performance or publication, which can only be accomplished when viewing the entire transcription.

♦ Re-copy your transcription with proper stem direction, enharmonic choices, appropriate spacing of each line, designation of sections—notational conventions that should be of no concern while sketching.

♦ Allow yourself the luxury of crossing out or erasing while sketching; produce a clean copy for permanence.

All of the decisions described above can be accomplished only after the sketch has been completed and you are in a position to assess the entire transcription.

Sketching is the domain of the pencil. While computer notation programs are fine for producing score and parts, they are not recommended for sketching for the following reasons:

♦ Pencil and paper notation is portable and immediate.

♦ Computer notation input requires two hands. Too much of your attention is focused on the device rather than the music.

♦ A printer must be available to produce a sketch.

RECOMMENDED TOOLS FOR SKETCHING:

◗ **SKETCH PAPER**   Single staff, 12 lines per page for maximum flexibility. Convenient size for duplication and faxing: U.S. letter (8.5 x 11") or European A4 (210 x 297mm). Staff papers from professional music services vary as to surface texture and weight. See page 383 for suppliers. You can design and print your own sketch paper with computer notation software.

◗ **PENCIL**   Mechanical or wood. Experiment with lead diameter (0.5mm, 0.7mm, 0.9mm) and softness (HB, B, 2B, etc.)

◗ **ERASER**   Soft type, non-smudging. Erasing must be clean—smudges are not only nonprofessional but demoralizing.

◗ **TRIANGLE**   6" plastic. Use as a straight edge for lettering, etc. If you form the habit of always using a straight edge when lettering, your work will have that professional flair.

◗ **CLIP BOARD**   Hold paper firm so you can use one hand for the audio player and one hand for sketching. (Try different surface textures on clip board or desk: wood, plastic, glass, sheets of paper, etc.)

It's worth the effort of trying different pencils, leads, erasers and paper to find the best combination for your hand. The right tools will help you establish a flow, optimum speed and *the look*. A professional looking pencil style is a great asset in the music business, especially for orchestrators.

If you don't have the artist's flair, you'll have to work harder to develop a style which can be read by others. A nice hand is appreciated aesthetically as well as for notational clarity by everyone involved in music production. Unsightly notation implies indifference and lack of respect for the work.

SKETCH SHORTCUTS

Save time by avoiding repetition while sketching. As your sketch technique develops, you'll be able to notate with maximum speed while maintaining accuracy. Your sketch is for your eyes only, or your trusted copyist who understands all your shortcuts.

Arrows pointing from chord symbols indicate the placment of "pushed" chords, those that are not on a beat. Chord symbols are discussed in section 9.

Use double bar lines at the beginning of each section and try to keep them at the left margin so you can easily see the overall form of the music as it unfolds. Sketch quickly by using as many shortcuts and repeats as possible. When the final copy is prepared, each line can be properly spaced to provide notational clarity. You can add your own shortcuts to your sketch technique.

FINAL COPY

Your final copy is published, in the sense that it is released to the world, to be read by musicians as performers or in some other capacity. Any piece of music that you distribute (whether pencil, pen and ink or computer generated notation) must meet certain minimal requirements of notation—standard music symbols on a staff with a designated clef and rhythmic values that add-up to the designated meter. Standard notation and special conventions are discussed in SECTION 10.

This notation has been rendered from the sketch on the opposite page.

Commotion

Ron Gorow

CHOOSING EQUIPMENT

A good transcribing technique depends on a reliable playback machine and the ability to develop a smooth pace with the equipment. Following are suggestions to guide you in purchasing equipment that will serve you most efficiently. A wise investment will save time and effort and help make your transcribing experience less tedious.

MEDIA:

Since sound quality is generally good in any media, our choice of equipment is predicated on compatibility, maneuverability and portability. When you receive music, you need to be able to transfer it to your audio format of choice. You may have to experiment to decide whether to transcribe from disc or tape. While digital media offers instant access to each track and real-time counters, you may find that audio tape players are easier to manipulate while transcribing.

PLAYER:

It is strongly suggested that you purchase a player that is designed for music transcription. The transports and controls of normal audio decks and most portable players are not built for the constant manipulation that is required for transcription. Portable MP3 players and multi-media software players should be considered, but measured with the same criteria as analog tape players. Select your transcription player with the same care you would use when choosing a musical instrument. Following are features to look for when purchasing a player.

MANIPULATION / ACCESSIBILITY:

◗ ONE-HAND CONTROL   Essential. Eventually, your fingers will memorize the controls, freeing your eyes and your writing hand.

◗ *CUE* AND *REVIEW*   Essential. The ability to audit while moving fast forward or reverse. You must be able to slide the music backward and forward without stopping the machine. Transcribing without this feature can be a frustrating experience.

◗ INDEX COUNTER/MEMORY   Preferable. Set beginning of music at zero to locate for next pass. Zero auto-stop is optional.

◗ LOOP   Optional. Repeat play for difficult passages. While this may seem like a good idea, the experienced transcriber will not linger at any particular spot long enough to bother setting the loop.

◗ PORTABILITY   Optional. You may have occasion to transcribe on location where batteries are your only source of power.

CLARITY / FIDELITY:

◗ HEADPHONE JACK   Essential to help you focus your hearing; keep out exterior noise.

◗ VOLUME CONTROL   Essential. Find a comfortable headphone level. A particular voice may be easier to define at a certain volume. Generally, there is better separation at lower volume levels. Changing the volume occasionally will give your ears a rest.

◗ STEREO   Preferable. Spatial separation helps to clarify sound.

◗ EQUALIZATION (E.Q.)   Preferable. Boost certain frequencies to help clarify a particular voice.

ACCURACY:

▶ PITCH CONTROL   Optional. (Essential if you have absolute pitch!) Adjust the pitch to compensate for difference in machine speeds. Those with relative pitch can transcribe at any pitch level; you need only determine the intended key/tonality. (See ESTABLISHING PITCH, page 191.)

All tape players vary in speed although most are accurate to within a quarter-tone. Every time a tape is transferred from one machine to another, the possibility of pitch error increases. Digital audio tape (DAT) players are known to be more accurate than analog tape cassette players. Digital disc media is virtually absolute.

▶ HALF-SPEED TAPE PLAYER   Optional. These models have an optional half-speed mode, sounding one octave lower. The current models, however, are not stereo. The half-speed feature is overrated. Music is intended to be heard at the original tempo and while half-speed could enable you to hear an occasional difficult passage, you should be comfortable transcribing in real-time. If you must slow down the music, normal variable pitch control (lowering the pitch as much as a minor 3rd) should be slow enough to hear a complex or extremely fast passage.

See TRANSCRIBING EQUIPMENT, page 384.

HEADPHONES:

20 or lower to 20,000 or higher Hz. Light weight; must be comfortable for long periods. Volume control adds unnecessary weight to the phones; headphone volume control should be controlled from the player.

PITCH SOURCE:

Tuning fork; electronic tuner; pitch pipe. Tuning forks and electronic tuners are accurate, portable, inexpensive, reliable and convenient. A pocket digital tuner/metronome is ideal for location work. Tuning forks are available at 440 Hz or other frequencies. A pitch pipe is convenient but may not be accurate enough for transcribing. They must be checked periodically. (See ESTABLISHING PITCH, page 191.)

EXPENSE should be the last consideration but is often the first. Consumer equipment is not built for frequent starting and stopping so we don't recommend using a low-end tape or disc player. Instead, purchase a player with the features discussed above that you will use only for transcribing.

SUPPLIES: See pages 155 and 383.

EXERCISE 72

Prepare your work space, equipment and materials and for your transcribing experience.

You are now ready to take action—to put notes on paper. The information, suggestions and tips provided are designed to make the process of transcription rewarding rather than tedious. When you get tired or discouraged, stop and do something else for a while. Remember that you learned to write each letter and eventually formed them into words and finally into sentences. Have patience and watch your progress. Once you have it, it's yours for life.

8

TRANSCRIPTION TECHNIQUE

8

TRANSCRIPTION TECHNIQUE

Transcription—in a word—is the ability to transform sounds into symbols, to "magically" pluck tones out of the air and capture them in notation.

Transcribing music has proven to be the best method of ear training. While traditional dictation exercises promote skills with intervals and rhythm, the transcription of real music is much broader. It is, in fact, training in composition and orchestration in that it requires the same decisions—the placement of all elements of notation on the page.

The use of a piano or any other instrument is unnecessary. It will slow you down, limit your perception and create a dependence on an instrument for this very important work. The tools you have developed thus far replace the need for an external sound to verify what you are hearing. If you've been using a keyboard or other instrument, you've been wasting time, dividing your concentration with the unnecessary step of playing notes or phrases that you obviously can hear. Now is the time to free yourself and train your primary instrument—your ear.

I wanted to establish the fact that thematic material
worked out away from the piano is better.
Prokofiev, on his *Classical Symphony*

When you learn to **trust your ear**, you will have gained the freedom to
notate anything, anytime, anywhere. If you are still insecure about trusting
your ear, review SECTIONS 5 and 6.

Music may be transcribed from several sources: your memory, recorded
media, live performance and your creative imagination. Although each source
emphasizes a slightly different approach, this training will prepare you for
any situation. The tools you've developed are the foundation of your ability
to notate any musical sound.

You are now ready for action, to put into practice
your skills of perception. Your dedication and
patience will be rewarded every day of your life.

BASIC TECHNIQUE

Primarily, we are concerned with the representation of each tone as a note on a staff. To place a note on a staff, you must determine its place in musical space and musical time. Its pitch has a relationship to the prevailing tonality or key, its duration has a relationship to the prevailing beat or meter. These are the primary attributes of the tone and all that we'll be concerned with at this time. Articulation, dynamic levels and other performance indications may be ignored during the initial stage of transcription.

Transcribing will bring your perception into focus, clarifying intervals and rhythms as familiar recognizable entities. If necessary, you may separate pitch and rhythm values, notating one then the other. You'll soon be transcribing both pitch and rhythm simultaneously, capturing tones, making immediate choices and notating with absolute accuracy.

PITCH TO NOTE

As you will see in the following pages, establishing the first note differs with each type of transcription. After the first note has been named, the procedure is the same whether transcribing from memory, recorded media or a live source.

METHODS OF IDENTIFYING NOTES:

There are several methods of proceeding from one tone to the next and identifying the new tone by note-name. Teach yourself to use all the methods. When you are transcribing, your subconscious will choose one initially and another as verification.

▶ INTERVAL RECOGNITION   Identify the new note from the interval between it and the previous note.

▶ TONAL RELATIONSHIP   Identify the new note from the interval between it and the tonal center or tonic note.

▶ SCALE DEGREE   Identify the note as a scale-tone (diatonic or altered).

▶ CHORD TONE   Identify the note as a chord-tone (if harmony is apparent).

▶ TONAL MEMORY   Associate the new note with a previous note of the same pitch.

The five methods are in no particular order; musical context will guide you in choosing one or the other. Soon, the choices will be entrusted to the subconscious and you will gain speed and confidence. The five methods are used to reinforce each other in a system of mutual agreement, guaranteeing the correct choice of notes.

When you determine the new note, there will be a choice of enharmonic spelling. Generally, all the notes of a phrase should form a diatonic relationship so that the reader (the performer, arranger, etc.) does not encounter awkward intervals. Keep in mind that you are putting notes on a staff for others to read, often to sight-read.

BASIC RHYTHM TRANSCRIPTION

Tonal identification, when combined with rhythmic perception, results in a technique that ultimately approaches the smooth flow of music. For many musicians, rhythm is not a problem; others have great difficulty assigning rhythm values to notes. Following is basic instruction to get you started. HEARING AND WRITING RHYTHM, in SECTION 9, addresses rhythm as applied to specific types of music.

▶ QUICK REVIEW OF TIME-RELATED TERMS:

▶ BEAT   The perceived pulse of the music.

▶ RHYTHM   Relation of tones (notes) to the beat.

▶ METER   Regularity of beats, divided into bars (measures).

▶ BAR (MEASURE)   Groups of beats, set off by bar lines.

▶ DOWNBEAT   First beat of each measure.

▶ TEMPO   Rate of speed of the beat.

▶ DURATION   Length of a note or phrase, measured in beats or bars.

▶ QUANTIZE   Average, or round-off, rhythm values to simplify notation.

Your task is to interpret what you hear and choose the best way to represent it. Transcribing rhythm is merely deciding where the tones begin and end in relation to the beat. Any rhythm can be represented as a multiple or subdivision of the beat.

Transcribing recorded music requires editorial decisions as to the intention of the performer or composer.

Musicians have been *quantizing* (rounding off durations) for as long as music has been represented in notation. We round off rhythm values for the sake of consistency and ease of reading, knowing that they will again become *human* (imprecise) when our transcriptions are performed. The degree of quantizing depends on several factors: style of music, tempo, and level of performers. More precise durations may be required for situations such as vocal choir, slow tempi or synchronization to film. Performance considerations always influence notational choices.

TIPS: RHYTHM TRANSCRIPTION

◆ Until you are comfortable with notating rhythm, transcribe note heads only, concentrating on pitches. When all the note heads are on the staff, listen again from the beginning, this time concentrating on placing bar lines and assigning rhythm values to the notes.

◆ Quantize rhythm, rounding off values to the nearest quarter, eighth or sixteenth, appropriate to the style of the music.

◆ When you encounter a problem, internalize or sing at a slow tempo so that each beat seems very "large" and you are able to perceive as many subdivisions as necessary to capture the desired rhythm. This technique, in conjunction with quantizing, will help you solve any rhythm problem.

◆ If you have trouble hearing a subdivision, internalize at a slow tempo, counting subdivisions so that an eighth note receives one beat, and sketch. Notate the figure in this expanded and simplified manner (eighths become quarters, sixteenths become eighths, etc.) Check the notation with the audio source at tempo. When the rhythm is clear in your mind, compress the notation (halve each value) to the original meter. Read your notation at tempo while listening to the source. Use this method to simplify complex rhythms.

◗ When you cannot discern the rhythm in relation to the beat, slowly tap four fingers (if the meter is in four) while singing the figure and watch the beginning of each tone in relation to your fingers tapping the beats.

Observe which tones fall on the beats and which tones fall between beats. Then, determine if those in-between tones are even or syncopated. Equal divisions of the beat produce eighth notes, triplets, sixteenths, etc. If there are five *even* tones between beats, they are quintuplets; if there are five *uneven* tones, you must determine which are of equal duration and which are further subdivided.

◗ Always notate for clarity. Group notes so that the eye perceives the divisions of the bar: 8th notes grouped per half bar; 16th and shorter notes grouped per beat.

◗ When the beat is divided, beam the notes within each beat.

◗ Rhythm values must always add up to the designated meter. Learn to recognize a rhythmically complete bar.

◗ Rhythms tend to consist of repetitious patterns. Develop an eye for rhythmic patterns. Soon you will recognize familiar recurring patterns.

Refer to HEARING AND WRITING RHYTHM, page 207.

TRANSCRIBING FROM MEMORY

Transcribing from memory is the ideal method for your first transcribing experience, as it requires no equipment, just a pencil and staff paper. It is but a step away from the ultimate technique—transcribing from your imagination: composing music.

> Transferring a melodic line from sound to notation is simply a matter of reversing the process of reading music. If you can read music, you can write music.

EXERCISE 73

Start with a song or tune that you know well enough to re-create with voice or instrument. Most pop songs, folk songs, children's songs, national, religious or holiday songs are simple diatonic melodies with an obvious tonality.

1 **Establish the tonality.** Sing or hum, starting at any pitch that is comfortable. As you sing through, notice which tone seems to be the tonal center, or tonic. Many songs start on the tonic and virtually every song ends on the tonic.

2 **Choose an arbitrary key.** Since you are not listening to a recording, you may place it in the key of your choice. Pick a key, any key.

3 **Determine the first note name.** Is it indeed the tonic or is it another scale-tone? The relationship of the first tone to the tonic determines the note name of the first tone. For example: if the first tone sounds a major 3rd above the tonic (*Georgia On My Mind* or *Ode To Joy* from Beethoven's 9th Symphony) and you choose the key of C, the first note is an **E**. (We're not concerned with the original key at this time.) If you are unsure of the interval, sing up or down a diatonic scale from the tonic to the first tone, in the example: **C, D, E.** The **E** is the third scale-degree in the key of **C**.

4   Place a clef, key signature and your first note on the staff.

5   **Determine the following notes.** Proceed, using any of the methods of determining the next note as described on page 167.

▶ If this first exercise seems obvious and easy, you will have no problem developing the transcription technique.

▶ If you are confused, review INTERVALS (section 5) TONALITY (page 118, 119) PERCEPTION OF A PHRASE (page 124) and NUTS & BOLTS (page 133, 134) as needed.

▶ If you understand how to establish your first note but had trouble continuing the transcription, proceed to the next page.

▶ If you had no problem and no hesitation in transcribing exercise 73, review pages 181-187 then skip to page 188, TRANSCRIBING RECORDED MUSIC.

TEST YOUR TRANSCRIPTION ABILITY

Use the following exercise to evaluate your transcription ability and discover any weakness in your technique that may need review.

If you are now able to distinguish the intervals and relate them to note names, you should have no problem transcribing any tune that you are able to sing or play.

EXERCISE 74

If there is one song everyone knows, it must be *Happy Birthday To You.* Write the song as you remember it on the staff below. Place the first note as **middle C** in the treble clef. Determine the tonality and place an appropriate key signature on the staff.

Complete the melody and lyric. The words will help us keep our place as we discuss each step on the following pages.

HAPPY BIRTHDAY TO YOU

Compare the printed notation with your transcription and discover where your strengths and weaknesses are. If your transcription matches, you're ready to proceed to page 188, TRANSCRIBING RECORDED MUSIC. If not, use the following description of the process to improve your technique.

Follow along as we go through the process of transcription, step by step. Since we have the words, we'll arbitrarily find the meter and rhythm first, although you may choose to place the notes first then assign the rhythm. Soon, you'll be transcribing both notes and rhythm simultaneously.

With practice, all the following steps will blend into one seamless technique.

1 Establish the meter. Tap a steady beat. As you sing, notice which beats are accented. Hap-py **birth**-day to **you**, hap-py **birth**-day to **you**, hap-py **birth**-day dear **some**-one, (pause) hap-py **birth**-day to **you**. Every third beat is accented, therefore the tune is in 3/4 meter. Since the first "Hap-py" is unaccented, it is a pickup to the first full bar. Place a double bar line between the first "happy" and "birthday." Place vertical bar lines before each accented syllable. You now have two pickup notes plus 8 bars.

>   >   >   >

3/4: Happy ‖ birthday to |you, happy |birthday to |you, happy

>   >   >   >

|birthday dear |someone, (pause) happy |birthday to |you.

2 Establish the rhythm. The rhythm of "Hap-py" is sometimes sung with a dotted feel or a triplet feel. We'll use the simple straight eighth rhythm, as it would probably be sung at a slow tempo. The rhythmic feel is usually consistent throughout a song.

Since we're using the simplified eighth-note rhythm, "Hap-py" is notated as two eighth notes. "Hap-py" starts on beat 3. Write "3 &" under "Hap-py."

Tap the quarter-note beat as you sing. After the pickups, "birth" "day" and "to" each receive one beat, while "you" has a duration of two beats. Using the lyrics above, place 1,2,3 under the words, indicating where each beat falls.

3   Sing through to find the tonality. Start singing at any comfortable pitch. Since we've already determined the key, the actual key you are singing in is irrelevant.

The tonic is the final tone, as is true of most songs. All the tones in the melody eventually gravitate to the tonic. In this assignment, the first note was given as **C**, therefore the last note of the song is **F**.

4   Designate the key signature. Since this melody is obviously in the major mode, place the key signature of F major in the treble clef. Song lead sheets are normally placed on a treble clef staff.

5   Establish first note. Since you were given the first note (**C**) we'll just confirm that the key is indeed **F**. After arriving at the last note (**F**) sing the interval between it and the first note, as if you were going to sing the song again. Is the first note (**C**) a 4th below the last note?

Another method of confirming the key is to determine the scale degree of the first note. Does the song start on the 5th scale degree? Is **C** the 5th of the key of **F**? There is always more than one way to confirm that your perception is correct.

6   Place the first note. In this song, both syllables of "Hap-py" are **C**s. Place two eighth-note **C**s as "middle **C**" in the treble clef.

7   Proceed to the next note as described in BASIC TECHNIQUE, pages 166-167. The next note (downbeat of the first full bar on the syllable "Birth") is a whole-tone above "Hap-py." You may verify this by counting from the tonic to the sixth scale-degree. Both methods determine that the note name is **D**. Place a **D** quarter-note on the staff because we've already determined that this syllable receives one full beat.

The next syllable "-day" is a whole-tone lower, the fifth scale-degree. Or you can use your tonal memory and hear that it is the same pitch as the first two notes "Hap-py." Any of these methods determine that the note name of "-day" is **C**.

The next word "to" is up a 4th; also the tonic note. Both methods determine that the note name is **F**.

The next word "you" is down a half-tone; also the seventh scale-degree. Both methods determine that the note name is **E**.

The next two words "hap-py birth-day" are the same four notes as the beginning. Our tonal memory tells us that they are **C C D C**.

This time the melody leaps up a fifth from **C** for the word "to." Or, we may hear the tone as the second (or ninth) scale-degree. Either method gives us the note **G**.

The next word "you" is down a whole-tone, also the tonic, **F**.

The next two syllables "hap-py" again return to the original **C** (tonal memory).

Now the mighty leap of an octave to the higher **C**, then down a minor third to **A**. If we confirm that this "birth-day" is the fifth scale-degree to the third scale-degree, it assures us that we are still on track.

The next tone "dear" is down a major third; also the tonic, **F** (tonal memory.) The next two syllables "some-one" descends a half-tone to the seventh scale-degree **E**, then a whole-tone to the sixth scale-degree **D**. Place a fermata over the **D** to indicate the pause.

The next two syllables "hap-py" are a minor sixth above the last **D**. This interval is sometimes difficult to hear, but it is easy to hear that the tones are the fourth scale-degree **B♭**.

The next note confirms this somewhat questionable **B♭**. It is down a half-tone, the familiar resolution of the fourth scale-degree to the third scale-degree, confirming that the note for 'birth' is **A**.

The next note "-day" is down a major third to the tonic **F** (tonal memory).

Next "to" is up a whole-tone to the second scale-degree **G**.

The final "you" is down the same interval, a whole-tone, returning to the final tonic **F**.

Check by singing or playing on an instrument. If you had difficulty notating "Happy Birthday," isolate the problem. If you could not decide where to place the first note **C** on the staff, you need to learn basic music theory then return to this work. If you had problems proceeding from one tone to the next, review the tools in sections 5 and 6. If you had problems establishing a note-name for each tone, review NUTS & BOLTS, pages 133-135.

Always verify your decision with more than one method of determining each note. The decisions will soon be made automatically by your subconscious.

If this process seems extensive and laborious, have patience. When your technique is fully developed, you will be able to transcribe a song of this length and complexity in about 20 seconds—approaching real-time!

Visualize *Happy Birthday To You* as a relationship of intervals.

- **INTERVALS BETWEEN NOTES:**

Unis., up maj2, down maj2, up p4, down half
Down maj3, unis., up maj2, down maj2, up p5, down maj2
Down p4, unis., up octave, down min3, down maj3, down mi2, down maj2
Up min6, unis., down mi2, down maj3, up maj2, down maj2.

- **SCALE DEGREES:** (Get used to second-octave intervals: 9th through 13th)

5 5 6 5 8 7,
5 5 6 5 9 8,
5 5 12 10 8 7 6,
11 11 10 8 9 8.

- **NOTE NAMES** IN KEY OF **F**:

C C D C F E
C C D C G F
C C C A F E D
B♭ B♭ A F G F

- **SOL-FA (MOVABLE DO):**

Sol Sol La Sol Do Ti
Sol Sol La Sol Re Do
Sol Sol Sol Mi Do Ti La
Fa Fa Mi Do Re Do

- **SOL-FA (FIXED DO):**

Do Do Re Do Fa Me
Do Do Re Do Sol Fa
Do Do Do La Fa Mi Re
Te Te La Fa Sol Fa

All of these methods produce the same result in notation. Your goal is to eliminate all words and numbers when perceiving music. Soon your hand will follow your inner voice as you transcribe.

EXERCISE 75

Transcribe *Happy Birthday* again, this time in the key of **G**. Compare it with the first transcription. Notice that while all the notes are different, all the intervals are the same. A song is an intervallic shape, a template that may be placed at any pitch level, in any key.

EXERCISE 76

Transcribe the song in the key of **D♭**. Each time you transcribe this song, you are perceiving the same intervals, merely changing the note-names.

If you feel comfortable so far, you're ready to transcribe recorded music, page 188. However, you may want to read through the following exercise, where you will encounter more problems and decisions that typically arise in transcribing music.

EXERCISE 77

Transcribe from memory *Auld Lang Syne*. Transcribe only the first eight bars. Originally a Scottish folk tune, this song is traditionally sung at midnight on New Year's eve. We'll notate the melody only, as most people know the tune but not the words. There are several interpretations of this melody. Notate the tune as you remember it. We'll work with a strictly diatonic version and discuss the chromatic variations later.

This time, we'll establish the note-names first, then the rhythm.

1 Tonality. Sing through. Notice that it ends on the tonic.

2 Choose a key. How about **A**? We'll use a key signature because, like most songs, it maintains one tonality throughout. Place a treble clef and key signature of **A** MAJOR on the staff below.

3 Name the first note. After singing through, the tonality is firmly in your mind. What is the relationship between the tonic (**A**) and the first tone? Translate this relationship into a note-name and place it on the staff. Use black note-heads without stems until the rhythms are determined. Tonal memory should tell you that the second note is the same as the last note (the tonic). Place the note on the staff.

4 Proceed, using intervals or scale-degrees to name each note. Notate the first eight bars of this song using a diatonic scale—no chromatic notes. Quickly check your work—hum through.

Here is the basic melodic contour. Your interpretation may differ. (Variations are discussed on page 187.)

G♯ OR A, DEPENDING ON WHICH VERSION YOU KNOW.

5 Determine the meter. As you sing and count, a definite four-beat meter is heard, therefore a 4/4 meter signature is required. Place a meter signature on the staff above and draw bar lines before each downbeat (accented note). Count the number of beats of the highest notes (F♯) so that you maintain the meter. Did your last note end on a downbeat? If not, try again.

Notate the song in **A major** on the staff on the opposite page, as we discuss each step of the process. If you feel confident, skip the discussion and add rhythmic values to the notes already established, then complete the song as you remember it.

6 Determine the rhythm of each note. The first note is a pickup because it is unaccented. It falls on a beat, so its duration is a quarter-note.

The second note is a definite downbeat, so place a double bar before it.

The next note does not fall on a beat but somewhere between the second and third beats of the bar. If you cannot decide where it falls, use four fingers to tap the beats and you will see that the note falls exactly halfway between the second and third beats. Therefore, it commences on beat 2½ and its value is an 8th note.

This is verified by the next note, which falls exactly on the third beat. Notice that there is no note on beat 2 of the bar but there are notes on beats 2½ and 3. The delayed note produces a rhythmic figure (dotted quarter, eighth) which is characteristic of this song.

The next note (C♯) falls on the fourth beat, completing the first bar.

The rhythm pattern has been established, so each time you encounter a similar figure, you already know what the rhythm values are.

When you get to bar 4, there is a climactic note (**F♯**). Assign a duration that corresponds to the number of beats you've allowed this note. The second **F♯** is the same rhythmically as the first pickup; it initiates the next phrase.

Bar 5 descends with the characteristic syncopated rhythm pattern.

The sixth bar contains the same notes and rhythm pattern as the second full bar. Proceed, finishing the phrase (8 bars).

Complete the song. The next section of 8 bars parallels the rhythm pattern with some bars containing the same notes as previous bars. Notice how much repetition you encounter. Remember that repetition saves you transcription time as well as providing an opportunity to verify your notation. See Sketch Shortcuts, page 156.

The duration of the last note of the tune is your choice. Early notation would assign a value of dotted half-note to the final note with no fourth beat, offsetting the pickup note. Modern notation would fill the last bar with four beats.

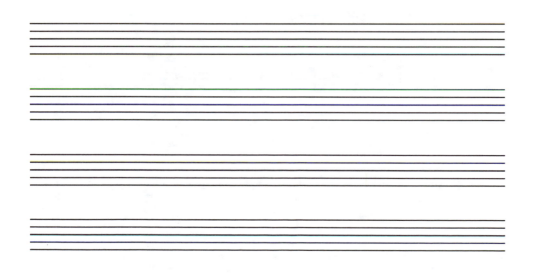

Your sketch should look something like this:

You may decide to notate the song in *half time,* where each note receives half the rhythmic value. The meter (4/4) is unchanged but the relationship between the beat and the meter is halved. The eight bar phrase is now 4 bars. Both versions may be played at any tempo.

The song may also appear in 2/4 meter. This time, we'll transpose it down a tritone to the key of E♭. In the first example, the durations are twice as long as in the second example.

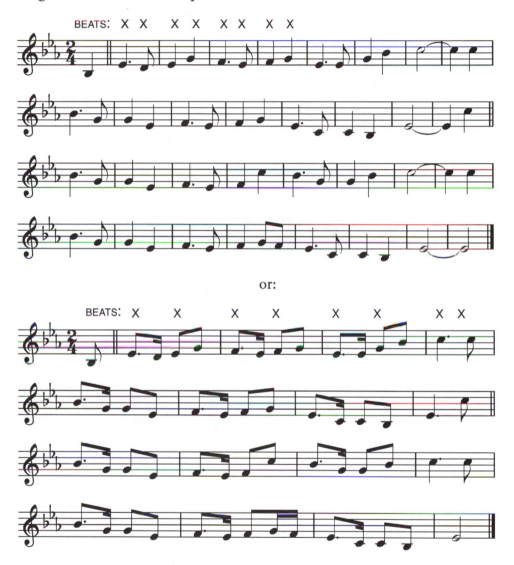

or:

The composer or transcriber has choices: A piece of music retains its identity in any key, any register, and in several different metric configurations. The relationships of intervals and rhythms that define the song are constant.

There is sometimes more than one interpretation of a song. You may have heard this song with embellishments, as interpreted by a soloist:

1 Diatonic embellishments (using notes only from a pentatonic scale):

2 Chromatic embellishments:

Many musicians interpret this song with this chromatic alteration.

3 Rhythmic variation:

EXERCISE 78

Transcribe *Auld Lang Syne* in B♭, simultaneously placing notes with their rhythm values on the staff. Check your work by singing or playing.

Each time you transcribe the same tune in a different key, the intervals will be a little more familiar and your transcription will be a little faster, a little smoother.

EXERCISE 79

Transcribe another familiar tune from memory. Pick an arbitrary key. Try to combine notes and rhythm simultaneously. Check your work by singing or playing.

There are many interpretations of songs, especially old ones in the public domain. Your decisions as to chromatic embellishments and rhythmic details as well as key and meter signatures are an important part of the transcription process. These choices help establish a style but do not alter the essence of a piece of music.

If you have mastered both the intervals and the diatonic matrix, you're ready to delve into more chromatic and complex music. If you have to stop and calculate each new note, the process can be tedious and you may feel defeated. That is why so much emphasis has been placed on instant recognition of the intervals and knowing the diatonic matrix. Now is the time to evaluate your progress and decide if you should review or proceed to recorded music, where you will finalize your technique.

TRANSCRIBING RECORDED MUSIC

Using recorded music, your technique will be refined and developed to its fullest. You'll find a certain satisfaction in capturing sound on paper. Unlike transcribing from memory, the perception of recorded music requires an open mind, free of preconceptions, ready to experience the unknown. When transcribing recorded music, you are actually re-creating a performance, making the same notational choices as the composer.

If you plan to transcribe directly to computer notation or simply convert MIDI files to notation, it is highly recommended that you first learn to transcribe from tape or disc to paper, where your attention will be focused on the designation and placement of each note.

When notating previously recorded music, it is normal to retain the original tonality, preserving the composer's choice of key. If the intention is to document the composition or a particular performance, then every detail, including the original key, is essential for an accurate rendition. However, a new arrangement of the music may require transposition to accommodate the requirements of a specific orchestration or performance.

As you learn to trust your ear, you can check your transcriptions simply by reading and internalizing while listening to your audio source. You no longer need to rely on an external instrument to verify melodic lines.

CHOOSING MUSIC

One person's music is another person's noise. The choice of music can make the transcribing experience very profound or very boring. Each piece of music you choose presents a unique challenge, a new puzzle to solve, an unknown journey. In a favorite piece, you can find something interesting or inspiring to transcribe—a solo phrase, duet, harmonic passage, a curious bit of orchestration. If you choose music that you love or that intrigues you, the process will be less tedious and more rewarding—you'll be personally involved from the first note.

Traditional ear-training exercises typically offer repetitive keyboard drills, out of the context of real music, whereas transcribing recorded music that interests you can be a revealing and rewarding personal experience. Even when transcribing music that you've listened to many times, you'll become intimate with each phrase, discovering details that otherwise would go unnoticed. Let your curiosity and passion guide you in selecting recordings.

Choose music that is suitable for your level of competence. Simple melodies are recommended until you are comfortable with the transcription process. As you develop your technique, you can assume more difficult music. In SECTION 9, we'll progress from melodic lines to counterpoint, chords and full orchestrations.

For your first transcription experience, choose single line instrumental music so pitches and rhythm will be clear and definite. If you prefer keyboard music, find material where the right hand is restricted to a single line.

Music of any style or period is transcription material. Generally, older music is simpler. Use this experience to gain insight into music that you value, as well as an opportunity to investigate something new. Your choice of music will make the difference between tedious training or exciting discovery.

TECHNIQUE AND PROCEDURE

The following technique—transcribing from recorded media—is an indispensable skill, used in the music business for day-to-day activities such as arranging and orchestrating.

Using a keyboard or other instrument when transcribing is a waste of time and destroyer of confidence. You need one hand for the source (player) and one hand for the pencil. As a composer, an instrument between you and the music will tend to slow you down, confine your writing to the instrument's predictable patterns and limit your imagination to your own instrumental technique. You may use an instrument to check your work but you'll soon find this unnecessary as you gain confidence in your ear.

USE OF EQUIPMENT

Whether transcribing from tape or disc, the technique is the same. Position your equipment and sketch paper so you can work comfortably. Learn to operate the player with one hand, freeing the other hand for sketching. Use a clip board to stabilize your sketch paper. (See SKETCHING, pages 153-157.)

Learning the equipment involves training your fingers to manipulate the controls (*play, review* or *replay, cue* or *fast forward, pause, reverse,* and *stop*) without looking at the machine, assigning specific fingers to each function. Eventually, you'll develop a pace, using only the *play* and *review* controls to move through the music. The technique is described in detail on page 196.

Caution: Avoid hitting the *record* control which is usually next to the *play* control. Some machines prevent this and some don't. If you are working with tape, punch out the safety tab. Prevent disasters—always make a backup copy before starting a transcription.

RELIABLE PITCH SOURCE

Your source of pitch is an indispensable tool that you must be able to trust when you need the correct pitch. Recommended: a tuning fork or electronic tuner for accuracy and portability. Musical instruments, with the exception of electronic and mallet instruments, are not reliable for accurate pitch, as they are built to adjust the tuning pitch. (See page 161 for pitch sources.)

Your pitch source is used to establish the key or tonal center when beginning a transcription and referred to thereafter only if you need to check a pitch. Keep it within reach of your work so that checking a pitch takes only a few seconds. Once you've attained complete confidence in your ear, you will need your pitch source only to set the key or tonal center before you begin a transcription.

ESTABLISHING PITCH

Since tape machines are subject to variation in speed, it requires care and good judgment to establish the pitch/tonal center of the music that you are about to transcribe. You may receive a tape that has been transferred several times with accumulated error in pitch. Even when you are transcribing from digital media, such as a CD, keep in mind that performers do not necessarily tune to A=440.

Usually, the pitch is right on or very close to a standard key but there is no way of knowing whether a particular recording was given to you at the original pitch. If the pitch seems to be "in the cracks," midway between keys, use your orchestration experience to provide the best guess. Suppose the key is midway between E and F. If the music is guitar oriented—pop or country, the key is most likely E; if it is keyboard oriented or jazz, the key is probably F. Music that features a vocalist could be in any key, as the primary consideration is always the vocalist's range.

Another consideration is the intent of your transcription. Music transcribed for copyright, publishing or archival purposes normally remains in the original key. Music that is to be arranged or orchestrated for a particular performance or recording may be transposed. If there is doubt as to the correct key or the preferred key, check with your client.

ESTABLISHING THE KEY OR TONAL CENTER

When transcribing from media, we usually notate in the same key as the recorded media. Of course, using relative pitch, it is just as easy to hear in one key and notate in another.

Listen to the introduction and a few phrases of melody, enough to decide where the tonal center (tonic) lies. Match the tonic with your voice or internalize. When the tonic is firm in your mind, find its pitch by comparing it to your pitch source (tuner or tuning fork). What is the intervallic relationship of the tonic to your pitch source? If your source is **A** and the tonic sounds a whole-tone lower, the tonality is **G**. If the interval is a tritone, your tonality is **E♭**. Once you understand this process, you can establish the tonality in one or two seconds.

After listening to several phrases, it should be obvious whether this particular music is diatonic or abstract. Diatonic music usually requires a key signature. Abstract music, such as a film underscore, often does not carry a key signature as the tonality may change frequently. Key signatures are merely a convenience to avoid repeating accidentals. Conversely, chromatic or modulating music is best notated without a key signature to avoid many natural signs. Occasionally, you will choose a key signature that seems appropriate at the beginning but it soon becomes apparent that a related key is indeed the correct one. When the tonality changes permanently, change the key signature appropriately.

Key changes help define the structure of the music. Whether transcribing or composing, the choice of key and meter signatures require careful consideration for the performer.

Not every tune is clearly major or minor; the music may be *modal*, perhaps Mixolydian or Dorian. This presents another choice: if you notate in a key signature that represents the mode, there will be a minimum of accidentals. If you notate in the nearest major or minor key signature, the tonality will be more apparent to the performing musicians.

In this example, a bluesy tune with a tonality of **D**, the third is always major (**F♯**) and the seventh is always dominant (**C♮**). Which key signature is your preference?

Modal signature: 1 sharp (**D** MIXOLYDIAN)

Nearest major/minor signature: 2 sharps (**D** MAJOR)

When using the nearest major or minor key signature, consider each scale degree. Is the third more often major or minor? Is the fourth more often natural or Lydian? The objective here is definition; the complete diatonic system is at your disposal to provide a clear melodic line.

Notate a key signature on your sketch if it seems appropriate. You can change it later when reviewing the completed sketch. Now that you have your tonal center and key signature, you're off and running.

ESTABLISHING THE FIRST NOTE

You've established the tonality and named the key. Listen to the source (tape or disc) until you hear a tonic. Match with your voice or internalize the pitch. When the sound of the tonic is firmly in your mind, listen to the first tone and compare. What is its intervallic relationship to the tonic? For example, if the tonic is **F** and the first tone is a fifth above, it is a **C**. If it is a minor third below the tonic **F**, the first note is a **D**.

Place the first note on the staff.

Establishing the first note may seem tedious at this stage, but the whole process up to this point will take about 5 seconds with a little practice.

After you've established the tonality, key signature and first note, the remainder of the transcription is routine. If you are comfortable this far, you may incorporate the rhythmic value (duration) of each note as you proceed. If this seems too much at once, just place note heads on the staff and apply rhythm values later.

PROCEDURE

Determine the next note by any of the five methods:

1   Identify the interval from the previous tone to the new tone.
2   Identify the interval between the new tone and the tonic.
3   Identify the tone as a diatonic or altered scale-tone.
4   Identify the tone as a chord-tone (if harmony is apparent).
5   Associate the tone with a previous tone of the same pitch (tonal memory).

Use the method that is most apparent to you then verify with one of the other methods.

PLAYING THE PLAYER

At first, use the *play* control, listening to a bit of phrase—only as much as you can retain in memory. *Stop* or *pause,* notate, then *reverse* just that much. Listen again as you proofread your notation.

Now that you have an idea of the length of phrase you can retain, you can move past this awkward and tedious stage and speed up the process:

Instead of using the *stop* and *reverse* controls, use the *review* or *replay* control to slide the music backward, listening, so that you move the music back only as far as necessary to continue your notation. Once you have a note on paper and you are sure it is accurate, there is no need to listen to that note again.

You begin notating as soon as you hear the first tone and continue to notate even as you slide the music back, listening a second time. While one hand is toggling *review,* the other hand is notating. Remember to use a clip board to secure your sketch paper.

Ultimately, you'll achieve a smooth flow, sketching a few notes at a time—some while listening, some while sliding the music back—advancing in small segments of melody. This pace amounts to two steps forward, one step backward, allowing only one listen to easy material and two or more listens to more difficult material. In this manner, you proceed at your maximum speed, yet take as much time as necessary to achieve accuracy.

When you encounter a difficult passage, *pause* or *stop* immediately after a particular tone/interval so that you may concentrate on only that sound. *Internalize* (playback via your inner voice). If necessary, sing or hum that part of the phrase until it is firm in your mind. Determine each note name, using a combination of the five methods (page 194). Headphones are recommended for maximum concentration.

Proceed at your own pace, gradually increasing the number of notes you are able to retain in memory. While this may be tedious at first, remember that momentous works are created one note at a time. Eventually, the decision of note naming and the assignment of rhythm values will be relegated to your subconscious; you'll simply listen and notate.

TIPS: TRANSCRIBING TECHNIQUE

▶ When transcribing, the tonality and the beat are always there, even when implied or silent; they are your constant points of reference.

▶ When in doubt, use your pitch source (tuner or fork) to check any note. Ideally, the pitch source is used only to establish the tonality. When you can proceed without it, you will be working at maximum efficiency.

▶ Review the five methods of determining the next note (page 194.) Be sure you are aware of all five. Get in the habit of using one to check against another.

▶ All intervals and rhythmic patterns are familiar to you—only the resulting melodic shapes are new.

▶ Keep your notation simple. Remember, you're notating idealized intervals and quantized rhythms. You can go back later to add articulation, phrasing, dynamics, embellishments, etc.

▶ Review SKETCH SHORTCUTS, page 156.

▶ Remember to take breaks; rest your ears, eyes, brain and body.

▶ Gear your transcription to your level of skill and experience. Start with a single line, a few phrases, eventually expanding your work to multiple voices, longer phrases, faster tempos, more complexity.

▶ Break the keyboard habit. If necessary, work in another room, away from your keyboard or other instruments. Use your voice, your pitch source when necessary and your tools acquired thus far.

▶ Choose simple but interesting music; have patience and a positive attitude; be willing to work. Your technique will soon be "second nature."

COMPLETING THE SKETCH

If you have not assigned rhythmic values to the notes while sketching, start from the beginning and determine the meter and where the bar lines fall. If the accented notes start to fall on weak beats, you may have omitted or added a beat, or the music may have changed meter. When the meter changes, let the phrase or harmonic structure determine where to place the bar lines. (Review BASIC RHYTHM TRANSCRIPTION, page 168)

Compare similar sections of the sketch for repetition of melody and rhythm. When there are differences, go back and listen to each instance and decide if the discrepancy was a performance variation, an intentional variation of the writer, or your error. If a performance variation, you may decide to notate each occurrence the same. Usually, the first occurrence is a good choice, as the artist is more aware of the composer's intent and is more apt to take liberties thereafter.

EXERCISE 80

Transcribe short, simple melodies until the process of establishing tonality, key and the first note is *second nature*.

See HEARING AND WRITING LINES, page 213, to continue developing your transcription technique.

TRANSCRIBING IMPROVISED SOLOS

Improvisation is perhaps the ultimate creative activity, as it combines performance, communication of emotions, instrumental technique, spontaneous response to other musicians, and immediate composition. Some musicians have never experienced improvisation; others have devoted their entire lives to perfecting their personal style of improvisation.

A recorded improvised solo that moves you is worth not only repeated listenings, but your time dedicated to its transcription. While transcribing a solo, you'll experience much more than casual listening can provide.

Choose solos that captivate you. The many styles and periods of jazz and rock provide a rich body of recorded work. Choose the style, particular instrument and artist that attracts you. Earlier works are usually simpler; as instrumental technique developed, improvising became increasingly complex both rhythmically and harmonically. Perhaps most rewarding are the solos of the great musicians of the classic bebop era—Charlie Parker, Bud Powell, Fats Navarro, Horace Silver, Clifford Brown, Bill Evans, early John Coltrane. Their solos are prime examples of creating lines over chord changes, yet they are accessible. Like Bach, the rhythms are usually even subdivisions of the beat and the lines are composed of melodic patterns that resolve in a traditional manner. Even fast passages are so logical that, once you have them on paper, they will seem inevitable. There are recordings of many jazz instrumentalists, any one of whom could provide years of transcription study. If rock is your bag, choose your favorite guitar or keyboard solos.

Since improvisations are usually based on harmonic structure, you may want to write out the chord changes before transcribing notes so that the sound of the progression is in your ear. Piano solos may be transcribed as right hand single lines with chord symbols. Later, you can add the left hand spelled out in notation. When transcribing avant garde or non-tonal solos with no chord structure, approach as any abstract music. Find the tonality in each phrase. Look for duplication, similar interval structures and sequential phrases.

Phrases in a quasi-rubato style may require some quantization when notating. For example, if Miles Davis chose to delay a few notes, an exact transcription would result in a very complex rhythmic figure. If notated in a simplified rhythm with *laid-back* or *delayed* written above it, the phrase would reflect the intent of the improvisor and be more accessible to the reader.

After completing a transcription, look for continuity of melodic patterns, rhythms, phrasing. Every improviser has a personal style that is evident in each solo. Recordings that include *alternate takes*, usually recorded just minutes apart, provide interesting comparisons of the soloist's variations on a particular chord structure.

Improvised solo transcriptions are rewarding in many ways. As you transcribe, you'll share the experience of the creator weaving melodic lines from chord tones and passing tones. You can gain insight into the process of spontaneous creativity, focusing on the particular stylistic choices of your favorite improvisor. You can trace the development of a style in successive generations of musicians.

Some musicians have learned to transcribe solely to collect material for study or practice. Pianist Jane Getz developed a personal technique based on transcribing Coltrane solos and adapting them for piano.

If improvisation is where your interest lies, you now have the training to concentrate exclusively on solos. Refer to HEARING AND WRITING LINES and HEARING CHORDS in section 9.

TRANSCRIBING "LIVE"

The ultimate challenge. You may have no need to develop the technique of transcribing *live* (while a musician plays) but if you work in the music business, you could be required at any time to transcribe from any type of source. The requirements of live transcription are: speed and, of course, accuracy.

Naturally, you must be prepared. If you plan to do this as a professional service, have an extra supply of pencils, sketch paper, eraser, clip board and tuning fork in a kit ready to go out the door. (If your kit includes an electronic tuner, have extra batteries.) To save time on location, use sketch paper (both single and double staff) with printed bar lines—4 bars to a line or system. This allows for arrow shortcuts. (See SKETCH SHORTCUTS page 156.) If you encounter a three-bar phrase, simply cross out a bar. 12-line sketch paper is the most versatile for any situation.

The most common scenario is a musician ("the writer") playing a keyboard or other instrument while the transcriber notates melody, chord symbols or voicings. The transcriber must be alert; the writer must be patient. If you work with the same composer or arranger often, you'll develop a pace.

Ask the writer to play through the material one time so that you can establish the key, the meter, and get an idea of the overall form, as to repeats, meter changes and key changes.

Ask to hear the first phrase and notate as much of it as you can. Ask for a repeat of the first phrase. During the repeat, check the notes that you have on paper, adding as many notes as you can. If necessary, ask for another repeat, checking and adding notes until you have a complete phrase.

Ask for the second phrase. If it appears to be the same, check each note against the first phrase. If it is indeed the same, use repeat marks, bar numbers or arrows. If it is slightly different, use arrows or reference bar numbers with cue notes to indicate differences in notation. If there is a slight discrepancy between the first and second phrases, this is the time to point out the difference and ask for clarification; the discrepancy may be a simple oversight or an intentional variation. Chances are that you won't be reviewing, so clarify everything as you proceed. Ask for repeats or clarification as often as needed; it is in the writer's best interest that you transcribe the music accurately.

On occasion, the author has been required to transcribe "live" during a rehearsal of a popular instrumental group playing a "head" chart, that is, using only a set of chord symbols. Transcribing a group, you don't have the luxury of stopping the musicians when you need clarification. The technique is here carried to the extreme, analogous to sketching a portrait of someone who is riding on a merry-go-round.

Prepare a comfortable place to write, supplies at hand. Have your sketch paper ready, barred (4 to a line) and page numbered. Since you don't know the length of each section of music, use a separate page for each section. Find the key and meter as soon as possible or pick an arbitrary key and change it later.

As the group starts to play, get as much as you can of the first section. When the music has left you in the dust, skip ahead to the next section, wait for the group, then get as many notes of the second section as you can. Then get ready for the third section. If it sounds like the first section, look at page 1 and verify repeated notes while indicating any differences. Each time a section repeats, verify the notes already on paper and get as many new notes as you can. At the end of the performance, you'll have an opportunity to look over what you have on paper, adjusting, clarifying or filling in notes. As the group starts another run-down of the same music, continue checking and filling in notes, hopefully completing each phrase before the group does.

When you are finished sketching, finalize all details and make a readable copy. Ideally, you should record the rehearsal and prepare a final copy later, if time allows.

TRANSCRIBING MIDI

Transcribing from audio to MIDI **sequencer or notation software** may be an option after you have mastered pencil transcription. Manipulating keyboard and/or mouse requires more attention than pencil and paper, whether you are playing in real time or step entering. You will have to experiment with equipment and software to find your optimum set-up to achieve a reasonable transcription speed.

Converting MIDI **sequences to computer notation** can be a great productivity booster, saving time and labor. Music notation software, after years of cumbersome trial and error, has finally approached traditional music engraving standards but will never achieve the sophistication of making decisions as only an experienced musician can.

Notational situations arise that cannot be anticipated—too unique to be delegated to predetermined software solutions. While software applications may be trained and automated to some extent by selecting preferences, there is always a certain amount of adjustment required to produce readable notation. Some situations are not always predictable, such as choices of enharmonic spelling, degrees of quantization, rhythmic beaming, the spacing and placement of peripheral information about the staff. Any limitations in your notation program require your personal attention, as there is no excuse for less than professional notation if it is to be placed in front of musicians.

Technology is not your replacement but your assistant. Whether or not you use computer-assisted notation, you are ultimately responsible for every mark on the page. If you are producing music for performance or publishing, you have an obligation to maintain notational standards, which have been developing for five hundred years.

See COMPUTER GENERATED NOTATION, pages 334-337.

TRANSCRIBING FROM THE CREATIVE IMAGINATION

The final step in the transcribing technique is simply replacing the source of music with your own creative imagination.

Composition is not just an intellectual activity. Let your ear guide you— let the music flow through you.

EXERCISE 81

Listen to your inner voice. It is probably "singing" right now. If not, make an effort to hear something—whatever comes in. Don't judge it or try to change it. Notate the phrase quickly. Don't deliberate over a key or meter. Just get the notes down. You can take years to refine an idea but only if you capture it while it resides in your inner voice.

Composing new music is a reordering of familiar components; the artist knows the materials before the work is conceived. You now possess the tools to compose, arrange, orchestrate, or write songs without a keyboard or any other instrument. You have the skills to define and notate your musical thoughts, broaden your artistic choices, embrace any style or system.

You've completed the basic procedure for transcribing melodic lines. Your technique will evolve over time; it will take x number of hours until you feel comfortable and confident, then more time until your technique is smooth and efficient. If you picked up a violin or a trombone for the first time, how would you sound the first day? The second day? After one week? As a musician, you already know about patience, persistence and dedication.

In the next section you'll refine your technique, with emphasis on hearing and writing specific elements of music.

9

PERCEPTION TO NOTATION

9

The previous section focused on the perception and notation of the melodic line as the basic element of music. Further refinement of your technique will include rhythm, counterpoint, chords and orchestration, applied to instrumental, vocal, solo, and ensemble music.

As you become more adept at the transcription process, you will be able to focus more of your attention on the details of notation—on how to best represent sounds from recorded media or from your creative imagination. Your notational choices will ultimately determine the success of your projects. If you can notate an audio recording faithfully, then you can compose, orchestrate or arrange with confidence—knowing that your notation is accurately reflecting your intent.

In this section, we'll remain in the sketch mode—fast and accurate. In section 10, we'll be concerned with finalized notation, to be read and interpreted by other musicians.

You are encouraged to find your own transcription material—music that is meaningful to you. Occasionally, you'll find suggested music for selected exercises. If you choose music from your own collection, listen for passages that interest and inspire you, so that your transcription experience will be rewarding on several levels. Start with simple, primarily diatonic tunes and work toward more complex, chromatic music. Transcribe only those phrases or passages that captivate you.

Your transcriptions are perceived through your ears first, then your eyes.

206

HEARING AND WRITING: RHYTHM

In section 8, we introduced basic rhythm transcription. As you progress, you will encounter many different rhythmic situations, all of which may be solved with a fundamental understanding of how music time is perceived and notated. If necessary, review basic rhythm transcription and time-related terms, page 168. Develop a clear picture of how these terms relate to each other.

MUSIC TIME   Music lives in sound and sound lives in time. *Real time* is objective; clock time. *Music time* is subjective, inherent in your perception. Music time is simply a series of pulses occurring against a background of real time. Since time is a continuum, marching on with or without our awareness, we must *tune in* when we actively listen to music, get in sync with the beat, get into the groove.

RHYTHM   is everywhere: your breath, pulse, the tides, days, seasons, life cycles, celestial motion. As in nature, rhythm in music is the measurement of events rather than clock ticks.

The casual listener may not be aware of the rhythms that drive and define phrases of music. If we turn our attention exclusively to rhythm, we'll discover that rhythm patterns are fundamental in describing music styles. Every style consists of one or two basic patterns.

BEAT   Intervals of time are as essential as intervals of pitch in defining music. Music time, like music space, is relative; we measure and notate rhythm in multiples and divisions of the beat. The beat is intrinsic in every phrase. It may be fast or slow, regular or fluctuating, pulsating or subtle—yet the relative duration of each tone remains constant, retaining the identity of the phrase. When notating, we are concerned with the commencement and duration of each tone in relation to the beat.

The beat is usually regular, occurring in multiples of two, as natural as walking. It is also natural to alternate accented with unaccented beats. Multiples of two seem to be a human trait; most music reflects this, spinning out phrases in 4, 8, 16, and 32 beats and measures. We expect rhythmic symmetry; when we hear the exception—an interruption of a pattern—it becomes a characteristic of the music. When some beats are accentuated, we have rhythm.

Music in three (triple meter) similarly occurs in multiple groups: 2 threes, 4 threes, 8 threes, etc. Complex polyrhythms can always be simplified into groups of 2 or 3 beats.

DETERMINING THE BEAT   When transcribing, the beat may be obvious or obscured. Listen from the beginning of the piece until you find the pulse of the music, which may be evident in the melody, the bass, or in the harmonic movement. The beat is physical; feel it in some part of your body. You may want to tap a foot or nod your head or just feel the pulse in your chest or stomach. You may find that conducting helps to establish the beat.

Dance music has a strong, steady beat, immediately apparent. Rubato type music usually contains a discernible pattern but it may be so subtle that you will have to second-guess the composer in designating bar lines. Use your experience as a performer or conductor to make the best notational choices. Clarifying phrases may require changing meters, adding ritards and accelerandos, or indicating changes of tempo.

METER, the ordering of music time, is defined by accented (stressed) beats. The grouping of notes with bar lines coordinates accented beats and functions to keep musicians together in performance. The placing of double bar lines defines sections of music.

DETERMINING THE METER   Once the beat is established in your mind, the meter should be apparent—relationships of accented and unaccented tones that usually fall into regular patterns. Determining the meter is a matter of making the best choice for the performer. The normal pulse of music is the quarter note, however, eighth note meters are used frequently and half note meters occasionally. When transcribing, look for repeated patterns and assign barlines and meter changes accordingly. Your experience as a performer will guide you in making these choices.

▶ **Choices of related meters:**

TEMPO, the speed of the beat, may be indicated by traditional terms, metronome rates, or click track indications. The beat (basic pulse) usually falls within a comfortable range of walking or running. Below are several methods of indicating a tempo; the choice is usually determined by the style of music.

▶ Traditional Italian tempo markings (Moderato, Allegro, etc.) may be found in scores, music dictionaries and orchestration books.

▶ Common tempo markings (Medium-up, Slow walk, Bright two) are idiomatic to the style, usually in the composer's native language.

▶ Metronome marks (♩ = 90) indicate beats per minute. More accurate than words, the metronome mark is often added to a verbal tempo marking. You may determine a tempo by playing the recorded music while adjusting a metronome until it is in sync with the beat of the recording. Or you may count beats as you run a stop watch, timing the number of beats for, say, 30 seconds. Subtract one beat (the first beat = 0 seconds) and multiply by 2 for the number of beats per minute.

▶ Click tracks correspond to the frame rate of visual media. Originally, clicks were produced by punching holes in film at increments of eight per frame. Traditional click notation represents the number of frames + eighths of a frame per second (Ten and two eighths frames per second is a 10-2 click.) Now that clicks are generated electronically rather than physically, there is no limit to the gradation of click rates. Absolute accuracy is required when synchronizing music to visual media.

EXERCISE 82

Develop a sense of tempo. Find a recording that is 120BPM and duplicate the tempo from memory. After you have memorized 120, you can arrive at 60 by halving, 240 by doubling the beat. Think of quarter-note triplets as you tap 120BPM to arrive at 180BPM. Half of that tempo is 90BPM. If you memorize these tempos, you can estimate any tempo.

Q<small>UANTIZING</small>   As you transcribe (or compose) you must decide on the placement and duration of each note, relative to the beat and to surrounding notes. Rhythmic values are quantized (averaged, or rounded-off) to produce a notation that is clear and consistent. Rhythm is notated accurately to the degree that is necessary to convey the *feel* of the music. In the reality of performance, rhythms are inexact, shifting, flexible—just as pitch fluctuates.

When transcribing music, we normally quantize imperfect or sloppy performances to produce a simplified notation that is easy to interpret. When that notation is performed, the musician(s) will add the natural subtleties of rhythm that makes every performance unique. A transcription of a specific performance would be notated "tightly" to preserve the subtle nuances of the artist, whereas a transcription for the purpose of a lead sheet would be in its simplest notational form, merely a guide for future performances.

Quantization values depend on several factors: the tempo, the style of music, and the intent of the notation. In actual performance, a tone is commenced rather precisely (perhaps to the nearest 16th) while it is terminated rather loosely (possibly to the nearest quarter-note). The exception is ensemble writing, especially choral, where the termination of a phrase must be notated precisely. *Be the conductor.*

song lead sheet

instrumental or choral ensemble

While a simplified (lead sheet style) notation is often sufficient, some styles require rhythmic detail to preserve the feel, such as anticipations, or "pushes."

There are always choices of rhythm notation—the best choice is determined by clarity and style. Let the nature of the music guide you in setting meters and quantization. Keep in mind that there are situations where your notation may be sight-read without benefit of rehearsal. Your choices should reflect the complexity of the music, the tempo, and the capability of the performers.

Review BASIC RHYTHM TRANSCRIPTION TIPS, pages 169-170.

EXERCISE 83

Find examples of drums or non-pitched percussion instruments to transcribe. Use standard percussion notation—notes or "**X**" note heads in the percussion or bass clef.

EXERCISE 84

Research various styles of music, notating the characteristic rhythms of each.

EXERCISE 85

Compose a series of short tunes using the rhythm patterns found in exercise 84.

As rhythm patterns become familiar, the transcription of tones and their rhythms will become simultaneous, a coordinated technique.

HEARING AND WRITING: LINES

The melodic line is our natural link to music. The perception
of the line is the means to hearing every element of a score.

The origin of melody is vocal; singing is the fundamental human expression
of music. Instruments add flexibility, larger intervals and extended registration
to melody. Virtuoso instrumentalists add even more elaboration, taking the
melodic line to extremes of complexity, speed and maneuverability. Orchestrally, a line may be produced by many different instruments in unison,
octaves, or other parallel intervals, but compositionally, it is but one line.

We perceive a line by its shape—relationships of intervals and rhythmic
patterns. This image is clarified as we define the size of ascending and
descending intervals and the duration of tones. When we have perceived a
line, defined its characteristics, we then apply actual note names and
rhythmic values to the successive tones, setting the line in notation.

While transcribing, we internally *play back* the line—or any portion of it—
at any tempo, slowing down as much as necessary to accurately perceive the
intervals and rhythm. Using your inner voice, retain the phrase in memory
long enough to notate it, then proceed to the next phrase.

Check your transcriptions simply by reading them while listening to your
recorded source. Sing internally or externally as if performing the line. You
do not need an instrument to help you transcribe, nor to check your work.
Have confidence in your ear. Your tools are with you at all times.

Listen, internalize, notate.

Refer to page 124 to review the PERCEPTION OF A PHRASE and section 8 to
review TRANSCRIPTION TECHNIQUE.

REVIEW: METHODS OF DETERMINING THE NEXT NOTE

◗ Identify the interval from the previous tone to the current tone.

◗ Identify the interval from the tone to the tonic (or prevailing tonality).

◗ Identify the note as a scale-tone (if diatonic/modal).

◗ Identify the note as a chord-tone (if harmony is apparent).

◗ Associate with a previous note of the same pitch (tonal memory).

Develop all five methods. Use the methods that are appropriate for the moment. As you proceed, arrive at each note with the most natural or intuitive method for that moment, then consciously verify the note with one of the other methods. Eventually, the combination of any two methods will operate on a subconscious level and guarantee that you will always hear accurately!

TIPS: ACTIVE LISTENING

◗ Visualize the contour of the line.

◗ Let your perception of tonality guide you, cementing the line. Remember that tonality is subjective and fluid; the tonal center of a phrase may change as you progress.

◗ Compare repetitions of the phrase when applicable; each time a melody is repeated, there is an opportunity to verify your accuracy.

◗ In orchestral settings, focus on the melodic source. Visualizing a specific performer may help to isolate the line.

> Your goal is immediate perception, then notation on the staff.
> Thinking interval names or note names is an intermediate step
> which should be relegated to the subconscious as soon as possible.

TYPES OF MELODIC LINES

Your notation should be tailored specifically for the type of performance intended.

ENSEMBLE LINES   Notation for ensemble players must be precise, as they are expected to perform as one. This requires careful notation of each phrase as to rhythmic placement, articulation, and dynamic markings. When wind instruments play in ensemble, phrasing and carefully placed rests coordinate the breathing of the players. Vocal choir music also demands precision in phrasing and dynamics with attention to breathing and the duration of each syllable.

SOLO LINES   A soloist may be given explicit notation if the composer is adamant about every detail, as if the composer is, vicariously, the performer.

Conversely, a soloist may be given a certain amount of freedom of interpretation and expression. The solo line may be notated with simple rhythm values, leaving subtleties of phrasing, articulation and tone color to the discretion of the performer. The soloist is given permission with words such as *freely* or *ad. lib.* to phrase with rhythmic shading, ahead or behind the beat, rubato style. Rests for breaths may be ignored in notation for a wind soloist if the phrasing suggests breathing points. When writing for a wind instrument, you can whistle the line in tempo to be sure it can be performed comfortably.

The distinction between solo and ensemble notation applies to both instrumental and vocal music. Particular attention must be paid to the specific techniques and idiomatic notation of each instrument. Refer to orchestration and music notation books, talk to performers and collect information pertaining to each instrument.

Listen....Remember what you hear.

NOTATING PHRASES

Use your ear rather than your eye. The ear perceives distinct intervals; the eye can be deceived by our notation system.

If the music is diatonic, primarily of one mode or scale, a key signature may be assigned for the convenience of both the writer and the reader. However, if the music is chromatic, or even diatonic with frequent modulations, a key signature may not be desirable.

Chromatic lines are often awkward in our notation system, which was designed for diatonic music. A general rule is: don't mix sharps and flats; avoid misleading intervals.

EXERCISE 86

Rewrite these awkward intervals by changing one of the notes enharmonically.

The best enharmonic spelling of a phrase may be determined by its musical context: the perceived tonality, the implied harmony or the tempo. If a line is fast, a "melodic spelling" (that is, as diatonic as possible) will enable the player to perceive it at a glance. A slow tempo might favor "harmonic spelling," where the player has time to adjust the intonation to the prevailing harmony.

Poorly notated phrases are especially hazardous for vocalists, as well as string and brass instrumentalists. Even when trying to maintain logical note spelling, you must occasionally change from sharps to flats or vice versa. Try to choose an interval of transition that will not deceive the player.

EXERCISE 87

Choose a short, simple single line passage from your collection of recordings—any type of music. There is no reason to start at the beginning of a piece.

Determine your own skill level; find a phrase that is challenging, yet not so difficult that you will get frustrated.

A chorded melody, such as a song, is the simplest type of line. Treat the vocal line as if it were to be played by an instrument, simplifying (quantizing) the rhythms and ignoring any vocal inflections. If you need something more challenging, find an unaccompanied instrumental solo, where you can concentrate on intervals without the influence of harmony.

Limit your transcription to a few bars; set the limit before you start. Perhaps you will be impelled to continue further.

When you have finished your sketch, read it with your audio source, as if you were performing. You could play it on an instrument but you don't need to because you now have confidence in your ear!

After you are satisfied that your sketch reflects what you heard, re-copy it (pencil is fine) with attention to enharmonic spelling (changing a sharp to a flat, or vice versa), correct rhythmic notation, stem direction and spacing. In other words, make it presentable for a musician to play.

Continue this process, each time challenging yourself a little more. As you do five, six, seven transcriptions, your speed will increase and you will start to experience a flow.

If you have difficulty, analyze your problem and review the appropriate pages to sharpen your tools.

When you feel comfortable with transcribing single lines, proceed to the next page.

HEARING AND WRITING: COUNTERPOINT

Music progresses with two basic types of motion:
contrary moving voices (counterpoint)
and parallel voices (chords).

HEARING POLYPHONIC VOICES

When listening to music passively, our ear may be attracted to the prevailing lead voice or wander freely among supporting counter voices, bass lines, harmonic pads or embellishments. However, when our ears are in active mode, we focus on one specific voice at any given moment.

All art forms, especially temporal, promote clarity of expression: a story has singular direction and intent; drama employs continuity and form; actors usually speak in turn. Good counterpoint allows each voice to be heard as an independent entity, no matter how complex the setting. When individual parts are not crafted with respect to the whole, music can quickly dissolve into randomness or chaos. The astute composer/orchestrator creates depth—layers of foreground, midground and background—allowing the listener to perceive a single line within the total environment of sound.

Students of traditional music theory are often confused by the "no parallel fifths" rule in writing Bach-type polyphonic voice-leading. Rather than learn a rule, it is better to understand a principle. The interaction of our ear with nature produces the concept of tonality. Quite simply: two voices a fifth apart are linked in a strong tonal relationship. If the two voices move parallel, the tonal relationship is maintained and the ear perceives the two voices as a single line. The same effect occurs with parallel voices moving at any interval. The interval(s) of separation help define the character of the line.

In Bartok's 4th String Quartet: I, ms. 26, 27, the husky sounding line consists of parallel major 9ths (the outer voices). The addition of the lower double stopped violin I produces minor 9ths with the top voice and both minor and major 2nds with violin II. The ear perceives these three voices as one line. The viola and cello echo the effect.

Conversely, if two voices in a fifth relationship move in contrary motion, the harmonic link is immediately dispelled as a new interval is formed. This guarantees that the ear will perceive two distinct voices. Bach was a master of moving several voices, each retaining its individuality.

Transcribing multiple voices usually presents no problem if you isolate each voice in turn. Simply focus on one voice and notate, then focus on another voice and notate. Each voice should have its own distinct register, timbre, melodic and rhythmic shape—all attributes of good counterpoint.

As you transcribe contrapuntal lines, a constant check of the vertical relationships will confirm the accuracy of your work.

Transcribing allows us to "freeze" music in time, increasing our perception of each line and ultimately of the totality of countrpuntal lines. After transcribing a passage of counterpoint, listen again in real time with your eyes closed.

COUNTERPOINT: CONTRAST OF ELEMENTS

Counterpoint achieves clarity of lines through the use of CONTRAST:

▶ **VOICE MOTION** Contrary motion promotes independence of voices, whereas parallel motion is perceived as one voice.

▶ **RHYTHM** Typically, one voice moves while another sustains. Rhythm figures, like entrances, attract the listener's attention. Repetitious rhythm soon fades into the background until the pattern changes. Notice how you suddenly become aware of a constant noise when it stops.

▶ **REGISTER** Each voice is provided breathing room, its exclusive space in the audio spectrum.

▶ **TIMBRE** The ear distinguishes differences in timbre, the characteristic voice of each instrument. The orchestrator uses timbre to contrast or blend voices.

▶ **DYNAMIC LEVEL** A balanced ensemble allows perception of each element.

▶ **TONALITY** Two or more voices that move within the same harmonic series tend to blend into oneness—they are harmonious. In order to perceive them as independent voices, other elements of contrast must be at work. The duality of harmonious and contrapuntal forces working simultaneously was Bach's genius.

A remote tonal relationship between voices (i.e., one voice centered around B♭ and another voice centered around E) virtually guarantees independence of lines.

These basic principles of counterpoint apply to all styles of music.

On a larger scale, some music forms and styles are designed to emphasize the contrast of elements:

◗ Solo instrument vs. orchestra

Orchestral concertos; jazz band arrangements featuring a soloist. The solo concerto and concerto grosso forms of the Baroque era emphasize the sharp contrast of the soloist or small ensemble alternating with the orchestra.

◗ Vocal vs. instrumental accompaniment

Opera, musical theater, song accompaniment. Skillful orchestration is required to enhance, yet not compete with the vocalist.

◗ Dialogue vs. underscore

Film composers and orchestrators utilize all the above techniques when underscoring scenes with dialogue, sometimes treating the actor's speaking voice as melody.

Clarity is a result of contrasting elements,
whether you are listening to natural sounds or music.

EXERCISE 88

Expand your transcriptions to include two lines, then three and four.

Continue to search your own collection for transcription material. Following are suggested recordings if you cannot find examples of your own. Choose a piece that you are attracted to, then find the phrase or passage that captivates you. Start transcribing at that point. When you have completed your sketch, decide if you will continue from there or start at the beginning or move on to another piece of music.

◗ Paul Hindemith: *Philharmonisches Konzert, Var. 2.* Extended oboe solo.
◗ Aaron Copland: *Quiet City.* Any solo passage for English horn or trumpet.
◗ Roy Harris: *Symphony #3.* Single line celli, string section chords .
◗ Hector Berlioz: *Symphonie Fantastique: III.* Oboe/English horn duet.
◗ Ralph Vaughan Williams: *Symphony #6: IV.* String unison, then *a2.*
◗ Maurice Ravel: *Trio in A minor: III Passacaille*
◗ William Schuman: *Symphony #3: I Passacaglia.* Viola unison, then *a2, a3, a4.*
◗ Paul Hindemith: *Nobilissima Visione: IV Passacaglia.* Brass unison, then *a2, a3, a4.*

HEARING AND WRITING: CHORDS AND VERTICALS

COMMON CHORDS AND ABSTRACT VERTICALS

Multiple voices that are sustained or move in parallel are perceived as one element, a chord or an abstract vertical. We'll designate those chords used throughout the world of commercial music as *common chords*. All other possible sonorities, including clusters, we'll designate as *abstract verticals*. Hearing chords is a matter of learning to recognize familiar sounds, whereas hearing abstract verticals requires more scrutiny—an analysis of each tone. Your familiarity with intervals will allow you to perceive and notate any sonority.

Chorded music probably originated in antiquity with the first strum of a multi-stringed instrument, perhaps a gourd or shell harp. The concept of harmony, however, was not formalized until the Middle Ages, as Western European music evolved from basic polyphony (unison, octaves, fifths and fourths) to multiple voices moving independently. Music that is constructed on the principles of harmony (modulating tonalities) may be perceived as a series of chords, even if the music moves contrapuntally and the chords are only implied.

Chords may be indicated by placing notes on a staff or with symbols. Common chord symbols may be found in printed sheet music, jazz fake books and production scores used in the recording industry. The parameters of "common" are a reflection of general usage—like a dictionary of common language—chords that are used everyday, rather than every possible conglomeration of intervals.

Chords are used extensively in all styles of tonal music, serving many variations of jazz, pop, rock, theater music, etc. Music that exists outside the diatonic tradition, however, is not supported by conventional chords and symbols. In order to represent sonorities of abstract or microtonal music, new or revised symbols must be invented to meet the needs of performance. As music continues to evolve, the common chord vocabulary will continue to provide a uniformity and functionality to serve as a basis for new styles.

Once you grasp the logic of traditional chord structure, you will have the means to harmonize any note; i.e. any interval between the top and bottom notes will encompass at least one common chord.

CHORD CONSTRUCTION

Chords are constructed of interval combinations, providing a rich harmonic language which is the basis of popular music of many cultures.

Diatonic chords are built on the basic triad, adding tones to create a variety of sounds. Altered chord-tones complete the chromatic spectrum, making it possible to harmonize any note with any chord.

Modern chord structures span nearly two octaves to the 13th. In theory, chords are built by stacking thirds. In practice, a chord may be arranged in many intervallic configurations, or voicings. Any chord may be voiced for two hands comfortably on a keyboard or for the full range of an orchestra.

Since chords are merely aggregations of familiar intervals, they are recognizable and retain their identity through changes of register, timbre, and orchestration.

CHORD COMPONENTS

▶ **ROOT** (also TONIC) The tone comprising the tonality of the chord, symbolized by the letter-name of the root note. In order to assign a symbol to a chord (while listening to or reading music) we must first identify the root, the tonal center of the chord.

▶ **CHORD BODY** The component tones of a chord. A chord is initially perceived in close voicing, that is, collapsed into one or two octaves so that the structure (interval content) may be easily assessed. Later, when finalized in orchestration, a chord may be voiced in an infinite variety of configurations.

Common chord-tones occupy **only one** diatonic scale position, as described below. A chord containing more than one tone in any scale position (i.e. a minor 7th **and** a major 7th) would be considered an abstract vertical.

BASIC TRIAD
3rd: major **or** minor **or** no 3rd.
5th: perfect **or** diminished **or** augmented.

EXTENSIONS
7th: major **or** minor.
9th: major **or** minor **or** augmented.
11th: perfect **or** augmented.
13th: major **or** minor.

These variations combine to provide the entire palette of common chords.

CHORD CONFIGURATION

▶ **BASS NOTE** The lowest sounding chord-tone. In many styles of music, the bass note is most often the chord root.

▶ **PASSING BASS** If the bass moves between chords, the passing tones are sometimes indicated with chord symbols:

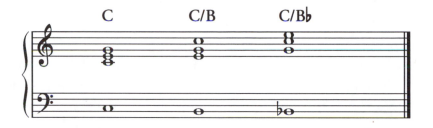

▶ **INVERSION** A chord is inverted when the bass is a chord note other than the root. A triad has two possible inversions, a 4-note chord has three possible inversions, etc. The basic color of the chord is preserved but the overall sound of each inversion is unique. An inverted chord may suggest a sense of movement or suspension, whereas a chord in root position provides a sense of stability or resolution.

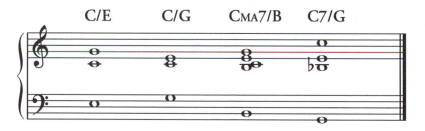

♦ **COMPOUND CHORDS** reflect a simplified voicing of extended chords. Typically, the 3rd and 5th are omitted, leaving the definitive chord-tones. (See ECONOMY OF VOICING, next page.)

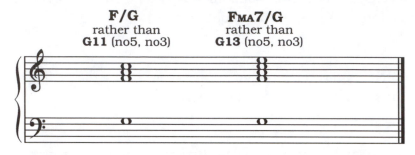

♦ **POLYTONAL CHORDS (POLYCHORDS)** are normally constructed of two simple triads or 7th chords, where each tonality is clearly perceptible. To distinguish from compound chords, a horizontal dividing bar, rather than a slash, separates the two chord members. Some polychords function as compound chords, while others are composed of remote tonal centers.

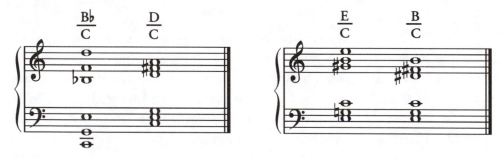

EXERCISE 89

Write a chord symbol that describes the "crunch" chord from Stravinsky's *The Rite of Spring,* as notated below. (Spell enharmonically if desired.)

VOICING

The voicing of a chord specifies the actual pitch of each chord-tone; the vertical arrangement represented by notes on a staff. Any chord may be voiced in a variety of configurations to produce maximum resonance (imitating the harmonic series) or to emphasize a particular color or register.

Chord voicings contribute to the sound of some styles of music: the piano voicings of George Shearing, Thelonious Monk, Red Garland; the orchestral voicings of Maurice Ravel, Igor Stravinsky, Aaron Copland; the band voicings of Duke Ellington, Glenn Miller, Stan Kenton, Gil Evans.

ECONOMY OF VOICING   A 9th, 11th, or 13th chord contains too many tones for most styles of music. However, the sound and function of these chords may be retained, using fewer tones. The essential tones that characterize the chord are usually the 3rd, 7th, and the uppermost extension. Even the root may be eliminated. For example, the most economical voicing of a dominant-type 13th chord requires only three tones:

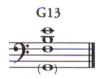

The root is implied and the 5th, 9th, and 11th are unnecessary to convey the function and color of the 13th chord.

Chords voiced in this manner enable arrangers such as Oliver Nelson to get a "big sound" using a small number of players. Economical voicing also defines the piano chord style typified by Bill Evans.

LANGUAGE OF CHORD SYMBOLS

A basic understanding of chord symbols will allow you to describe virtually any vertical structure with a symbol.

The representation of a chord with a symbol provides us with a shorthand system of harmony. Chord symbols, like the figured bass notation of the baroque era, serve as a guide for improvised accompaniment. The figured bass system consisted of a written bass line with numerals indicating the remaining chord-tones to be played above the bass. Modern chord symbols, however, indicate roots and related chord-tones without specifying the placement of each chord-tone. Chord symbols do not define chord voicings or registration. Think of a chord symbol as a collection of harmonically-related tones—a sound environment—rather than a literal description of a vertical sonority.

Ideally, a chord symbol represents a complete harmonic sonority— the basic chord structure and any added or omitted notes. In actual performance, a chord symbol does not necessarily reflect every tone that is sounding; there may be non chord-tones (passing tones, appoggiaturas, or other embellishments) at any given time. Chord symbols are only a guide—usually for improvised solos or accompaniment figures. Chord progressions *(changes)* are often simplified for expediency in performance, allowing musicians the freedom to voice and enhance at will. Many studio musicians are hired for their ability to interpret chord symbols and adapt to a particular style of music.

Common chord notation is found throughout the world with regional or stylistic variations. If you have an understanding of tonality and have mastered the nuts and bolts of key relationships, you'll have no problem designating chord symbols.

A *chord chart* is a bar line layout of the form of an arrangement, usually chord symbols over a blank staff line which is provided for musicians to sketch notes or instructions. Rhythm figures may be included in the bar layout. Chord charts—sometimes called *roadmaps*—are commonly used as simplified rhythm section arrangements for recording or live performance.

A score functions with or without chord symbols. On the other hand, a *chord chart* can function without notes, or even a staff. Many songs have been recorded using chord charts exclusively.

Chord symbols may be used for analysis: a harmonic overview of lines or voicings. Often, the symbols are assigned in retrospect—after the music has been composed or performed—by the composer, an arranger, editor or student. The chord symbols may reflect a detailed summary of voice movement or a general observation of the harmonic flow.

The language of chord symbols is subject to the influence of those who use it. A composer, songwriter or performing musician will choose specific chords to create a definite mood or texture. The style of music is determined by the selection of chords as much as any other element.

We would all benefit from a uniform language of chord symbols. However, there have always been many inconsistencies throughout the industry. Brandt & Roemer's *Standardized Chord Symbol Notation* (now out of print) illustrates 24 unacceptable symbols for a major seventh chord! Occasionally, a new symbol emerges to gain acceptance in the recording studios and eventually in print media, while other symbols remain in limited usage.

EXERCISE 90

Listen to various styles of music and list the chord types found in each style (i.e. minor; MAJOR7; mi7♭5). Notice how a limited selection of chord types contributes to the sound of each style.

DESIGNATING A CHORD SYMBOL

The logic of chord symbol notation reflects the evolution of harmony, from simple diatonic sonorities to complex chromaticism. A chord symbol implies tonality: a governing tone, or root. All other tones are indicated by their relationship to the root. Even complex chords can be reduced to a single tonality.

Chord symbols are constructed from five components: The root, a modifier, extensions, alterations, and a bass note if the chord is inverted. A simple major triad is symbolized by the root (letter name) only; the other components expand the symbol to represent a multitude of sonorities.

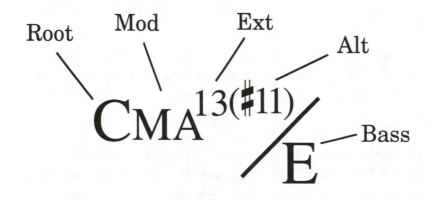

This symbol represents a 7-tone sonority—a major triad with the 3rd in the bass, a major 7th, an implied 9th, an augmented 11th and a 13th.

Extensions and alterations may be configured linearly or stacked. See page 315.

The correct use of chord symbols, as well as accurate notation, will assure a faithful interpretation of your music in performance.

COMMON CHORD TYPES AND SYMBOLS

◗ ROOT

SYMBOL	CHORD TYPE
(Letter Name)	MAJOR TRIAD

The root (a letter name with sharp or flat when appropriate) represents the tonal center, its fifth and major third, which implies the primary overtones of the harmonic series and embodies the Western European concept of tonality. All other chord types are derived from the major triad through the use of additional symbols.

◗ MODIFIERS

SYMBOL	CHORD TYPE
m or **mi** or **min**	MINOR TRIAD

A triad is understood to be major unless modified with one of these symbols. The use of the dash (-) is not recommended as it is simply too difficult to see. The single lower case "m" is widely used; however "mi" or "min" are more specific and easily distinguished from upper case "MA." **"Minor" always refers to the 3rd** of the chord and is not used in any other context.

SYMBOL	CHORD TYPE
MA or **MAJ**	MAJOR 7th

The use of "M," "+" and other symbols only lead to confusion. The worst offense of all is using the slashed 7 (7̶) to represent a major 7th chord. Since both types of seven (7 and 7̶) are used throughout the world and music is truly international, the use of either seven should be confined to the dominant 7th or minor 7th chord. To use anything other than MA7 or MAJ7 to represent a major 7th chord invites harmonic disaster. **"Major" always refers to the 7th** of the chord and is not used in any other context.

SYMBOL	CHORD TYPE
+	AUGMENTED TRIAD

The PLUS sign should be used exclusively for the augmented triad and its extensions (C+) (C+7) (C+Maj7) (C+9). Other raised chord-tones are indicated by the ♯ sign. ♯5 is commonly used in conjunction with other altered extensions, as (♯5♯9) or (♯5♭13).

SYMBOL	CHORD TYPE
°	DIMINISHED TRIAD

The small circle (degree sign) denotes a diminished triad, although musicians often add the diminished 7th when reading this symbol.

SYMBOL	CHORD TYPE
°7	DIMINISHED 7th

The diminished symbol with a seven denotes a diminished 7th chord. Note that this is a four-note symmetrical chord. Since the diminished triad is rare, the diminished 7th chord is often indicated with the ° symbol.

SYMBOL	CHORD TYPE
sus4	SUSPENDED 4th

The 4th replaces the 3rd—the traditional suspension. In modern music, the suspension is recognized as an independent sound, not necessarily compelled to resolve.

The sus4 is so common that it is often notated simply **sus**. However, if the music also contains sus2 chords, **sus4** should be specified to avoid confusion.

SYMBOL	CHORD TYPE
sus2	SUSPENDED 2nd

The sus2 functions like the sus4, replacing the 3rd. Not to be confused with the 2 (add2) chord. (See ADDED TONES.)

▶ EXTENSIONS

The extended chord symbol carries the name of the largest interval (highest chord-tone). Lower extensions are implied. If the next lower extension is not part of the chord, parentheses are used.

SYMBOL	CHORD TYPE
7	SEVENTH (triad, add dominant 7th)
9	NINTH (implies dominant 7th chord, add 9)
11	ELEVENTH (implies dom. 7th chord, add 9 and 11)
13	THIRTEENTH (implies dom. 7th chord, add 9, 11 and 13)

All extended chords are dominant chord types unless specified with "MA" or "MAJ," indicating a Major 7th. Therefore, MA9 indicates a major 7th, add 9 chord.

▶ ALTERATIONS

SYMBOL	CHORD TYPE
♭5	FLAT FIVE
♭9	FLAT NINE
♯9	SHARP NINE
♯11	SHARP ELEVEN
♭13	FLAT THIRTEEN

♯ (not +) is used for a raised 9th or 11th.
♭ (not -) is used for lowered 5th, 9th, 13th.

An altered extension is added to a lower extension, such as: C7♭9 or C9♯11.

Less common alterations: ♭2, ♯4, ♭6. While these symbols are sometimes used to indicate condensed voicings, the corresponding extensions ♭9, ♯11 and ♭13 are more familiar. The fifth is sometimes omitted from the higher extended chords; the symbol need not reflect this omission.

SYMBOL	CHORD TYPE
mi7(♭5) or **Ø**	HALF-DIMINISHED 7th

The **Ø** symbol is okay for sketching but **mi7(♭5)** is recommended for studio or publication.

◗ ADDED TONES

SYMBOL	CHORD TYPE
2	ADD2
6	ADD6

2 indicates a triad with an added 2; 6 indicates a triad with an added 6. Any other added tones should be preceded with "add" to avoid confusion: **add4**; **add9**. Parentheses ( ) are sometimes used, rather than **add**. It is important to distinguish between **2** (2 *added* to a triad) and **sus2** (2 *replacing* the 3rd.)

SYMBOL	CHORD TYPE
*	WHOLE-TONE

The asterisk, proposed by the author, is a convenient symbol to represent a six-tone symmetrical chord which, when collapsed, amounts to a whole-tone scale. The symbol C✳ would eliminate the cumbersome symbol C+9 ($\flat$5), a whole-tone chord with a C root.

◗ OMITTED TONES

SYMBOL	CHORD TYPE
5	TRIAD, NO THIRD

The "power chord" is notated as simply **5** rather than **NO3** or **OMIT3**. This streamlined notation was devised by studio musicians and eventually appeared in published music. Some rock-style songs contain **5** chords exclusively. A **C5**(**add9**)chord may be notated **C59** or **C⁹**.

◗ BASS

If no bass is specified in the symbol, it is implied that the chord is in root position; the root and bass note are the same.

SYMBOL	CHORD TYPE
/	INVERSION or COMPOUND
—	POLYTONAL

REVIEW: CHORD COMPONENTS AND SYMBOLS

COMPONENT	SYMBOL	CHORD TYPE
ROOT	*Letter Name*	MAJOR TRIAD
MOD	**m** or **mi**	MINOR TRIAD
	MA or MAJ	MAJOR 7TH, 9TH, 11TH or 13TH
	+	AUGMENTED TRIAD
	o	DIMINISHED TRIAD
	o7	DIMINISHED 7TH
	sus4	SUSPENDED 4TH
	sus2	SUSPENDED 2ND
EXT	7	7TH
	9	9TH
	11	11TH
	13	13TH
ALT	♭5	FLAT 5
	♭9	FLAT 9
	♯9	SHARP 9
	♯11	SHARP 11
	♭13	FLAT 13
BASS	/	INVERSION or COMPOUND
	—	POLYTONAL

▶ **DIAGRAM OF A CHORD SYMBOL**

$$Cm^{9♭5}/_{Eb} \quad \text{or} \quad Cm^{9(♭5)}/_{Eb}$$

▶ **LINEAR CHORD SYMBOL (word processor configuration)**

$$Cm9♭5/E♭ \quad \text{or} \quad Cm9(♭5)/E♭$$

SUMMARY OF CHORD SYMBOL CONVENTIONS

▶ The **letter name** alone implies a major triad.

▶ "MINOR" always refers to the 3rd of a chord.

▶ "MAJOR" always refers to the 7th of a chord.

▶ 7   Dominant type 7th.

▶ +   Reserved for the augmented 5th—a symmetrical chord.

▶ The sharp (♯ not +) is used for other raised tones (♯9, ♯11).

▶ The flat (♭ not -) is used for lowered tones (♭5, ♭9, ♮13).

▶ o   Minor triad with flat 5th.

▶ o7   Full-diminished 7th (symmetrical) chord.

▶ mi7(♭5) or Ø   Half-diminished 7th.

▶ Sus 4 and Sus 2   Both replace the 3rd.

▶ 2, 6, Add4, Add9   Tones added to a major or minor triad.

▶ 5   Triad with the 3rd omitted. "Power chord."

▶ **Parentheses** are used when necessary to clarify.   (♭5)(♯9) etc.

▶ **Parentheses** are sometimes substituted for "add."   C5(9), Cm(9)

Chord symbols do not indicate voicings—the actual vertical configuration or spacing of chord-tones. However some symbols may imply a voicing. **C(9)** implies a triad with a 9th added at the top of the chord, while **C2** implies a triad with an added 9th in close voicing, below the 3rd. An omitted 5th is not always reflected in the symbol.

ALTERNATE CHORD SYSTEMS

While chord structure seems to be generally understood and accepted, chord notation varies widely. Several systems of chord symbols persist, each reflecting a period, region or style. Within each system there are variations of style and personal preference.

▶ **ROMAN NUMERAL SYSTEM** The Roman numeral system was developed in the nineteenth century for the purpose of harmonic analysis. Numerals I through VII (or i through vii representing minor) indicate a chord's relationship to the tonal center, or key, and its harmonic function. Arabic numerals are added to describe component tones and inversion.

The Roman numeral system is limited to classical harmony (closely related diatonic chords and key centers). However, the concept of functional harmony has remained a valuable tool for communication among musicians. A "four chord" is immediately understood as the chord whose root is the 4th scale-degree of the prevailing key. While Roman numerals may be valuable for understanding functional harmony, they are of little use outside the domain of diatonic key centers.

▶ **NASHVILLE NUMBER SYSTEM** or "Nashville notation" is a functional variation; a hybrid of common chords and the Roman numeral system. Although limited to the recording of American *country* music, the concept is applicable to any chorded music. Nashville notation simply replaces letter-name roots with numbers. The chord root is designated by a diatonic scale-tone number (1 through 7) with sharps and flats added for chromatic alterations. Modifiers and extensions are notated in the same manner as common chords. A Nashville chord chart has the flexibility of being played in any key—musicians translate numbers to chord names as they play. If there is a key change, the new key center becomes "1." The Nashville system is especially useful when accompanying vocalists.

▶ **JAZZ CHORD LANGUAGE**   Chords reflect all styles of music. However, the short history of jazz capsulizes the evolution of chords from very basic to very sophisticated. Early jazz groups of 5 or 6 musicians played tunes with simple chord changes that were easily memorized. As jazz groups grew to larger ensembles, written notation became necessary and with it the notation of chord symbols. Larger ensembles provided opportunities for arrangers to explore more complex harmony—extended and altered chords. Jazz harmony has continued to expand harmonic textures while preserving a sense of tonality.

TOWARD A SIMPLIFIED SYSTEM OF SYMBOLS

The following symbols are suggested for your personal use, as they are not yet accepted as common.

1 (omit 3 and 5—root only) rather than "pedal" or "bass only" or "no chord"

57 (7th chord, omit 3)   **24** (sus 2, sus 4, omit 5)

3 or **mi3** (omit 5)   **37** or **mi37** (7th chord, omit 5)

4 (sus4, omit 5)   **47** (7th chord, sus 4, omit 5) a "fourth" chord

* The asterisk is a convenient symbol to represent a whole-tone chord which, when collapsed, amounts to a whole-tone scale.

Common chord symbols are a product of traditional tonal music. Other symbols may be adapted to represent verticals of chromatic, microtonal or alternate tuning systems as the need arises. Intervals may be measured with equal parts of an octave or as harmonic ratios. Verticals, even specific voicings, can be specified by frequency in Hertz or MIDI key numbers. Microtonal "detuned" intervals can be represented with conventional notation if they approximate tempered intervals or with cents for explicit tuning.

Intelligent software can interpret verticals, define chords and generate chord symbols. However, computer assisted music production is, at best, an unretouched photograph. The experienced ear and eye of a trained musician must always oversee and override computer generated notation.

NOTATING CHORD SYMBOLS

▶ CONSIDERATIONS IN DESIGNATING A CHORD SYMBOL

INTERPRETATION   Every symbol must be specific and unambiguous: include each note of the chord, no more and no less.

SIMPLICITY   Chords symbols should reflect the total sound of the ensemble or rhythm section; they generally do not reflect nuances of vocal or instrumental melodic lines. Passing tones or even passing chords are sometimes omitted. Soloists and certain accompanying instruments may have a simplified chord chart while other instruments, such as keyboards, may have a more detailed set of chord symbols. Keep in mind the musicians that will be reading your chord symbols, the instruments involved and the possibility that they may be sight-reading.

STYLE   Consider the style of music as you are designating chord symbols. Every style consists of a limited selection of chord types.

STYLE	TYPICAL CHORD
primitive; earthy; hard rock	C5
folk; anthem; reggae	C
blues; rhythm 'n' blues	C7
romantic; pop ballad; jazz ballad	CMa7
jazz blues; funk	C7(♯9)
country; pop ballad	C2
1940s swing	C6
bebop; lush ballad	C13(♯11)

Organize (in your mind or on paper) all the tones of a chord, assigning a function (root, fifth, seventh, etc.) to each tone. Evaluate the result and configure a concise symbol that describes the complete harmonic setting. Considerations of structure, tonality, and functionality contribute to the chord symbol. Abstract verticals may be assigned symbols using the principles of chord construction with altered or added tones. As with everything else, this process will become fast and intuitive with practice.

EXERCISE 91

Circle the chord-tones:

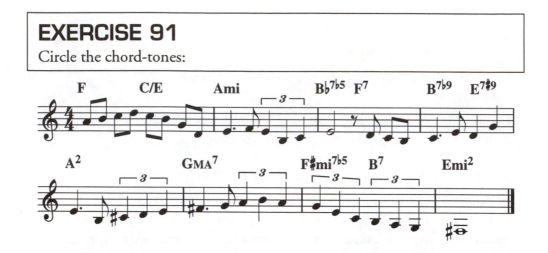

ENHARMONIC SPELLING   When voicing chords on the staff, choose spelling that reflects the diatonic nature of chord construction—the scale position of each chord-tone.

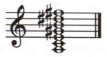

When notating abstract verticals or clusters, try to maintain diatonic scale positions, thereby minimizing accidentals.

EXERCISE 92

Place a chord symbol above each chord type:

INVERSION   COMPOUND   POLYCHORD

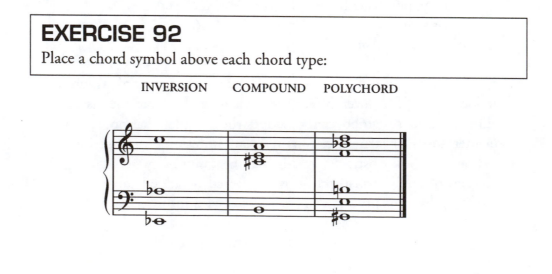

EXERCISE 93

Designate a chord symbol for the following common chords. If the symbol is not immediately apparent, collapse the chord to a stack of thirds. Use enharmonic spelling if necessary. There are often two or more chord symbols to describe a chord. Try to use the simplest chord symbol here.

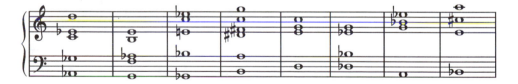

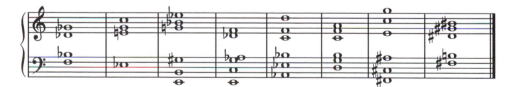

Once you know the sound of a chord, you should be able to notate the chord in every tonality.

EXERCISE 94

Notate, in the treble staff with close voicing.

MODIFIERS:

    F   F+   F   F°   F

    G   Gsus4   G   Gsus2   G

    Dmi   Dsus4   Dmi   Dsus2   Dmi

ADDED TONES:

    A   A2   A   A6   A

    Emi   Emi2   Emi   Emi6   Emi

EXERCISE 95

Here, the progressions in exercise 94 have been transposed at the interval of a tritone. Transpose the notes up or down, using proper spelling to maintain the intervallic relationships:

MODIFIERS:

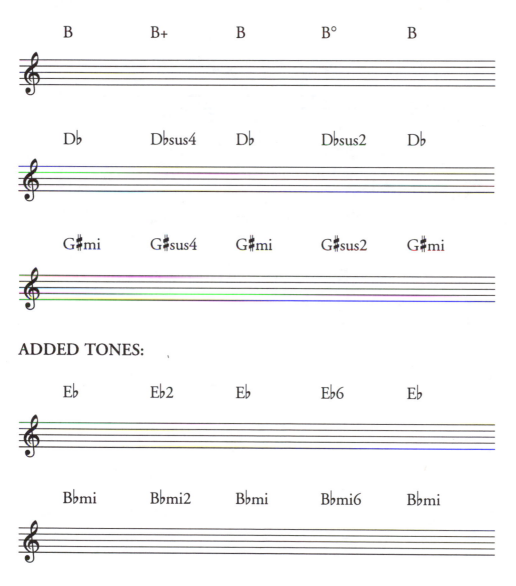

ADDED TONES:

EXERCISE 96

Voice the following chords in the treble clef, root position, close voicing.

G9   Gadd9   G2   Gsus2

B♭MA7   B♭7   B♭mi7   B♭mi MA7

EXERCISE 97

Voice the same chords on a double staff, open voicing.

G9   Gadd9   G2   Gsus2

B♭MA7   B♭7   B♭mi7   B♭mi MA7

HEARING CHORDS

As your chord vocabulary grows, you'll recognize most chords instantly. Your familiarity with common chords provides a vocabulary that will enable you to identify any sonority. If recognition is not immediate, play back the sound; match each tone with your voice to verify, transposing tones up or down octaves when necessary.

Hearing chords amounts to mentally compressing the tones into a range of two octaves—a chord structure's compacted range. Mentally organize the tones into a chord that falls within a two-octave range. When you have sorted out the structural intervals and the modal intervals, you'll have the means to compose the symbol that best represents that sound.

A keyboard instrument is of great value in learning the sound of each chord. Allow the chord to sustain as you absorb its particular resonance and recreate each component tone with your inner voice. Even chord clusters are distinguishable after a few minutes of listening and comparing. When you have the sound of each chord in memory, you will no longer need the keyboard. You will quickly expand your chord repertoire.

EXERCISE 98
Distinguish between these similar chords. Use a keyboard if necessary.

- C2; Csus2
- C(9); Cma9; G/C
- Gsus4; G11; F/G

CHORD IDENTIFICATION
1   Determine the bass note.
2   Determine if the bass note is the root or an inversion.
3   Identify the chord type, noting any extended or altered tones.

Eventually, you'll make these decisions simultaneously, hearing and writing the symbol without conscious thought.

HEARING COMPONENTS OF A CHORD

▶ **BASS** Identify the bass note as you would any note—as a scale tone, or relative to the previous note, or relative to the key center. Determine if the bass is the root, an inverted tone or a non-chord (passing bass) tone. It is not necessary to identify the bass tone first, but it may be helpful in establishing the chord's function in relation to the key and the surrounding chords.

▶ **TONALITY** The presence of a chord-root suggests tonality. Locate the root and establish the relationship of each chord-tone. Look for clues such as 5ths that will help you determine where the tonality lies.

▶ **MODALITY** 3rds and 7ths (major or minor) determine the modality of a chord. Four possible combinations of 3rds and 7ths produce the (dominant) 7th, major 7th, minor 7th and minor/major 7th chords.

▶ **EXTENSIONS** Since chords extend through a two-octave range, there is a distinction between a 2nd and a 9th, a 4th and an 11th, and a 6th and a 13th. Extended chords (9ths, 11ths, 13ths) are normally voiced with the extended tones above the 7th. If the chord contains no 7th, these tones are usually perceived as added tones (2nd, 4th, 6th.)

▶ **ALTERATIONS** Any chord-tone may be altered by a half tone to support a melodic tone or to produce color or tension. Most common are altered 5ths and 9ths. Once you are familiar with each altered chord, your ear will recognize the particular resonance that characterizes it. Altered tones are conspicuous in a diatonic setting.

▶ **ADDED TONES** Normally, tones are added to simple triads to provide color, weight, or to accommodate more voices in part writing.

▶ **ABSTRACT VERTICALS** are chords with non-diatonic added tones, such as a chord containing both a dominant 7th and a major 7th or a chord containing both a suspension and its resolution.

Abstract verticals are found in the music of jazz artists Duke Ellington, Thelonious Monk and Bill Evans, as well as various styles of pop, rock and folk music. When you encounter a chord that seems to defy common structure, identify the basic chord then isolate the added tone by pinpointing the source of additional tension. Even the most abstract cluster may be symbolized if you are able to perceive the relationships of tonality, modality and chromaticism.

TIPS: HEARING CHORDS

❭ Notate the tones that are clear, then fill in missing tones according to your *impression* of the chord. Consider the qualities of the chord: the resonance, the density, the color.

❭ Use *matching* to verify each chord-tone if you cannot immediately identify the chord. Arpeggiate up and down the chord with your voice.

❭ Compare with similar sonorities in the recording. Consider the type of chords inherent to that particular style.

❭ If you cannot identify a chord immediately, write each chord note on a staff. After you've identified the tonality, stack all the chord notes in a two-octave range. When a chord is stacked in thirds, tonal elements (root, 5th) alternate with modal elements (3rd, and 7th).

❭ The voicing or inversion of a simple triad is sometimes difficult to hear, as it blends, by nature, into one sound. Conversely, added tones, altered tones, and extensions are easier to hear, being harmonically more distant.

❭ When verticals are muddy—poorly recorded or so dense that it is impossible to isolate each tone—use extreme EQ (electronic equalizing, boosting or subduing specific frequency ranges). Try listening at a very low volume.

❭ Abstract (non-chorded) music: estimate the qualities of resonance, density and color as you would with a common chord. When you've notated every tone that you can hear, fill-in by *matching,* using resonance to affirm the presence of additional tones.

HEARING AND WRITING: CHORD PROGRESSIONS

A chord symbol represents a vertical sonority;
a series of chord symbols describes the flow of
harmony, the sound environment.

A good chord progression is the songwriter's secret weapon. Some hit songs
have caught the public's ear with a strong chord structure, arguably stronger
than the melody. *Sunny; *Since I Don't Have You; Hey Jude; House Of The Rising
Sun; Lay, Lady, Lay; Sittin' On The Dock Of The Bay* and *Just The Two Of Us*
come to mind.

Many classic jazz tunes of the bebop era are based on chord changes of
Broadway show tunes. The songs of George Gershwin, Jerome Kern, Cole
Porter, Richard Rodgers, etc. offered smooth diatonic progressions with
interesting modulations, usually a brief excursion to a remote key center—
ideal for improvisation. Many jazz lines have been composed over the chord
changes of "standards"—as many as five or six tunes on one set of changes.

The particular sound of a song's chord structure results from a pattern
of chordal movement within a specified meter—its harmonic rhythm.
The sound is not dependent on the relative elements of music; the chord
structure of *I'll Remember April* is recognizable in any key at any tempo.
A jazz musician can easily identify a familiar tune by listening to only
the "changes."

An awareness of style is helpful when identifying harmonic progressions.
While traditional Western European music is usually categorized in terms
of centuries, jazz styles seem to have evolved each decade and various styles
of pop music even more frequently.

*NOT TO BE CONFUSED WITH *SINCE I FELL FOR YOU*

HEARING CHORD PROGRESSIONS

Hearing chords is an extension of hearing intervals—the recognition of familiar sounds. Hearing chord progressions is an extension of hearing phrases—perceiving horizontal patterns. Just as the interval of an ascending 4th is a predictable sound, a triad followed by a triad a 4th higher is a recognizable sound, regardless of register, timbre or voicing. The same tools used in the perception of a phrase are employed when hearing a chord progression: intervals, tonality, scale-tones, chord-tones and tonal memory. The combination of tools guarantees accuracy.

When listening to chord progressions, there are three elements to consider: bass line, chord roots, and chord colors. If you get into the habit of identifying the bass first, you will get a sense of the direction of the progression. Bass lines tend to follow patterns which may include inversions.

- Perceive the bass line as you would any melodic line.
- Identify each chord, including inversions, extensions or alterations.

When transcribing a chord progression, your familiarity with chords should lead to immediate recognition. Until that occurs, use *matching* to verify all chord-tones. If a chord is not immediately apparent, slow down, use your voice and *match* chord-tones, arpeggiating up or down the chord. Check your progression by singing each line through the voicings.

EXERCISE 99

Sing each line (the voice leading) through the progression—first the top line, then the second, then the third. Accompany yourself with a keyboard, then sing *a cappella*. Play the bass notes in root position.

EXERCISE 100

Play exercises 94, 95, 96 and 97 on a keyboard while matching with your voice each line (bottom, top, etc.) in turn. After you are secure with this exercise, abandon the keyboard and listen internally to the progression of chords, starting on any arbitrary pitch. Again, sing each line while listening (internally) to the chord progression.

◗ Diatonic Chord Progression

In diatonic harmony, the chords share the same mode and many common tones. Diatonic chord progressions are therefore smooth, familiar and easy to hear. Try to hear the following progressions internally. If necessary, play them on a keyboard. Sing each line (voice leading) through the progression.

Diatonic chords that are third-related (with roots a minor or major third apart) share a close vertical relationship, having two chord-tones in common.

A diatonic progression with inversions draws the listener's ear to the bass line:

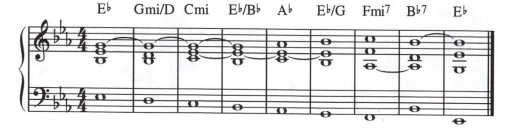

▶ MODAL CHORD PROGRESSION

We'll use the term "modal harmony" to describe the prevalent harmonic language of the Renaissance: primarily major and minor triads, moving in a free, non-diatonic motion; that is, the chord roots are not necessarily of the same diatonic key or scale. The result is an occasional chromatic surprise. We now have a label to describe a particular harmonic motion—neither diatonic nor chromatic. Modal harmony can be a breath of fresh air to ears that have been inundated with diatonic harmony.

Dmi G Dmi Ami F Emi C Dmi F A E

We have recognized modal effects when they appear in lines. (Review MODAL EFFECTS, page 113.) We may apply modal effects to chord progressions:

LYDIAN:	C	D	C
MIXOLYDIAN:	C	Gm	C
DORIAN:	Cm	F	Cm
PHRYGIAN:	C	D♭	C

Typical of modal harmony, third-related major triads share one common tone:

Examples of modal harmony: *Greensleeves; The Exodus Song;* Ralph Vaughan Williams: *Fantasia on a Theme by Thomas Tallis.*

▶ CHROMATIC CHORD PROGRESSION

When a chord is altered, the sound of the progression at that point changes from diatonic to chromatic.

Ami G F E Dmi7♭5 G7♭9 C

When a progression consists of mostly altered chords, it is truly chromatic.

D F♯7+ Gmi7 C9♯11 F9 Emi7♭5 A13♭9 D2

EXERCISE 101

Concentrate on hearing the following progressions. Listen internally to each, then play on a keyboard. Notice how each progression makes a different musical statement.

1) Diatonic	C	Ami7	Dmi7
2) Modal	C	A7	Dmi
3) Modal (all major)	C	A	D
4) Modal (all minor)	Cmi	Ami	Dmi
5) Chromatic	C	A7b9	DMA7

EXERCISE 102

Notate the following progressions, close voicings. Assume the bass is in root position in the bass clef. Tie common tones. Sing each voice through.

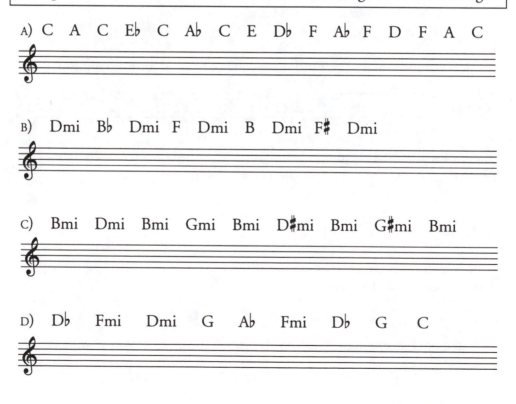

A) C   A   C   Eb   C   Ab   C   E   Db   F   Ab   F   D   F   A   C

B) Dmi   Bb   Dmi   F   Dmi   B   Dmi   F#   Dmi

C) Bmi   Dmi   Bmi   Gmi   Bmi   D#mi   Bmi   G#mi   Bmi

D) Db   Fmi   Dmi   G   Ab   Fmi   Db   G   C

EXERCISE 103

The following pop tunes contain "hook" chord progressions. All have been transposed to the same tonality for comparison. Identify the unique quality in the sound of each progression. Find two characteristics these progressions have in common.

Sittin' On The Dock Of The Bay	C	E	F	D
Lay, Lady, Lay	C	Emi	B♭	Dmi
Since I Don't Have You	C	Ami7	Fmi	G7♭9
Sunny	Cmi	E♭7	A♭7	G7

EXERCISE 104

6 STYLES OR MOODS. Using chord symbols only, write a chord progression (at least 8 chords) to describe each of the following styles or moods. Use modality, alterations or inversions as needed:

1) Serene   2) Majestic   3) Bluesy   4) Excitement   5) Terror   6) Sadness

EXERCISE 105

Write out chord changes to familiar standard tunes. Internalize: try to hear the melody and the roots simultaneously.

EXERCISE 106

Transpose those same chord changes to various keys until you are comfortable transposing at any interval.

Progressions are built on logical bass lines, functional harmony and smooth voice leading. As you write out chord changes, you'll begin to see patterns. Chord progressions may be easily memorized through the awareness of patterns.

HEARING AND WRITING: LEAD SHEETS

A lead sheet is a minimal representation: a single line sketch—the skeleton of a song, instrumental tune or larger work. Normally, a lead sheet will consist of a melodic line (lead line) with chord symbols above the staff and a lyric, if applicable, below the staff.

Lead sheets typically depict a melodic line in simplified (quantized) rhythm values, allowing a performer or arranger freedom to interpret phrasing. Songs are usually notated in the key of the original recording although many situations require transposition. Elements of expression are usually not included on a lead sheet. The form may be minimal: intros, interludes and repeated sections are often omitted. Repeats and *D.S.* signs are used to minimize the length of a lead sheet. It is not necessary to label sections of a song (verse, chorus, etc.) as not everyone agrees on the definitions. However, it is helpful to set off each section with a double bar.

Music can be memorized more easily with the aid of a lead sheet. The simple form (line and chord symbols) provides a convenient outline. Once you memorize the essence of a piece of music, the details can be added when you are improvising or arranging.

People often say "lead sheet" when they mean something else. If someone asks you to prepare a lead sheet, always ask why. Is the purpose of the lead sheet to document, perform or copyright? Is it a new work or a transcription of an existing work? Is it a recording, and on what media? Perhaps what they really want is an arrangement for live performance, recording, sheet music publication or some other purpose. If you understand the difference between a lead sheet and a complete arrangement, you can educate your client, as well as save yourself and them a potentially costly misunderstanding.

Review SKETCHING, page 153-154 and see LYRIC SKETCHING, page 259. Examples on pages 256, 257 and 351.

The form and content of a lead sheet varies according to the intended use:

▶ SKETCH A quick and convenient layout; an overview of an arrangement, medley, transition, timing map, etc.

▶ RECORDING Many recordings are made with lead sheets in lieu of arrangements, where detailed information is not required, such as bass lines and counterlines.

▶ COPYRIGHT A lead sheet submitted for copyright is a document of a musical work, containing legal as well as musical information: the title, writer's name, affiliation (ASCAP, BMI, etc.) at the top of the first page and the copyright notice at the bottom of the first page. (See examples on following pages.) Prior to 1978, a lead sheet was necessary for copyright registration; today, a sound recording is also acceptable. (See COPYRIGHT INFORMATION, pages 354-362.)

▶ SONG PROMOTION Many publishers include a lead sheet when submitting a song demo to an artist who may be interested in recording their song. The lead sheet provides the essential information: melody, chords, lyric—the basis for a new arrangement designed for that artist.

▶ FAKE BOOK A collection of lead lines used for practice or performing brief jobs, such as one-nighters (*casual* gigs). Musicians who are adept at *faking* are able to create the effect of a specific arrangement simply by reading a lead sheet, sometimes transposing at sight. Many styles of music such as dance tunes, pop songs, jazz and songs of celebration require no more than a lead sheet when performed by a small ensemble. Published fake books are available in collections, usually in editions for transposing instruments. Some musicians create their own fake books, altering or transposing lines and chords as desired.

TIPS: CREATING LEAD SHEETS

▶ Try to center the melody in the treble clef staff. Find the highest and lowest pitch in the song and place it in the register with the least number of leger lines.

▶ A melody note in a song is not necessarily a chord note. When transcribing chord symbols, listen to the rhythm section (track) only.

LEAD SHEET FORMAT

Below: SONG LEAD SHEET, with lyric and chord symbols.
Opposite page: INSTRUMENTAL LEAD SHEET.

COPYIST'S NIGHTMARE

LYRIC BY WORD SMITH   MUSIC BY TOON SMITH

MORE IN-STRUC-TIVE THAN PO-ET-IC   SOME BE-LIEVE THAT THE PHRAS-ING OF THE MU-

-IC   RE-PLAC-ES THE NEED__ FOR PUNC-TU-A-TION

MU-SIC NO-TA-TION MUST BE   SPREAD WHEN NEC-ES-SAR-Y

TO AC-COM-MO-DATE THE WORDS

LYR-I-CIST'S DREAM COULD BE   A   COP-Y-IST'S NIGHT-MARE

SOME-TIMES A   WORD CAN LOSE A   SYL-LA-BLE__WHEN SUNG   'CAUSE

EV-'RY - ONE'S TRY'N TO SING ONE

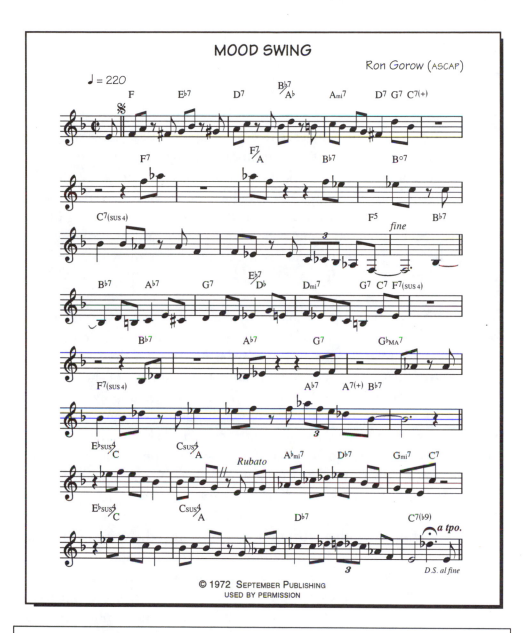

MOOD SWING

Ron Gorow (ASCAP)

EXERCISE 107

Transcribe songs or tunes of your choice. Build a collection of lead sheets for study, practice or work. Sight-reading your lead sheets, transposing to various keys, is excellent practice for situations where you are required to transpose at sight. Memorize the tunes in your collection. Be ready to play any tune in any key.

HEARING AND WRITING:
LYRICS

Lyric transcription is usually executed on a separate pass, after the notes are placed on the staff. All your attention can then be focused on the words. If a word is obscure, play it back several times. Often, the context of the sentence will clarify the word. You may have to search for a repetition of the phrase containing the word later in the song; another reading of the lyric may be enunciated more clearly. If you still cannot hear a word, change the EQ or the volume. Sometimes, another person with a fresh set of ears can hear it immediately.

Words with more than one syllable are hyphenated. There are several methods of dividing a word—as it looks, or as it sounds, or as the dictionary divides it. They may all agree or you may be faced with a choice of how to divide a particular word. Your choice should reflect the use of the music. If you are transcribing a lead sheet or the music is to be sung by a soloist, a word may be divided for its visual recognition: "Child-ren." If the music is to be sung by several people or a choir, the word may be divided as it sounds, so that all singers enunciate together: "Chil-dren." When hyphenating for sound, sing the word slowly and listen to how it divides. When a three-syllable word is sung as two, mark accordingly. ("ev-'ry" "diff-'rence")

When a note is tied within a bar or across a bar line, the word receives an extension line which corresponds to the tie. When a syllable is sung with more than one note, the notes are slurred and the syllable receives an extension line which corresponds to the slur. When both a hyphen and extension line occur, the extension line is omitted in favor of the hyphen. A long syllable over several notes or several measures may receive several hyphens or one hyphen centered between syllables. (See example on page 256.)

LYRIC SKETCHING

When sketching a lead sheet for a songwriter, request a lyric sheet. This will save time, as well as relieving you of the responsibility of interpreting every word correctly. Mark the lyric sheet with the following sketch system, rather than writing the lyrics on your sketch. This will save much time and guesswork on the part of the copyist, even if you are your own copyist.

Draw vertical lines where barlines occur. Draw a diagonal line when a note is tied across a barline.

```
    MORE INSTRUCTIVE THAN POETIC
    SOME BELIEVE THAT THE PHRASING OF THE MUSIC
    REPLACES THE NEED FOR PUNCTUATION
  ‖MUSIC NOTATION MUST BE |SPREAD WHEN NECESSARY
  |TO ACCOMMODATE THE |WORDS
   A‖LYRICIST'S DREAM COULD BE A COPYIST'S NIGHTMARE
  |SOMETIMES A WORD CAN LOSE A|SYLLABLE WHEN SUNG
   BECAUSE|EVERYONE'S TRYING TO SING ONE
```

Additional verses: The lyrics may be written under a previous verse using cue size notes when additional notes are required. Additional verses may also be written out as text at the end of the song.

Hand copyists traditionally draw all upper case letters, sometimes using larger upper case for caps. A computer copyist may continue the tradition, using small caps. However, normal (sentence case) lettering requires less space. Some computer copyists use a narrow typeface. Script lettering, although harder to read, is sometimes used for special occasions.

When copying music with lyrics, either by hand or with computer, the notes are copied first, then the lyrics. Since lyrics are added after the notes, spacing of notes must be opened considerably to allow enough space for the lyrics. Music that would normally lay out at four measures per line may have to be spread to two or three measures per line to accommodate lyrics.

HEARING AND WRITING: ORCHESTRATION

Orchestration is a lifetime study; a continual quest to bridge the illusion of music symbols and the realization of musical sound.

Orchestration is committing a composition to sound, the designation of specific instruments to produce specific tones, the awareness of the total sound environment at any given moment. As a job description, orchestration covers the gamut from transcribing to fully orchestrating from a sketch, MIDI file or audio source. All of these activities involve reading and writing music notation while listening internally or to an external source. Your training thus far has been directed toward the essence of orchestration— representing sounds with notation.

Hearing and writing for each instrument requires knowledge of its playing technique, its peculiarities of iteration and expression, its sound throughout the registers, and its use as a solo instrument and in combination with other instruments. Intimate knowledge of an instrument can only be obtained by learning to play it and perform with it in ensemble.

Since we cannot hope to play every instrument, we must observe instruments in live performance at every opportunity, memorizing the sound of articulations, registers, and typical passage work. Instruments of the same family are similar in technique but each brings to the orchestral palette a unique sound. For specific information about an instrument, go to the source; most musicians welcome the opportunity to discuss the particular characteristics and problems of their chosen instrument.

The study of instruments is only a prelude to the art of orchestration. Combining instruments is a skill that can be attained through careful listening and remembering details and impressions. Look for various combinations of instruments in scores while listening to recordings. The mixing of timbres is limited only by the imagination.

You can learn to hear, and therefore to write, orchestral music by listening to live music, listening to recorded music, reading scores while listening to music, reading scores while listening internally and, of course, listening internally as you write. Transcribing offers additional insight into orchestration; you'll experience the orchestrator's choices as you transcribe recorded music.

When transcribing orchestral music, focus on one line, whether a single instrument or several instruments in unison or octaves, isolating and concentrating on that line. If the composer/orchestrator produced good counterpoint, the line should be easy to follow.

If the line becomes obscure, listen for clues in the surrounding orchestration—doubling, harmonic context, repetition of phrases. If you were the composer or orchestrator, what would you have written at that instance? If there does not seem to be a solution, leave it and continue. Perhaps a following phrase will contain the answer. Or take a break; a fresh ear may perceive the problem in a different perspective.

We recommend that you purchase several orchestration books. Browse through all that are available and choose those that appeal to you. Each orchestration book, while covering essentially the same material, presents its own method of organization, emphasis and specific information as to each instrument. Always have with you a range and transposition reference to supplement your collection of orchestration books on the shelf. (See page 382 for recommended references.)

Composing is drawing; orchestrating is painting.

♦ TIMBRE

When an instrument or human voice produces a tone, a set of harmonics (overtones) in varying intensities results which shapes that instrument's particular sound, or tone color, or timbre. The shape of a tone's pattern of harmonics may be described as a wave form. (Refer to page 31.) Timbre enables us to identify an instrument family, a particular type of instrument, an individual instrument and, yes, even a particular instrumentalist.

Each note generated by an instrument produces a unique wave form which is effected further by changes in dynamic intensity. The result is a discernible change in tone color throughout an instrument's range, and a distinct sound in each register.

The simplest tone, a sine wave, is devoid of harmonics—flat, sterile, not desirable for music. You've heard sine waves used for audio and video test tones. When sine waves are combined, more interesting sounds result. When sounds of musical instruments are combined, complex mixtures of various wave forms result. Yet we are able to discern individual instruments within the mix.

Instruments are built to emphasize certain overtones which contribute to the instrument's overall characteristic sound. Associated noises are integral to the sound of certain instruments: keys clicking, air hissing, external vibrations, buzzes, strings squeaking. The ability to recognize characteristics of timbre, attack and expression is essential when deciphering complex sounds or contrapuntal textures.

It is the complexity of wave form that creates beautiful and interesting musical sounds. The different acoustical properties of each instrument produce the palette of orchestral colors.

When we are writing, we perceive a simple (idealized) tone. In the reality of performance, that tone is actually a complex pattern of sound waves containing a rich mixture of harmonics in a dance of various frequencies and amplitudes. When orchestrating, we are either writing for an *idealized* instrument or for the unique sound of an individual soloist.

EXERCISE 108

Collect recorded examples of each instrument in solo and in combination with other instruments. Broaden your own experience of each instrument, adding to your memory of live performances and recordings.

EXERCISE 109

As you listen to an instrument, describe its timbre. How does the tone color change with varying dynamic intensity? How does it change throughout its register?

EXERCISE 110

Transcribe small ensembles of mixed instruments where the timbre of each voice is distinctive. Woodwind or brass trios, quartets or quintets are a good place to start, then larger ensembles such as the Brandenberg Concerti.

Orchestration involves an awareness of detail;
an orchestrator must cultivate a love of detail.

◗ DURATION

The wave form of a single tone changes constantly throughout its duration. The shape of the tone's evolution is referred to as its envelope. An instrument's characteristics are most apparent during the *attack* or commencement of a tone. During the remainder of a tone's duration, the *sustain* phase, the instrument loses most of its identifying attributes. After the attack phase (perhaps one-quarter second), the duration of tones produced by different instruments playing in the same register sounds remarkably alike.

When focusing your ear on a particular instrumental voice, it is essential to listen carefully to the entrance, or *attack,* of each tone in order to isolate that voice. It is amazing how we can identify the sound of a familiar instrumentalist or vocalist in an instant.

EXERCISE 111

Listen again to each instrument from your collection of recordings (EXERCISE 108). Isolate one tone. Describe the envelope. Is it immediate or slow to speak? Is the velocity hard or soft? How does the sound change as it sustains? Is there modulation within the sound, such as vibrato? Listen to other tones produced by the same instrument. How does the envelope change throughout the instrument's register?

◗ ARTICULATION AND DYNAMICS

An effective performance depends on careful orchestration. Clarity, perspective, balance and control of the orchestra are maintained through a consistent placement of dynamic and articulation marks so that all elements are balanced. There must be vertical agreement as well as uniformity throughout the score. Always check your scores both vertically and horizontally for continuity. See ARTICULATION, page 318.

◆ REGISTER

In order to discern pitch and register accurately, we must consider differences of timbre. In terms of composition, *middle C* is an idealized pitch of which we have some sense. In terms of orchestration, *middle C* represents an actual sound somewhere in the vicinity of 262Hz. However, each instrument playing *middle C* produces a different sound, for the tone is produced with various harmonics.

Even though all brass instruments are constructed similarly, a different intensity and timbre results when *middle C* is produced by each type of instrument. Below is a comparison of the natural harmonic series (through the 8th harmonic) of common brass instruments and how each produces *middle C.*

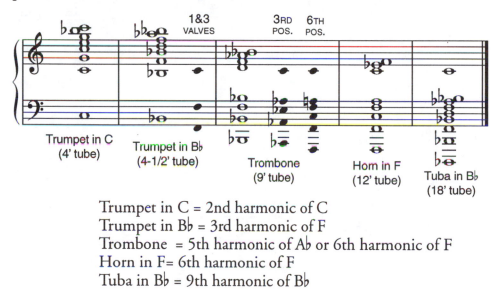

Trumpet in C = 2nd harmonic of C
Trumpet in B♭ = 3rd harmonic of F
Trombone = 5th harmonic of A♭ or 6th harmonic of F
Horn in F = 6th harmonic of F
Tuba in B♭ = 9th harmonic of B♭

As you can see, not every brass instrument is capable of playing *middle C* with its natural harmonics. The trumpet in B♭ and trombone must use a lower harmonic series (obtained with the use of valves or slide).

The same phenomenon is true of woodwinds and strings: *Middle C* (or any other tone) constitutes a different position in the harmonic series of each type of instrument.

RANGES OF ORCHESTRAL INSTRUMENTS (CONCERT PITCH)

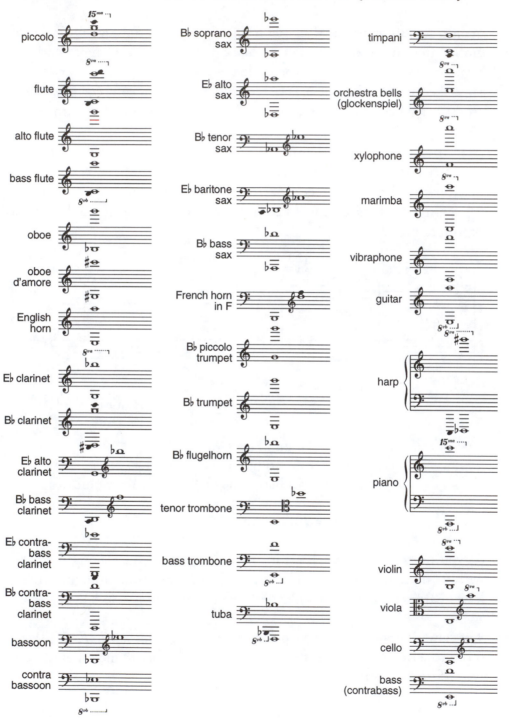

EXERCISE 112

Study the ranges of instruments on the opposite page. Listen internally to each instrument. As you listen, concentrate on the unique (idealized) timbre of that particular instrument. Use a tuning fork or keyboard to establish a starting pitch as you:

▶ a) Mentally play a scale (chromatic or diatonic) throughout the entire range.

▶ b) Mentally arpeggiate a chord throughout the entire range.

▶ c) Mentally play a slow melody, first in the lowest register, then repeat an octave higher.

EXERCISE 113

Within each instrumental family, find recorded examples of unison/octave melodies and combinations in ensemble.

EXERCISE 114

Transcribe melodic lines from your recorded examples as played by each instrument. Again, note the range, articulation, dynamics, tone coloration and effects. Reflect all this information in your notation so that the recording could be faithfully reproduced.

EXERCISE 115

Buy yourself a series of instrumentation lessons. Seek out a professional instrumentalist for each instrument family. Prepare questions. You may be able to learn enough in one hour to last a lifetime. If you are writing a solo piece for a particular instrument, you'll need to investigate much more thoroughly.

CHOOSING THE BEST KEY FOR AN ARRANGEMENT

1 Obtain the range of your vocalist or instrumental soloist.
2 Create a lead sheet of the song you are about to arrange, including modulations.
3 Find the high and low notes of the solo line.
4 Shift the music to fit within the range of the vocalist or instrumental soloist. There will probably be a choice of several keys.
5 Narrow the choice to one key after considering the soloist's timbre— do you want to emphasize higher or lower tones?

TRANSPOSING INSTRUMENTS

Become familiar with all transposing instruments and the extent of their ranges as they appear in both concert and transposed scores. Be able to read both directions—concert to transposed and transposed to concert pitch. Always be on the alert for lines that exceed an instrument's range, especially when orchestrating for acoustic instruments from MIDI patches which, of course, have no such restrictions.

Learn transposition by instrument families. Once you understand the relationship of a B♭ clarinet to concert pitch (the clarinet sounding a whole-tone lower, therefore the clarinet player reading a whole tone higher) you will have a guide to the whole clarinet family. The bass clarinet in B♭ sounding an octave lower than the clarinet ordinaire, has the same relationship to concert pitch plus an octave. The contrabass clarinet in B♭ is the same plus two octaves. The E♭ clarinets, similarly, share a common relationship. The E♭ soprano clarinet, being smaller than the B♭, therefore sounds higher and reads lower to compensate. The difference between E♭ and C is a minor third, therefore the E♭ soprano clarinet sounds a minor third higher than concert and reads a minor third lower. The E♭ alto clarinet then, sounds an octave lower than the E♭ soprano clarinet, or a minor sixth lower than concert (same as an alto sax). The E♭ contrabass clarinet (also known as the contra alto clarinet) sounds yet another octave lower and therefore reads an octave plus a minor sixth higher than concert. If you are reading or writing a concert score, both bass clarinet and contrabass clarinet would appear in bass clef as they sound. In a transposed score, all clarinets are written in treble clef, as are the musicians' parts.

Sometimes it is necessary to perform a double transposition—when transposing a score to a new key while notating a transposing instrument. Double transposing is easily accomplished if you hear relatively, transposing by melodic/key relationships. Your training in the first half of this book has prepared you for such challenges.

EXERCISE 116

Visualize the relationships of transposing instruments to concert pitch and to each other. Learn the intervals of transposition in both directions—sounding to written and written to sounding. Note that all except the soprano clarinet are written higher than they sound.

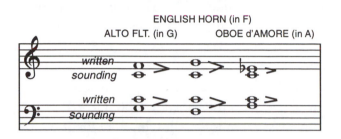

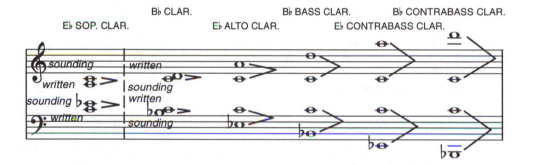

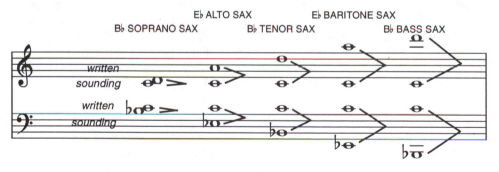

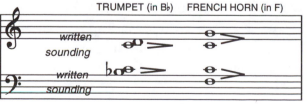

CONVENTIONS OF ORCHESTRATION

Non-transposing instruments of extreme registers are normally transposed by an octave to avoid many leger lines. The piccolo, xylophone and celesta are written an octave lower than they sound. The orchestra bells (glockenspiel) are written two octaves lower than they sound. The bass flute, contra bassoon, guitar, string bass and men's tenor voice (in treble clef) are written an octave higher than they sound. The only exception to this convention is a sketch or keyboard reduction, where these instruments may be written at actual pitch. Some instruments owned by professional musicians have extended ranges, such as: low C string on the bass; low C (concert) on the bass clarinet; F extension on the bass trombone, allowing low E♭ down to B♮, a chromatic bridge to the pedal register.

EXERCISE 117

Memorize the intervals of transposition:

INSTRUMENT	WRITTEN	INSTRUMENT	WRITTEN
Alto Flute	4th higher	B♭ Soprano Sax	MA 2nd higher
English Horn	5th higher	E♭ Alto Sax	MA 6th higher
E♭ Clarinet	mi 3rd lower	B♭ Tenor Sax	MA 2nd+8va higher
B♭ Clarinet	MA 2nd higher	E♭ Baritone Sax	MA 6th+8va higher
E♭ Alto Clarinet	MA 6th higher	B♭ Bass Sax	MA 2nd+15ma higher
B♭ Bass Clarinet	MA 2nd+8va higher	French Horn in F	5th higher
E♭ Contrabass Clar.	MA 6th+8va higher	Trumpet in B♭	MA 2nd higher
B♭ Contrabass Clar.	MA 2nd+15ma higher	Trumpet in D	MA 2nd lower

EXERCISE 118

Study each family of instruments. Learn the scheme of key or fundamental pitch relationships. Memorize the range, transposition and appropriate clefs of each instrument in the family. Note the common traits, overlapping of registers and subtle differences of timbre.

EXERCISE 119

Write the following phrase in unison (no octaves) for the instruments listed. Find the tonality of the phrase; internalize; sing as you write the phrase in the appropriate clef and key.

EXERCISE 120

Create a personal orchestration notebook, dedicating a page or two for each common instrument. Leave extra pages for less common instruments as you encounter them, such as exotic flutes, the recorder family, bagpipes and miscellaneous percussion instruments.

Describe each instrument's range, transposition, clefs, fingering technique, performance characteristics, idiomatic notation and list of recorded examples. Listen to recorded solos; study scores featuring the instrument. Pay particular attention to the difference of register, articulation, dynamics, tone coloration and effects. Consult with musicians as to the possibilities and limitations of writing for each instrument. Your personal experience as a listener is more valuable than information gathered from orchestration books.

EXERCISE 121

Choose a recording of a short orchestral passage. Focus on each compositional element: foreground line, counterlines, vertical sonorities. Next, focus on each orchestral timbre and its influence on the whole sound. Note the texture, the dynamic balance, perspective, the effects of doubling.

Transcribe the passage, one line at a time. Isolate each voice (one or more instruments playing one line). Focus on the character, the *personality* of the voice. Visualize the performer(s) as they produce that particular line.

If you compare your transcriptions with a printed score, remember that there are several ways to notate any one phrase. Compare any differences between your notation and the composers. Yours may be just as valid.

EXERCISE 122

Orchestrate your chord progressions from exercise 104 (page 253), "6 STYLES OR MOODS" for woodwind, brass or string ensembles of any size. Keep it simple—primarily sustained tones. Remember to give wind instruments phrases that breathe. Use timbre, register, articulation and dynamics in conjunction with the chord sonorities to produce the desired style or mood.

NOTATING ORCHESTRATION

Music editors have labored to maintain meticulous standards of music notation through print publications. While computerized desktop publishing has opened the publication and distribution of printed music to "the rest of us," we are obligated to carry on the notational practices that have been developed over the last millennium. It is in the interest of your own music that your notation be understood and interpreted correctly by musicians across the world and perhaps long after you've left the world.

Music notation, as well as idiomatic notation of each instrument, is discussed in section 10. Also consult orchestration books and published scores. Notational variations according to style, period and region must be taken into consideration. Keep in mind the caliber of musicians you are writing for, the style and purpose of your music, and notate accordingly.

Both transposed and concert scores are common today and you must be comfortable with both. The traditional published score is transposed but you will also find concert scores in print. Each has advantages and limitations. The transposed score, preferred by many composers and conductors, depicts each instrument's notation as the performer sees it. The concert score presents an overall harmonic picture. Most film score orchestrators prefer concert scores, as much time can be saved by writing a line only once and specifying that the copyist transpose the line for various instruments.

An orchestrator who uses innovative sounds must be aware of the performance requirements, as well as the symbols that represent those sounds. If you wish to write special effects for a particular instrument, the violin for example, you can educate yourself by consulting with a professional violinist to hear each effect, see how it is produced and how long it takes to prepare and then return to normal. You must be able to visualize the performer at tempo to know how many beats to allow for the preparation of an effect or device such as a mute. Then when you notate a symbol for an effect, you'll not only "hear" it but you'll have the confidence of knowing it is a reasonable request to ask of the performer.

HEARING AND WRITING: COMPLETE SCORES

If you can transcribe a single line, you can transcribe a full score. It is a matter of concentrating on one voice at a time. Even a complex score breaks down to a number of single lines, each of which is a series of familiar intervals and rhythms.

Each voice consists of one or more instruments playing in unison, octaves or other parallel intervals. When transcribing a voice, focus on a specific musician playing an instrument. That musician is a face in a crowd but once singled out, you will be able to follow that voice through polyphonic textures. The personality of the voice includes characteristics of attack, articulation, vibrato and timbre. Visualizing helps, even when the individual voice is a section, such as 2nd violins.

Isolating a single line may be difficult or impossible in complex music or a poorly mixed recording. When the line you are focusing on disappears, listen to the overall vertical texture and use your composing and arranging experience to fill in notes logically, completing the phrase. Look for stylistic patterns that occur in other parts of the piece.

Situations arise in the music business when a score or part must be reconstructed from a recording. Music that has been lost or destroyed may need to be replaced. Frequently, previously recorded music is re-recorded for use in a film when the original master is of poor quality or when the producers discover that it would cost more to license the original recording. (Either way, the publisher is paid for use of the composition and/or the arrangement.) These "soundalike" recordings require exact takedowns in order to recreate every detail of the original sound.

A score may be configured in several formats—full score, condensed, or conductor's score, compositional sketch, orchestral sketch, keyboard reduction.

The following exercises are designed to integrate your perception with your notational skills. Be willing to dedicate the time required to complete the exercises. When you are in a working situation, you will then know exactly how to proceed.

EXERCISE 123

Select a passage in a fully orchestrated score of a favorite work. Copy the printed score on blank score paper. This may seem tedious and unnecessary, but it is worth doing one time.

Hint: scan the first bar vertically to find the busiest part. Copy this part first. Draw vertical guide lines (at the left side of the note head) for each beat. Align all the other parts vertically. Repeat this for each bar. This will assure that no part will be too crowded. Vertical alignment is essential for representing the rhythmic relationship of all parts in a score.

Following is a short excerpt from Stravinsky's *The Rite of Spring* in full score, followed by an orchestral sketch of the same passage on page 278 and a compositional sketch on page 279.

Read with your ears. As you discern the vertical relationships, mentally transpose the alto flute, English horns, clarinets and horns to their concert pitches. Visualize the orchestra as you listen (internally) to the score. The vertical relationships on the score page become three dimensional on the stage.

If you've never played in an orchestra, find an excuse to put yourself in the orchestra (or on the floor) during a rehearsal. Feel the resonance.

◗ ORCHESTRAL SKETCH Concert (non-transposing); all instruments shown at actual pitch. Organized by woodwind, brass, percussion, string choirs.

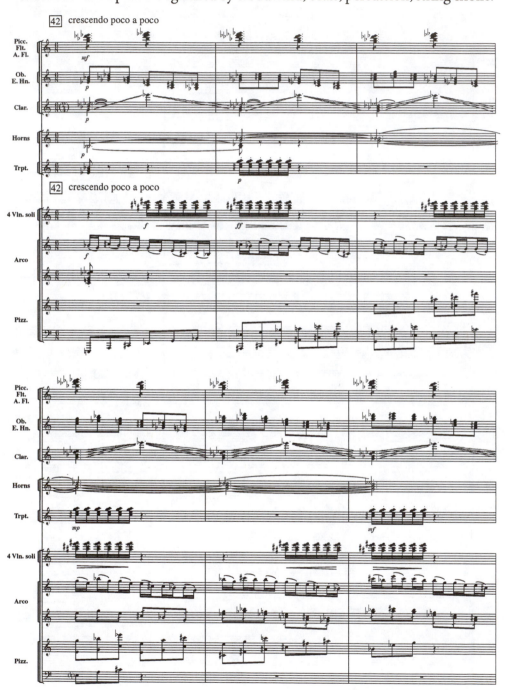

◗**COMPOSITIONAL SKETCH** Concert (non-transposing); all
instruments shown at actual pitch. Organized by compositional elements;
the orchestration has been stripped away.

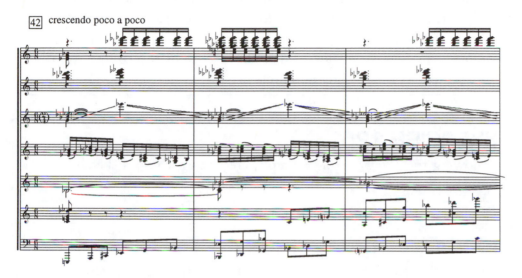

EXERCISE 124

Create a keyboard reduction from the *Rite of Spring* sketches on the previous pages, to be played by four or six hands. Use a grand staff for each of the two or three players. Notate every line at the original pitch, to reflect the actual sound of the orchestrated version. Stravinsky's arrangement for two pianos renders the essence of the composition but does not reflect the full orchestration.

EXERCISE 125

Following the *Rite of Spring* example, create an orchestral sketch of your score from exercise 123.

EXERCISE 126

Create a compositional sketch from your orchestral sketch (exercise 125).

EXERCISE 127

Write a short composition in sketch form.

EXERCISE 128

Expand your composition to an orchestral sketch.

EXERCISE 129

Expand your orchestral sketch to a full (transposed) score.

EXERCISE 130

1 Find a recorded work that interests you. Transfer a portion of it to tape or disc. A few bars may be enough for your first experience. You can always add more later. For this first assignment, we'll make a full concert score, then a transposed score. You must be comfortable with both.

2 Listen through and make a list of the instruments that you hear. The list may change as you progress.

3 Sketch a lead sheet so that you can see the scope of your project, notating a prominent single line as a guide. Choose a meter signature that will allow the music to be notated comfortably for musicians and conductor. Find the pitch and tonal center and determine a key signature, if appropriate.

4 Make a compositional sketch, designating one or two staff lines for each compositional element. Disregard the orchestration and focus on the notes of each line. Indicate chord symbols if applicable.

5 Make an orchestral sketch, grouping each instrumental choir on two staves or more, if necessary. During this phase, while you are concentrating on each instrument family, determine which instruments are contributing to the sound of each voice.

6 Make a full concert score. Never force too many instruments on a line. Combine instruments of the same family on one staff line only if they play together rhythmically and can be notated clearly on one staff. It is always preferable to choose staff paper with extra lines; you may need an extra staff above the violins or below the tuba so that notes in extreme registers do not run into neighboring staff lines. Extra staff lines can be utilized for bar numbers, sketching, timing notes, breakout divisi, solo or ossia lines. (See page 346, SCORE LAYOUT.)

7 Make a transposed score. This may require a few more staff lines than your concert score to accomodate woodwinds of various transpositions.

After you gain experience, you may eliminate intermediate sketches. However, it is recommended that you always start with the lead sheet format, where you make critical decisions of meter, tonality and form.

EXERCISE 131

RECREATING A COMPLETE SCORE FROM AUDIO:

Sometimes it is necessary to duplicate an existing recording—when the original music has been lost or destroyed, for placement in a film, or for archival purposes.

1   Listen through the recording and create a list of all the instruments that you hear. Check liner notes or other reference sources to verify the exact instrumentation of the original recording.

2   List the instrumentation requirements of your recording project. If your instrumentation differs from the original recording, you will have to adapt. Decide if you will re-orchestrate as you transcribe or after your initial transcription. It is suggested that you transcribe the original instrumentation, than decide how best to orchestrate with the new instrumentation.

3   Before transcribing, listen through again and decide how your transcription can best represent the material—an orchestral sketch or a full score.

4   Sketch a single-line (lead sheet) to determine the layout, duration, form. Will your transcription maintain the original form or be modified? Will your transcription remain in the original key or is there a reason (such as vocal considerations) to change it? Determine the meter, any changing meters, tempos, key centers, and whether or not to use a key signature.

5   Select appropriate score paper, considering divisi or single line parts, transposed instruments and the amount of activity in each bar. Allow extra staff lines for extreme registers, bar numbers, etc.

6   Lay out your score. Instrument names, key signatures, meter signatures, double barlines, bar numbers, page numbers. Your lead-line sketch provides information for a complete score layout. Take the time to lay out as much as possible before transcribing.

(CONTINUED)

7　When you begin transcribing, concentrate on one voice at a time and move ahead. Transcribe lead lines, chord symbols (if appropriate), significant events. Skip any obscure parts—keep moving ahead. Don't get bogged down with details that can be filled in later. Whether you transcribe linearly throughout or vertically, bar by bar, often depends on the style of music.

8　After completing your first pass, start from the beginning and fill in missing details.

9　Check your lines against the vertical or harmonic texture.

10　Finalize your score. Add dynamics, phrases, articulation, performance instructions. Check for continuity of all markings.

11　Check continuity of pages. Match the end of each page to the beginning of the next page for continuation of lines, ties, reiteration of accidentals, etc.

12　Check your work: follow (internalize) each voice through the score as you listen to the recording. Have you allowed enough time for breathing, instrument changes, mute changes? *Be the performer.*

EXERCISE 132

Re-copy your score from exercise 131. While this may seem like a waste of time, you will be surprised at the results. Not only will you have the opportunity to clean up and align the notation, you'll view the music in another light, perhaps more vertically, more orchestrally or more compositionally. Your own compositions and orchestrations, also, will benefit greatly if you develop the habit of re-copying your scores.

The payoff is greater insight, accuracy and clarity, which will prove invaluable to your future projects. You probably will not have time to do this under the duress of real working conditions but your time invested now will prepare you to turn out quality scores in one pass. What better way to spend your time? Is this not your work, your life?

A transcription of only a few bars can be an education. As you get up to speed, you'll be able to transcribe more music at one sitting. Always transcribe in two steps: sketch first, then final copy. Let your inspiration, passion and curiosity propel you to greater challenges.

This completes your training. You are now ready for new experiences. In the following section, you'll have an opportunity to refine your notation skills.

10

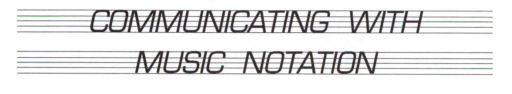

COMMUNICATING WITH
MUSIC NOTATION

10

COMMUNICATING WITH
MUSIC NOTATION

Now that you can "hear anything," how can you
best represent those sounds in music notation?

Symbols become sounds, as music notation is interpreted by musicians in the
moment of performance. Notation enables us to compare music of various
cultures, periods and styles, and to distribute our own music for performance,
publication and preservation. In this section, we'll look at how notation evolved,
became standardized, altered to accommodate chromatic tones and how it
may be adapted to serve contemporary music.

LANGUAGE OF MUSIC NOTATION

Music notation evolved over many centuries, simultaneously in different parts of the world, coinciding with other innovations such as printing with movable type and the concept of representing time graphically from left to right. The idea of using symbols to represent sounds elevated music to a high art. Music notation freed performers from the limits of memory, enabling more complex polyphonic lines, polyrhythmic figures and longer forms.

Modern music notation has roots at least 3,000 years old. The early Greeks devised various systems of notation using alphabetical letters to represent scale-tones. During the middle ages, letters were replaced by shapes indicating upward or downward motion, which later evolved into crude square shapes, neumes, the prototypes of our modern note heads and stems.

An innovation occurred during the ninth or tenth century when a horizontal line was drawn above the text, representing the first tone of the mode. This line was an indication of tonality; it established a reference with which to measure all intervals, a horizon for melodic contour. The pitch was, of course, relative—adjusted up or down to accommodate a comfortable range for the singers.

Eventually, a second horizontal line was drawn above the first. The distance between the two lines represented the interval of a 5th. In order to gain more precision, a line was drawn between the two, representing intervals of a third. More lines were drawn to create staves of 6, 10, as many as 15 lines—too many for the eye to differentiate. This process of trial and error extended over several centuries. The eventual solution was to split a *grand staff* of eleven lines into two 5-line staves, the middle line replaced with a space. Each portion received a signature clef (treble and bass).

Soon after the invention of the printing press in the sixteenth century, music notation become standardized, settling on the familiar five line staff, rounded note heads and rhythmic note values. Bar lines made possible the modern score and the performance of more complex music.

MUSIC TO THE EYE

The eye is able to quickly gather information from symbols—shapes and proportions—if the language of those symbols is understood.

Our notation system was designed to optimize the interpretation of melodic lines and vertical sonorities. When hearing music, the octave is your reference for all tones. When writing music or reading music, the staff is your visual reference, the grid upon which melodic and vertical shapes unfold. The musician's eye moves along an almost invisible staff, absorbing a maximum of information in tempo. We scan groups of notes—linear and vertical patterns—just as we read groups of words, rather than each word or each letter. We tend to hear, see and think music in phrases.

The sounds and rhythms of music, moving freely in music space and time, must necessarily be constrained to the two-dimensional space defined by the staff, the bar line and the page. The lines and spaces of the staff accommodate the 7 tones of the diatonic scale and, when altered with accidentals, provide for the 12-tone chromatic scale. The accuracy of pitch and rhythm is set by our notational system. A note represents an idealized pitch, accurate to the nearest half-tone. Rhythmic values are usually simple multiples or divisions of the beat. Each performance provides a new rendition of a notated work, as discrete intervals of pitch and rhythm on a staff are transformed into an infinite variety of pitches and tempos, subject to subtle adjustments and fluctuations of the moment.

> Just as tonality is the gravity of music,
> the staff line is the horizon, the visual grid
> where intervals of space and time describe
> melodic motion and vertical sonorities.

SYMBOLS OF SOUND

Music notation uses static (digital) symbols to serve a dynamic (analog) medium. Modern music symbols, the product of centuries of refinement from medieval monks to Renaissance engravers, are aesthetically pleasing, as well as highly efficient. Each character is proportional to the staff and has a distinctive, almost three-dimensional shape, immediately recognizable to the eye.

The beauty and continuity of the music character set is achieved by uniform proportions and the *italic* effect of each shape. When a curved line is drawn with an italic (wedge shaped) pencil or pen point, a graceful shape results. The same weighted line is seen in the drawings of the Disney artists.

Hearing and writing music involves interpreting sound as symbols.

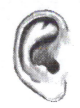

tones/intervals (pitch)   ⟺   note heads on staff
duration (beats)   ⟺   rhythmic note values
timbre   ⟺   instrument/patch names
performance attributes   ⟺   articulation/phrasing

You can become a better reader, and therefore a better writer, as you become adept at instantly recognizing intervals on the staff. Hear what you see.

 TONAL STRUCTURE

GENERIC INTERVALS

Train your eye to recognize instantly the span of each interval as it resides on the staff. We'll start with generic intervals—without clefs, therefore without specific notes.

EXERCISE 133

Space to space or line to line intervals. These intervals are the primary elements of chord structure.

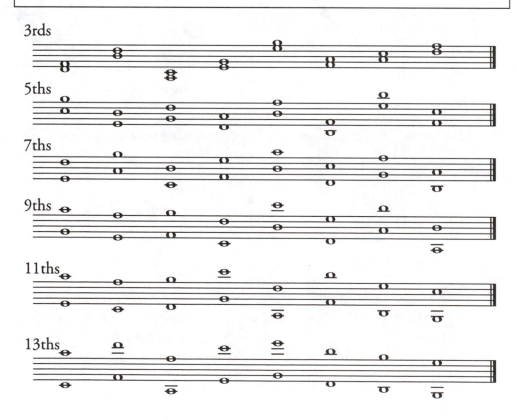

Space to line or line to space intervals.

2nds

4ths

6ths

Octaves

10ths

12ths

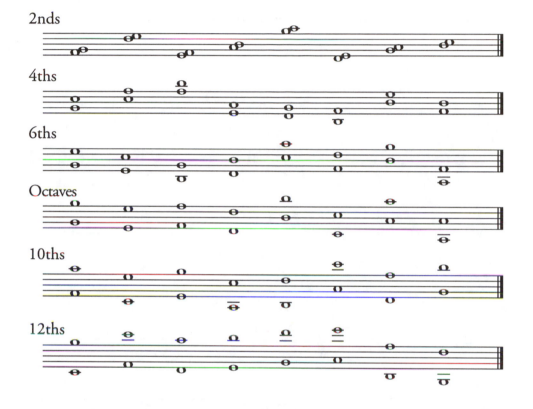

Find the uniqueness and the tonality in each interval.
If necessary, review section 5, HEARING INTERVALS.

SPECIFIC INTERVALS

A clef (with or without a key signature) defines a specific interval.

> ## EXERCISE 134
> Quickly identify the following intervals (minor or major 2nd, etc.)

2nds

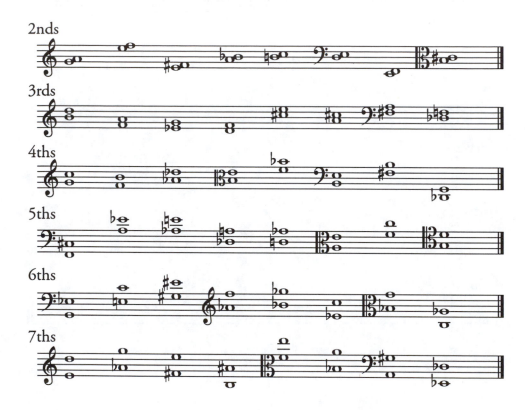

3rds

4ths

5ths

6ths

7ths

EXTENSIONS

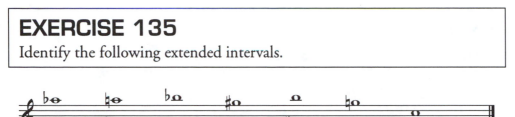

EXERCISE 135

Identify the following extended intervals.

ENHARMONIC INTERVALS

EXERCISE 136

Mentally change one of the two notes enharmonically, then name the common interval.

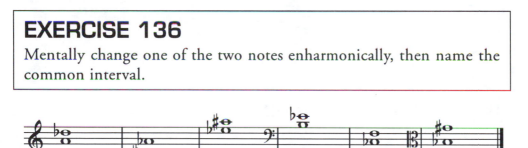

RECOGNIZING STRUCTURES:

EXERCISE 137
Learn to recognize the shape of a triad in any inversion.

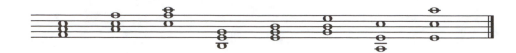

EXERCISE 138
Quickly identify these major or minor triads.

SYMMETRICAL STRUCTURES:

EXERCISE 139
Label the following diminished or whole-tone chords, disregarding roots.
Use only the symbol ° (for diminished) or * (for whole-tone).

BASIC RHYTHMIC PATTERNS

Even the most complex rhythms are multiples or divisions of these basic patterns. As you learn to recognize rhythm patterns at a glance, your eye will immediately spot rhythmic errors, bars that don't add up.

Bar ÷ 2 (duple)

Bar ÷ 3 (triple)

Beat ÷ 4

Beat ÷ 3

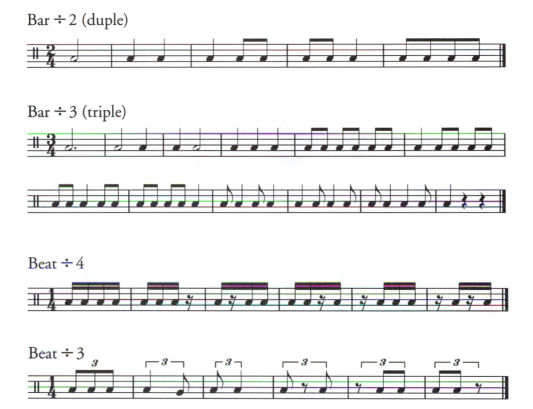

"Swing" style refers to uneven eighth note figures, the note on the beat receiving a longer duration than the upbeat note, which may be as long as an eighth-note triplet or as short as a 32nd. The precise notation is not practical as it is too detailed for the reader. More significantly, the writer cannot anticipate the exact ratio of swing, as the "feel" is often determined by the moment of performance: the tempo as well as the style. This is a good example of one word sparing needless notational detail; "swing" or "swing eighths" tells the musicians to listen and adapt.

STANDARD MUSIC NOTATION

The musician depends on proper notation; any deviation will slow the reading process and risk a faulty performance. This is especially true when minimal rehearsal time forces performers into a sight reading mode. Standard notation enables familiar intervals and rhythmic patterns to be interpreted spontaneously as phrases.

The present notation system is the product of centuries of refinement and is used throughout the world to represent the music of various cultures. Bela Bartok spent years recording, transcribing and adapting folk music of Hungarian and Rumanian villages. His compositions contain many examples of ethnic styles notated and performed with standard notation.

Music notation—like verbal language—is maintained by tradition, yet adapts to accommodate new uses. Notational problems can be solved by adapting the logic of standard notation, by looking at examples of printed music, or by consulting notation references such as *Music Notation* by Gardner Read, *The Art of Music Engraving and Processing* by Ted Ross or the *Essential Dictionary of Music Notation* by Tom Gerou and Linda Lusk.

> Standard music notation enables composers and conductors to function internationally and musicians of diverse cultures and languages to perform together.

CHROMATIC NOTATION

Our music notation system was designed for diatonic music and serves it well, but it falls short of representing chromatic music. Altering notes with sharps and flats may be awkward at times but the experienced musician adjusts, mentally substituting enharmonic spelling when necessary.

An intelligent notation must reflect musical phrases as we hear them, respective of tonality or some perceptible method of tonal organization. Since we conceive and perceive music in terms of intervals, we prefer to see those intervals in their "correct" spelling, both linearly and vertically, in order to interpret phrases and verticals accurately. An interval is more apparent if written F - B♭ rather than E♯ - B♭ or F - A♯.

Equal temperament, championed by Bach as a symbol of human equality as well as the freedom to move from one key to another, incited an ongoing argument of intonation—whether an A♯ is played the same as a B♭. Of course, the answer is both yes and no, depending on the instrument and the musical context. If an A♯ is played as a leading tone to B, it has a tendency to be played higher than a B♭ moving downward. The ear guides the intonation of vocalists as well as string and wind instrumentalists. When performing with keyboard or mallet instruments, however, the subtleties of intonation must be compromised. Your notational choices—even when writing for keyboard—help the performer's interpretation, by reflecting such melodic or harmonic tendencies. Nevertheless, there are some contemporary composers who seem to ignore the diatonic/chromatic relationship and notate as if music had always been 12 equal tones, leaving the performer to interpret phrases without the benefit of familiar intervals.

The best notational choice is always dependent on the context. We usually spell phrases diatonically with chromatic notes treated as alterations according to some criteria—direction of movement, resolution, or chord voicing. There are situations where you may want to make an enharmonic adjustment, such as a G7(♯9) chord. The ♯9 is an A♯ but may be more intelligible as a B♭. Or it may look best as an A♯ in a vertical and B♭ in a linear part. While scores usually reflect the vertical spelling of chords, those same notes may be changed enharmonically when extracting parts to facilitate the performance of individual lines.

Keys are sometimes changed enharmonically for a transposing instrument.

Concert key

Transposed (B♭ instrument)

Keys with many sharps or flats tax the musician's perception. When confronted with a choice of six flats or six sharps:

Use six flats if the phrases lean toward the major or Lydian side;
Use six sharps if the phrases lean toward minor or Phrygian.

A choice such as this will also minimize double sharps and double flats.

Occasionally, we experience the "chromatic crossover" where the tonality changes from sharps to flats or from flats to sharps. This is the equivalent of crossing the international date line; there is an adjustment, then a return to normal. Use your good editing sense to choose the least awkward interval to make the change.

The same type of problem occurs in modulation; a common tone sometimes looks best when two enharmonic tones are tied to each other in a score or keyboard part.

A sequencer simply plays back numbered notes but a musician needs more information. It is often necessary to convert uncommon spellings to recognizable (diatonic) intervals in the interest of clarity and expediency in performance. Music software should be savvy enough to do the same but cannot anticipate every situation. A spelling such as this should allow you to sing or play this phrase without difficulty.

Learn to quickly transpose enharmonically the awkward intervals that you may encounter.

EXERCISE 140

Rewrite the following to create a line that is easy to hear. Change notes enharmonically at will, add bar lines, meters and beams. There are many possibilities; if it sings or plays well, it's right.

MICROTONAL NOTATION

Microtones, as performed by acoustic instruments, are perceived as variations of the familiar 12-equal intervals. Likewise, microtones are best notated as altered tones, usually as an equal fraction of the whole-tone. Microtonal intervals are typically used for effects of tension or otherworldliness in film scores. Following are some of the more commonly used symbols used for the quarter-tone.

You may indicate a microtonal interval with text or a number just above or below the arrow (4 for quarter-tone or 3 for one-third-tone).

Both text and symbols are necessary to describe an effect, such as:

▶ MEASURED INFLECTION

▶ UNMEASURED INFLECTION

▶ RANDOM INFLECTION

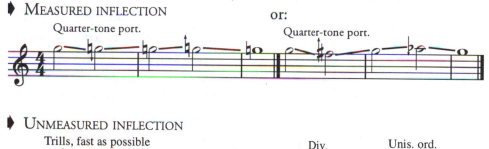

If you notate your effects carefully, you will save valuable rehearsal time.

EDITING

Every step of the music making process requires constant scrutiny and instant decisions; a series of "best" choices when composing, arranging, orchestrating, copying or proofreading. All of these jobs share the responsibility of every mark on the page. If you are capable of performing every job in the chain, you are better equipped to perform any one job. Your understanding of the total process enables you to communicate to others with maximum efficiency, preserving the original intent of the music.

While notating music, you are compelled to make editing decisions. Some decisions may be made spontaneously; some must be postponed until your sketch is complete, when you have a sense of the style, the duration, the form of the music.

Wise choices depend on knowing the purpose, style and performance particulars of the music at hand. What is the intent of this music? It may be to inspire, calm, excite; to serve live drama, visual media, person or product identification, play-on, play-off; to accompany a sport or patriotic event, to set a mood for exercise, dance, romance, healing or meditation. Will it be recorded or performed live? Acoustic or electronic instruments? What level of performers? Your notational choices should express clear musical thought with the least ambiguity, resulting in the best possible performance.

Be the artist—taking a step back to view the work at arm's length, checking for continuity and consistency, as well as examining the finest detail. Because deadlines often make editing a luxury, you will eventually cultivate the ability to edit as you notate. However, it is always beneficial to take the time to look over your work before releasing it.

Composition is like architecture, but it is also like sculpting—removing and refining through the editing process.

STYLE

A style is a convenient word to identify a set of characteristic elements of music. Choices of rhythmic figures, scales, modes, chords, instruments and forms are the recognizable elements that ultimately define a style. Composing or arranging within a style requires the consistent use of those attributes.

Styles are generally identified with a particular time and place, reflecting cultural rituals, local or national tradition, and shaped by indigenous instruments. There may be many sub-styles, defined by eras, regions and innovators. Folk styles are commonly perpetuated by rote, whereas classical or ensemble styles are more apt to be preserved in some form of notation.

If we are familiar with a particular style of music, editing becomes second nature; we know what sounds and rhythms are typical. If we are unfamiliar and want to be true to the style, some research is required—listening to recordings or finding examples in notation.

Film scores often contain *source music,* that is, music from a source within the film, such as a group of musicians or a radio, either on-screen or off-screen, in the vicinity of the scene. Creating source music requires researching a particular style, then incorporating that style into appropriate music for the scene.

With the emergence of the electronic age, music styles of various cultures have become accessible to all and shared mutual influences have been artistically combined. Composers are no longer confined to a regional or national style. A piece of music may be created from scratch, the style integral to the composition itself.

EXERCISE 141

Make a style matrix: list vertically all styles that come to mind. Make columns for GENRE OR INNOVATOR, PERIOD, REGION, CHARACTERISTIC INSTRUMENTS, SCALES OR MODES, RHYTHMIC PATTERNS, FORMS.

WHAT IS GOOD NOTATION?

> These things go out into the world and I want not to
> be ashamed of myself when I see my name on them.
>   Mozart

Out of the practices of composers and copyists, music engravers formalized rules of notation. Every rule is founded on logic and contributes to consistent, well-spaced and intelligible scores and parts. Proper notation produces clear, smooth phrases, giving the performer a sense of security and familiarity. Any deviation risks a potential hazard—the musician must slow down and scrutinize. For example, a note with the stem drawn in the wrong direction could be misinterpreted as a pitch a third higher or lower. Like every other discipline, there are inevitably situations where rules may be bent or broken. If you understand the basic principles of notation, you'll know how to best represent each musical moment.

Good notation is laid out so that the music "jumps off the page". Music symbols are never crowded; peripheral information does not interfere with notes; phrases flow; sections are clearly indicated. There are bar numbers and/or rehearsal letters. There are page turns during rests. There are no surprises: warnings of key and meter changes appear at the end of lines. Performance mistakes are anticipated: there are courtesy accidentals at places where the player may be in doubt. Be the performer.

> By practicing, you struggle throughout your life to make your
> communications more direct and concise, so that a person hearing
> you play receives emotional impressions in as pure a form as possible.
>   Mark Salzman: *The Soloist*

While writing music, strive for the same refinement of detail. Perform the music as you notate.

TIPS FOR GOOD NOTATION

▶ **Be specific** in your notation. Good notation is playable at sight.

▶ **Leave no doubt** Questions from musicians interrupt the flow of rehearsals and recording sessions, costing time and money. Often, these questions spring from unnecessary oversights by the orchestrator or copyist: questions of accidentals, articulation, dynamic markings, transposition or instrument changes. Spare your valuable rehearsal time for matters of performance, rather than questions of notation. Proofread.

▶ **Attention to details** of notation ensures a performance that reflects the composer's vision. Every detail must be conveyed from the composer to the performer through the orchestrator and copyist.

▶ **Avoid clutter** Too much verbiage or over-articulation will confuse the eye; the performer will see the essential information—pitch and rhythm—and may not have time to absorb peripheral marks. Notate for sight reading.

▶ **Absolute clarity** of intention is the goal. Every mark on the page should serve that end. Good spacing, correct stem direction and beaming produce familiar, performer-friendly phrases.

▶ **Develop your hand** When sketching, strive for straight vertical stems (drawn quickly). Noteheads carefully placed so there is no doubt as to the pitch. Use a straight edge (plastic triangle) for horizontal lines, beams, and as a guide for lettering.

▶ **Music is created** for many purposes. Your notation should reflect the style of music and type of musicians that will perform it. Notation choices reflect the end-use of the music. Consider performance venue, the allotted rehearsal time, level of musicians, instruments required.

▶ **The "best" notation** is the best choice for the situation at hand.

▶ **A credible composer, orchestrator or copyist** is one who possesses the experience of a performer.

ESSENTIALS OF NOTATION

Rules of notation help the musician to interpret phrases by presenting familiar patterns of symbols. Of course, every situation cannot be anticipated. Computer generated notation, especially, must be scrutinized and tweaked to communicate your music clearly. Following are basic rules for your review.

STEM DIRECTION contributes to the correct perception of a phrase. Notes above the middle of the staff extend stems down; below the middle, stems up. Notes on the middle staff line are normally down-stem.

STEM LENGTH is normally an octave. Notes extending to leger lines have stems lengthened to reach the center of the staff.

BEAMS help rhythmic perception. Notes are beamed together to divide a measure or to divide a beat.

BEAMS are slanted in the direction of the line. Stem lengths are adjusted accordingly.

BEAMING should clarify rhythms for the performer, dividing the bar into groups of notes relating to the beat. Beams are also used to indicate accentuation or phrasing.

Generally, dotted values are preferred to tied values, resulting in a less cluttered notation, easier to sight-read. However, a tied note across the center of a bar helps the reader to subdivide the bar. Syncopated rhythms over the entire bar are sometimes notated without ties.

Consider the level of performer when you notate. Generally, the inexperienced player needs to see more subdivision (tied notes) in the bar, whereas the professional will recognize rhythms with fewer notes (and more dots) per bar.

ACCIDENTALS are placed according to rule so even a cluster has a sense of familiarity. Two notes at the interval of a 2nd are grouped in the direction of the slant; the accidentals follow. Clusters are built in the same manner. Try to spell clusters diatonically, that is, only one alteration per scale-tone.

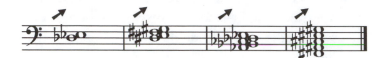

PERIPHERAL SYMBOLS are placed opposite the stem side of the note in the general order of: ARTICULATION; TIE; ACCENT; PHRASE.* Slurs appear outside of accents and articulations except at the beginning or end of a phrase. If all notes in a phrase are upstems, the slur goes under; if notes are downstems or mixed, the slur goes over. Bowing marks always go above.

* Jazz and pop arrangements: it is common practice to place all articulation marks above the staff, especially in hand-written scores.

VERBAL INDICATIONS of tempo, effects, etc. are placed outside of symbols:
    Above the staff: instructions; set tempo.
    Below the staff: dynamics; alter tempo.

BAR NUMBERS are usually placed below the staff for instrumental parts; above the staff for vocal parts. Bar numbers should never interfere with music symbols.

HORIZONTAL SPACING of music symbols on a staff creates familiar shapes—rhythmic patterns, intervallic leaps and melodic contour; a visual guide for the reader. Proper spacing is critical in sight-reading situations.

The spacing of music characters on a staff line is a simple concept, yet often misunderstood. There are two kinds of horizontal spaces, fixed and variable. Fixed spaces, such as the distance from a bar line to the first character, are measured in increments of a staff space. The variable spaces between notes are distributed proportionally.

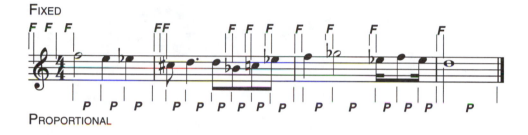

FIXED

PROPORTIONAL

PROPORTIONAL SPACING—sometimes referred to as engraver's spacing—positions the notes according to their relative duration, yet economizes staff space, resulting in an efficient, aesthetically pleasing layout. All notes are placed according to their rhythm values, each successive note value increasing or decreasing on a curved scale, rather than a scale of equal units. Even though a half note has twice the rhythmic value of a quarter note, the half note is allowed somewhat less than twice the space of a quarter note. The engraver's scale of proportion is similar to the harmonic series or the golden mean, an approximate ratio of 3:2.

Music manuscript copyists, like music engravers of the past, have developed the artist's eye—all notes on a line or system are distributed proportionally. Music notation software follows, proportioning music symbols automatically, but sometimes needs manual adjustment. (See software evaluation, page 336, 337)

VERTICAL ALIGNMENT   All music symbols within a system are aligned so that we may view the sequential or simultaneous relationship of every note. In a score or multi-staved part, the staff containing the most activity determines the minimum spacing for each beat.

Detail from Charles Ives *Symphony #4,*
engraved by Herman Langinger

NOTATIONAL PRACTICES

Music engravers, copyists and editors have tried to maintain standard practices, but since music notation was developed over centuries by people in different parts of the world and continues to evolve, there are in some cases several ways to notate the same sonic result. In the following pages, we attempt to present notational practices currently used in the recording industry. We have also consolidated and simplified the current sources of music notation texts. We'll focus on problems that occur on a daily basis, comparing and differentiating similar notational symbols and effects. Subtle differences in notation can result in vast differences in performance.

Standard music notation includes a set of assumptions, generally understood by those who read and write music. The performer assumes a normal manner of playing an instrument unless an instruction specifies otherwise. The designated instrument, clef, key, meter, articulation and style are maintained until a change appears in the part. When an instruction (such as *sord.* or *mute)* is written above the staff, the performer incorporates the instruction until it is negated *(senza* or *open).*

The word *simile* or *sim.* is often used to avoid repeating an instruction or articulation (such as staccato marks). *Simile* should be used only after the effect has been clearly established, so that the performer understands the instruction exactly. The conclusion of the effect or instruction may be indicated *ordinaire, ord., naturale, nat., normale, norm.* or *senza.* The word *sempre* (always) carries an instruction to the end of a movement or piece.

CLEFS   In order to accommodate the registers of various instruments without using many leger lines, the staff may be positioned in several locations on the pitch spectrum, each designated by a clef. Visualize *middle C* as a constant pitch while the staff moves up or down, as designated by a clef.

The octave treble clef (sounding one octave lower than written) is used for the male (tenor) voice as an alternate to bass clef.

Following are normal clefs and alternate clefs for common instruments.

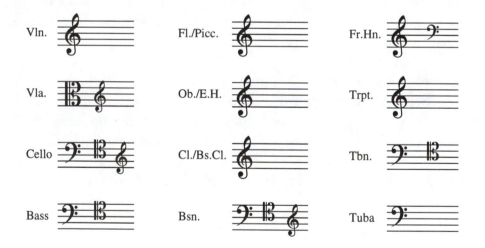

CHANGING CLEFS Generally, the need to change clefs arises when a part extends to more than four leger lines. Clef changes should be made where the performer has ample warning. Avoid frequent clef changes. Avoid changing clefs in the midst of fast passages.

Phrases in extreme upper registers are sometimes written an octave or two lower (in the staff) with the indication *8va.* or *15ma.* Similarly, phrases in extreme lower registers are sometimes written an octave higher with *8va basso, 8vab* or *8vb.* The return to normal notation is termed *loco.* These changes in notation should occur at places in the phrase where the performer can easily adjust.

CONVENTIONS OF TRANSPOSITION Instruments sounding in extreme registers are normally transposed by an octave or two in scores and parts in order to avoid many leger lines. Only in sketches or keyboard reductions are these instruments notated at actual pitch.

- Instruments sounding *8va*; one octave higher than written:
  PICCOLO, XYLOPHONE, CELESTA.
- Sounding *15ma*; two octaves higher than written:
  ORCHESTRA BELLS (GLOCKENSPIEL.)
- Sounding *8vb;* one octave lower than written:
  BASS FLUTE, CONTRABASSOON, BASS MARIMBA, BANJO, GUITAR, ELECTRIC BASS, CONTRA (STRING) BASS.

Review pages 268-270, TRANSPOSING INSTRUMENTS.

KEY SIGNATURES are a product of the diatonic system and serve to establish tonality as well as to minimize accidentals.

When faced with the dilemma of choosing between F♯ or G♭, read through to determine which way the music is leaning. If on the minor side, F♯ is preferable, yielding A♮ and E♮, rather than B♭♭ and F♭. If the music is more major or Lydian, G♭ is the preferred key, with F♮ and C♮, rather than E♯ and B♯.

The decision to change keys is another notational choice encountered while composing or transcribing. A temporary modulation to another tonality may not require a key change. An eight-bar bridge in a song, no matter how remote, is usually accommodated with accidentals rather than a key change. However, a 16-bar bridge in a remote key that maintains one tonality for most of the 16 bars would contain so many accidentals that a temporary key change would be appropriate.

When the music maintains a tonality or modality, a key signature is preferred. However, music that is abstract (chromatic or continually modulating) is best with no key signature, as frequent cancellation of signature sharps or flats is counterproductive. When music is free of a key, it is said to be in the *neutral key*—with no key signature. When copying parts from a concert score that is in the neutral key, leave transposing instruments also in the neutral key. Don't make the mistake of putting a B♭ instrument in two sharps, as you would if the music were in the key of C. Abstract music reads best when in the fluid tonality of the neutral key.

The familiar major/minor system of key signatures may also be used for other modes, i.e. 2 flats for E♭ Lydian; 2 sharps for E Dorian, etc.

CHORD SYMBOLS are aligned with the corresponding beats. A chord continues until the next chord symbol, but should be restated at the beginning of each line and at each double bar.

Chord symbols, as well as melodic and vertical spelling, should lean to either sharps or flats. The following chord progression:

> F♯ E D C♯7 B   would be awkward in flats.

> G♭ F7 B♭mi7 E♭7 A♭   would be awkward in sharps.

Staying true to either the sharp or flat side conveys an accurate interval perception.

F♯	C♯/E♯	A♯mi7	D♯mi7	DMA7	F♯/C♯
G♭	D♭/F	B♭mi7	E♭mi7	DMA7	G♭/D♭

Chords and verticals should be notated to reflect their tonality and interval content. Consideration must be given to enharmonic choices.

B♭m7(♭9) would normally be spelled:

In this case, C♭ is preferable to B♮, as a chord containing both B♭ and B♮ could cause confusion.

The notation of symmetrical structures transcends diatonicism, often mixing sharps and flats. The first diminished seventh chord suggests the key of **D** or **D minor**, while the second chord suggests the key of **B** or **B minor**, yet the third chord suggests the key of **F** or **F minor**.

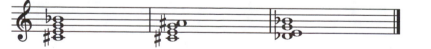

A seven-tone chromatic cluster spelled diatonically.

METER may be used to emphasize particular accent patterns or to characterize a traditional style. The best choice of meter signature requires considerations of phrasing, clarity of rhythmic figures, tempo, the performer's comfort and perception, the conductor's beat and the relationship of other meters throughout the score.

The same phrase, notated in various meters:

Various choices of tuple meters (multiples of 3):

WHOLE RESTS are recommended for all meters with the following exceptions: Rests in odd meters (3/8, 5/8, 7/8) or odd 16th meters should reflect the actual values, divided as the music sounds.

COMPOSITE METERS are merely combinations of simple meters. Phrases or accents may determine a choice of composite metering. The following example contains shifting patterns of 3/8 and 2/8 which are emphasized by beaming, phrasing, or articulation marks.

Since the following is a constant pattern, the 3+3+2+3/8 meter was used, rather than 11/8. The pattern is further emphasized by the beaming.

When the beat changes (i.e. from quarter note to eighth note) the symbols are indicated above the meter. Traditionally, the symbols are written as "new = old" or (♪ = ♩). Many contemporary musicians prefer "old = new" (♩ = ♪), reflecting the progression of time from left to right. Unfortunately, composers and orchestrators are not consistent in this notation. Be aware that both systems are in use. Additional hints, such as *half time, double time, meno mosso* or *piu mosso,* are helpful in determining the change of meter.

When a change of meter occurs and the beat remains constant, *L'istesso* (the same) or (♩=♩) or (♪=♪) or any appropriate value may be written above the new meter signature.

ARTICULATION AND ACCENT SYMBOLS may be interpreted by the performer in various ways, depending on the type of instrument and style of music. An eighth note with a staccato may be played lightly by a woodwind or stringed instrument, yet accented by a brass player. Since staccato refers to duration, a staccato with an accent or dynamic mark clarifies the intent. Generally, two duration symbols (staccato and legato) are used in combination with two accent symbols (medium and strong).

Other common symbols:

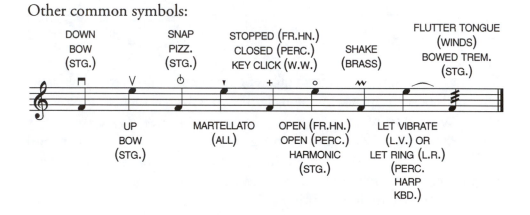

(See page 308 for placement of articulation and accent marks.)

Your careful choice of articulation and dynamic marks is your final opportunity to convey to the performer the direction of the performance. If you "listen" to each instrument as you notate, your marks will instruct the musician to produce the desired sounds with the intended manner or attitude. However, over-articulated notation tends to bog down a performance. There is a trade-off, a balance. The use of styles and words like *simile* contribute to notation that is precise, yet economical and flowing.

INFLECTION OF PITCH All stringed and wind instruments are capable of bending tones sharper or flatter. A tone may bend into or away from the normal pitch. Use directional symbols, portamento lines and/or language to describe the effect. Be specific in your notation: indicate the nature, direction and rhythm of the inflection.

When transcribing, you may hear a tone that is midway between half-tones, "in the crack." This may be notated as the nearest perceived half-tone, or more accurately, as a microtone. (See microtonal notation, page 301.) The nature of your transcription will determine the level of accuracy.

VIBRATO is normally specified with words: *slow* or *fast*; *slight* or *wide*. A "straight" or "dead" tone is designated *non vibrato* or *N.V.*

ORNAMENTS If you have studied the classical literature, you are familiar with turns, mordents and appoggiaturas. Jazz musicians also incorporate these ornaments, spontaneously and with personal variations. Since we are exposed to many styles of music, it is wise to notate an ornament precisely, at least the first time it appears, then perhaps use a symbol and the word *simile*.

GRACE NOTES have no rhythmic value, as they are usually played so fast as to be perceived as an embellishment of the destination note. They are notated preceding the destination note, on either side of the bar line. How they are performed—starting before the beat or on the beat—is a matter of the prevailing style. Single grace notes appear as an eighth note, usually with a slash through the flag. Two or three grace notes are double beamed; four or more grace notes are triple beamed. Normally, all grace notes are notated with stems up, sometimes with a slash. Grace notes and their accompanying accidentals, accents and slurs, are cue note size, approximately ⅔ normal size.

TRILL *(tr)* AND TREMOLO *(trem.)* A source of confusion, because of the similarity of terms as well as traditional versus modern interpretations. Both terms indicate a rapid alternating of two notes—the trill a half-tone or whole-tone and the tremolo a larger interval.

TRILL The starting note is normally below the auxiliary note, although sometimes above. The trill symbol is placed above the note, with an extended wavy line if the note is held longer than a beat. The accidental is placed to the right of the note, but may be placed above a short note. Traditionally, the auxiliary note is the next diatonic scale tone unless altered with a sharp or flat. However, the traditional rule is ambivalent when the music is non-diatonic. There will be no doubt if the auxiliary note is notated with a small note head in parenthesis.

MEASURED TREMOLO A beam connects two alternating notes, each of whose rhythmic values equals the total value. The beam corresponds to normal beaming, indicating eighths, sixteenths or thirty-seconds; however, the inner beams do not touch the stems.

UNMEASURED TREMOLO Similar notation as for measured tremolo. Two beams for fast tempos, three for medium, four for slow, with the word *tremolo* or *trem.* above the first note.

BOWED TREMOLO The rapid alternation of the bow on one note, either measured or unmeasured. (See example on page 318.)

GLISSANDO, PORTAMENTO, ARPEGGIO are similar but each has specific applications.

GLISSANDO *(gliss.)* The execution of a *gliss.* is determined by the nature of the instrument performing the effect. Instruments producing a *gliss.* with rapid fingering, usually a chromatic, diatonic or whole-tone scale, are woodwind, valved brass, mallets, harp, and keyboard. *Gliss.* is also used to designate a smooth slide for those instruments capable—the trombone and timpani. A *gliss.* may be notated with a wavy line or a straight line, depending on the instrument

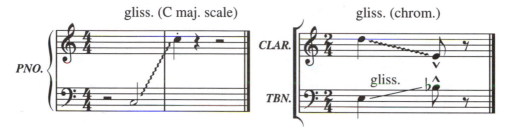

PORTAMENTO *(port.)* A stringed instrument can perform both a glissando and a portamento. *Gliss.* is specified for rapid fingering and *port.* for a smooth slide on one string. In order to distinguish the two effects on a stringed instrument, *gliss.* is usually indicated with a wavy line and *port.* with a straight line.

ARPEGGIO is similar to *gliss.* but composed of intervals of a 3rd or larger, rather than scale-tones—often "broken" chord-tones. Arpeggios are normally played upward unless indicated with a down arrow.

NON ARPEGGIO   A vertical, when played simultaneously, may be notated with the bracket symbol or designated *non arp.* so that it is not mistaken for an arpeggio.

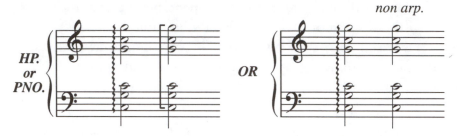

DOUBLE STOP   The same symbol is used to designate a double, triple or quadruple stop for stringed instruments.

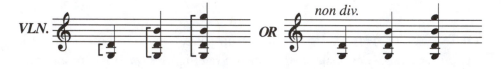

Since the bow travels across the strings in an arc, three or four notes cannot be played simultaneously. However, a rapid arpeggio effect can be played across all four strings and the top two strings may be sustained if desired.

DIVISI   Two or more instruments may share the same staff if the role of each is clearly notated. The notes share the same stem if rhythmically the same, or opposing stems if rhythmically diverse.

Notice that the B♭ in the first bar is restated. A common error in copying or extracting divisi parts is omitting an accidental when it occurs in both parts.

When two wind instruments share the same staff, *a2* indicates unison. However, stringed instrument divisi is also indicated *a2,* meaning "divide by 2." (Also, *div. a3, div. a4,* etc.)

COURTESY ACCIDENTALS (also known as cautionary accidentals) are essential reminders of previous accidentals.

Traditional notation employs a simple rule: an accidental applies to recurring notes at the same pitch within a bar and is carried over the bar line by a tie. Courtesy accidentals should be reiterated during a complex chromatic passage with a recurring note at the same pitch, at the octave, or to reaffirm a naturalized note in a new bar. The accidental is sometimes enclosed in parentheses but modern studio notation often eliminates the parenthesis in favor of a less cluttered page.

There are also instances when a courtesy accidental clarifies a questionable interval, such as an augmented second or a tritone.

Courtesy accidentals prevent hesitation when there may be doubt in the performer's perception. They save valuable rehearsal time, eliminate questions and prevent mistakes. Musicians under the pressure of performance appreciate courtesy accidentals.

LEGER LINES The accepted maximum number of leger lines is five. Phrases that extend above or below that limit require octave transposition and the designation 8va or 8vb (see page 313). Adjacent leger lines must not touch; notes above or below the staff need to be spread a little more than usual, as the illusion of other staff lines would be created, disorienting the performer.

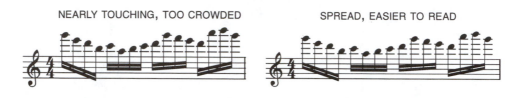

DOUBLE BAR LINE The placement of a double bar line provides an occasional landmark in the continuous flow of music. Often they are omitted in the media they are most needed: film score recording. Film scores are, by nature, seamless accompaniment to an evolving drama. Double bar lines help define the structure of the music for the conductor and musicians. Particularly hazardous are long rests with no cue notes for the musician. The careful placement of double bar lines serve to break up long rests into smaller sections which are audible as well as visible. Double bar lines should be placed where there are significant changes in texture, tempo or tonality. Changes in meter are usually too frequent to warrant double bar lines.

A double bar should be placed between a pickup (incomplete) bar and the first full bar of a piece. Music that begins with a rest, then pickup notes, invariably causes confusion. When a tempo is counted off (verbally or with clicks) some musicians will begin playing in the first bar of the count-off while others will assume there is a full bar of count-off before the pickup bar. This confusion can be eliminated if the parts are marked. In the example, "2 free" is normal count-off for a slow tempo or "6 free" for a fast tempo. Often, a (partial) pickup bar is numbered "A" rather than "1." If a sequencer insists on starting on a full bar, select a meter for that bar to match the pickup notes. Film scores may indicate "clicks" instead of "free." Here are three solutions:

Cᴜᴇ ɴᴏᴛᴇꜱ are approximately ⅔ size, although they may be notated full size if the music is clearly marked *cue*, followed by *end cue* or *play* at the appropriate place. A cue should always be transposed for the musician reading the part. If a bassoon part contains french horn cues, the line should appear in the bass clef, in concert, rather than a 5th higher. If a clarinet part contains a viola cue, it should be notated in the treble clef and transposed for the clarinet.

Cues have several functions:

1) A musician counting a long rest before an entrance should have a cue—a phrase played by a prominent instrument, clearly audible. This serves as security in counting, as well as helping to establish the pitch of the entrance.

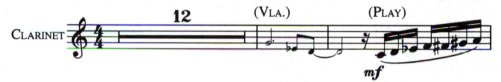

2) Alternate or *ossia* parts may be notated in cue size or normal size notes on a staff, above or below the normal staff.

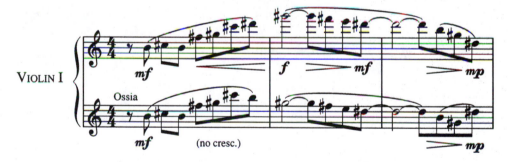

3) Film score recording is often subject to spontaneous rewriting on the sound stage. Much time may be saved if certain phrases are cued for alternate instruments, to be played at the discretion of the composer. Sometimes a solo line will be played by a different instrument for a change of texture, or two french horns may be augmented by adding two more.

CONVENTIONS OF FORM

With just a few symbols, a musician is able to travel around the landscape of music, negotiating repeats, alternate routes, etc. and arrive at the final destination simultaneously with the other players. Whether one is reading published scores and parts, recording studio manuscript, jazz band arrangements, lead sheets or chord charts—all music notation adheres to the same signs.

REPEAT	1-bar repeat sign	2-bar repeat sign

ENDINGS

Repeated sections may include multiple endings, labeled 1°, 2°, 3°, etc. Instructions may be included, such as:

3Xs—play 2°X ONLY or

6Xs—play 1°3°5°Xs ONLY or

REPEAT TILL CUE—TACET 1°X ONLY

Notice the ° symbol, used to distinguish "first" (1°) from "one" (1.) or "second" (2°) from "two" (2.) The distinction is subtle, but important for correct interpretation.

D.C. *Da Capo* "cap" or top of the music.

When a piece starts with pickups (that is, an incomplete bar) a D.C. would return to the pickups. However, modern notation requires a complete bar including the pickups, then a return (with a repeat sign or D.S.) to the first complete bar. Therefore, D.C. is used only when the piece starts with a full bar.

𝄋 *Segno* "the sign" is always placed at the beginning of a bar or line.

D.S. *Dal Segno* "from the sign"

Modern notation always places the D.S. at the end of a bar or line.

𝄌 CODA SIGN

Modern notation always places the coda sign at the end of a bar or line.

fine "the end" A *fine* may occur at any part of a bar.

come sopra "as above" Refers to musical material above or before.

VERBIAGE—SUPPLEMENTAL WORDS

A word is worth a thousand notes.

While music is the universal language, words are needed to supplement music symbols, to describe performance instructions and to indicate styles. Describing music with words is approximate at best. We use Italian or our native language for traditional performance instructions. We may use dramatic and emotional terms when discussing music for film or theater, and common language when discussing music with non-musicians. It is becoming increasingly important to communicate internationally; a dictionary of musical terms in several languages is an essential reference.

The composer was once the image of the social recluse, scribbling away feverishly, isolated in squalor, driven by mystic powers to transform the world into romantic splendor. In today's world, the composer is more likely to be found at work among many other people in related crafts: technicians, producers, directors, artists in various media. Whether you are a purist, producing art of your own design, or creating music to enhance other media, you must communicate with other people in order to bring your music to its intended purpose. Communicating with musicians requires a knowledge of traditional terms as well as the lingo of a particular style of music. Communicating with non-musicians, such as producers and directors, requires a general knowledge of their technical language as well as finding common nontechnical words to express musical thoughts, such as "intense," "smooth," "subtle," or "abrupt."

Today's commercial music often designates styles, rather than traditional performance indications. A stylistic word such as "shuffle," "swing," "funk," "cocktail," or "Baroque" is enough to steer an experienced performer to the appropriate interpretation of even a single-line lead sheet with chord symbols. Even more specific are styles that reference innovative musicians, such as "Basie," "Garner," "Dr. John," "Krupa," "B.B.King," "Wes Montgomery," "Van Halen," "Miles," etc. Studio musicians specialize in emulating various styles.

WRITING FOR SPECIFIC INSTRUMENTS

Following are reference pages; consult orchestration books for more detail.

WOODWINDS

While string and brass sections have a somewhat uniform timbre throughout their ranges, a woodwind section varies in the combination of instruments, number of players, and tone colors. Traditional woodwind sections consist of flutes, oboes, clarinets and bassoons, grouped in twos, threes or fours, with the respective third chairs doubling on piccolo or alto flute, English horn, bass clarinet, and contrabassoon. Studio orchestra woodwind sections are chosen for the requirements of a particular recording project and may include saxophones, as well as ethnic instruments. Most studio woodwind players double on several instruments.

Each family of instruments—flutes, oboes, clarinets, and bassoons—has its own timbral palette. Each instrument has its own tone color, which varies through-out its register. The differences in timbre may be learned (remembered) by careful listening and evaluating at every opportunity. Woodwind instruments have a limited dynamic range.

Woodwind notation consists of lines, as solo melodies or as part of the ensemble. The facility of woodwind instruments allows rapid arpeggiation, trills and tremolos. (See page 320, 321.)

ARTICULATION: All woodwind instruments are capable of sharp staccato to smooth legato phrasing. (See page 318.)

EFFECTS: Flutter tongue, key pad clicks. (See page 318.)

RANGES: page 266; TRANSPOSITION: page 269.

BRASS

Brass instruments are constructed in basically two shapes: *conical bore,* a gradual increase in diameter, and *cylindrical bore,* a straight pipe until it reaches the flare of the bell. Conical bore instruments, the horn and tuba, are darker, rounder in timbre, while cylindrical bore instruments, the trumpet and trombone, are brighter, brassier, due to a prominence of harmonics. Other instruments on the conical side are the flugelhorn, baritone horn and euphonium. For a brassier sound, *tuben* are sometimes used on film scores, played by hornists, and *cimbassi,* played by trombonists and tubists. All brass instruments are capable of great contrast; generally, the louder the tone, the brighter the timbre. Wide interval leaps are hazardous—think vocal when writing for brass.

Traditionally, the brass fortified other instruments, usually playing only roots and fifths, changing instruments for each change of key. Valves were added to the trumpet and horn during the mid 19th century, liberating the melodic line from the limitations of the harmonic series. During the 1960s, Don Ellis introduced the four valved, quarter-tone trumpet, advancing the trumpet from a chromatic instrument to a microtonal instrument.

Most scores are written for B♭ or C trumpet and horn in F. Piccolo trumpet in B♭ may be written *8vb* or *loco,* depending on the readability of the part. The trombone is unique, in that its fundamental tone (first position) is B♭, although it is written in concert, as if it were a C instrument. The tuba is a concert instrument, sounding as written.

EFFECTS: Mutes—straight, harmon, cup for trumpet, trombone and tuba; fiber or wood for horn. Stopped horn notes (with the hand) are marked + ; open marked o. Wa-wa with plunger for trumpet or trombone. Trill (valved instruments). Gliss (trombone). All brass instrumentalists can bend at least a quarter-tone with the lip.

A normal sized orchestra contains 4 horns, 3 trumpets, 3 trombones, 1 tuba. A large film score orchestra may require 6 or 8 horns, 4 trumpets, 4 to 6 trombones and 2 tubas. Brass divisi, especially 4 or 6 parts, may be notated in various configurations on the score, for clarity of voicings. Six horns on three staves could be configured 1&2, 3&4, 5&6 or 1&4, 2&5, 3&6. Traditionally, the odd-numbered horns are given the higher notes. Use the configuration that is best for each situation.

RANGES: page 266; TRANSPOSITIONS: page 269.

PERCUSSION

Common orchestral percussion instruments are listed here, although there is an endless array, fashioned from every material imaginable. Film scores, especially, call for ethnic and exotic percussion of every variety. Composers and percussionists are always searching for new and unfamiliar sounds, escalating the fear of the unknown for the audience. Emil Richards has collected and invented many percussion instruments, listed in his book, *Emil Richards' World of Percussion*. Hollywood percussionist Mark Stevens invented the now famous MARK TREE in 1976. You can add to your repertoire by observing, investigating recorded sounds that you hear and spending time with a percussionist. Electronic percussion has proven valuable for MIDI mockups, but has found limited use in the studio orchestra.

Percussion instruments are classified as pitched or non-pitched. On a score, the timpani traditionally occupies the first percussion staff, just below the brass. When there are several percussionists, one plays the timpani exclusively while the others divide up the remaining instruments. Allow time to change instruments. A live performance orchestrator may assign a staff to each player and divide the instruments in an efficient manner. Film score orchestrators tend to place all percussion instruments (except the timpani) on a minimum of staves and let the percussion section divvy up the chores among themselves, according to the particular situation. A (sit down) set drummer is likely to have an individual staff line.

Timpani In classical orchestras, the timpani enhanced the horns and trumpets, playing tonic and dominant notes. Today, it is used primarily in conjunction with the low brass and low strings. EFFECTS: Chromatic glissando with pedal.

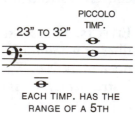

Mallets (pitched percussion)

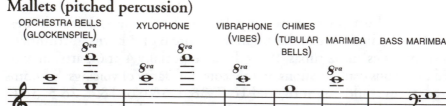

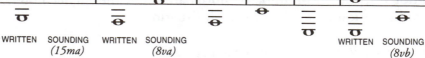

HARP

The harp is unique in that it is a truely diatonic modal instrument—limited to seven of the 12 notes at any given time. All strings, except the bottom string, have three pitch settings, regulated by pedals. The middle position produces the C♮ major scale, the upper pedal position produces the C♭ major scale and the lower position the C♯ major scale. Double sharps or double flats are not possible. Enharmonic pedal configurations enable *glissandos*, whole-tone and pentatonic scales. Rapid modulation or chromatic chords may require two harps.

The pedal diagram may be confusing, as flats are high and sharps are low. Think of a foot pushing a pedal down, tightening the strings, therefore raising the pitch.

The harp, like the piano, is capable of playing melodies, chords and arpeggiated figures. *Gliss.* may be notated with a pedal diagram or by placing the first seven notes on the staff. See page 321-322 for glissando, arpeggio and non-arpeggio notation. Limit four notes for each hand. Range: See page 266.

KEYBOARDS

Piano, celesta, harpsichord, clavichord, accordion, organ and an endless array of sounds from synthesizers are all notated in essentially the same manner. The main consideration for orchestration is the distinction between acoustic and electronic instruments. Acoustic keyboards, as well as harp, should be carefully notated as to the duration of each note. Following are three methods:

A note or chord that is to decay for its natural duration is marked *l.v.* (let vibrate) or *l.r.* (let ring).

Do not exceed the span of a 9th for each hand. If you mentally "play" as you notate, you will create a playable part, even if you do not have keyboard technique. Range: See page 266.

STRINGS

A string section, regardless of size, is a balanced entity (with an occasional exception—a violinless film score; another with only celli). Typical string sections (both concert and film score) are: 30+12+10+8 or 26+10+8+6 or 22+8+6+4. The number of staves allocated to violins, violas, celli and basses is an orchestration decision. Violins may be on one, two or more staff lines. When divisi parts become too cluttered or complex, more staff lines are added.

Divisi is normally by desk (the right-hand player plays the top line); other divisions (a3, etc.) must be specified. When divisions are unequal, it is necessary to specify the number of players on each part (see page 322).

Bowing Bow markings are important for live performance; optional for studio. Up-bow and down-bow symbols are placed over the notes, regardless of stem direction (see page 318). Bowing is often changed to suit the concertmaster or conductor. It is best to not mark bowing unless you play a stringed instrument.
Legato Full value. Each change of bow is marked with a slur.
Detaché Non-legato; alternate bowing; separate but longer than staccato.
Staccato Bounced off the string. Also: *spiccato, martellato, saltando, jeté.*
Effects   *Sul tasto* On the fingerboard (soft, floating); *sul ponticello* near the bridge (glassy, metallic); *col legno* struck with the wood of the bow (dry staccato); *modo ordinario,* or *naturale* (return to normal).

Trills Quickly alternating the stopped note and a note a minor second or major second above with another finger. Avoid trills on open strings. A trill by a solo instrument is precise; a trill by a whole section is undefined, shimmering (see page 320).

Tremolo *Bowed tremolo* (single note or double-stopped). Bow is alternated quickly; measured or random (see page 320).
Fingered tremolo. Like a trill but interval is larger than major second.

Portamento Smooth slide on one string, indicated with a straight line drawn between notes (see page 321).

Glissando Fingered; each note written out with a time value, or a wavy line between the first and last, specified as "chromatic" or "diatonic" (see page 321).

Accent (>) *sf, sfz, sffz, fp, fpp*
See accents, articulation and bowing symbols on page 318.

PIZZICATO (*pizz.*) Open strings sustain tone longer than stopped strings. Allow a beat to return to *arco. Snap pizz. (Bartok pizz.)* is snapped against the fingerboard (see page 318).

HARMONICS *Natural harmonics* are a result of dividing the string—lightly touching at the node—producing a resonant overtone. The 2nd, 3rd, 4th or 5th harmonic replaces the sound of the fundamental note. Since natural harmonics are produced only with open strings, vibrato is not possible. There are several methods of notating a natural harmonic. Placing a small circle over the *sounding* note is recommended.
Artificial harmonics are produced by lightly touching the string above the stopped position. A perfect fourth above the stopped note produces a harmonic which sounds two octaves above (the 4th harmonic). Touching a perfect fifth above will produce a harmonic sounding a 12th above (the 3rd harmonic). Less common are a major third above, producing the 5th harmonic, and a minor third above, producing the 6th harmonic. Artificial harmonics are notated with a diamond head at the interval above the stopped note. The sounding note head may be shown in parentheses.

DOUBLE STOPS *(non-divisi)* Bowing or pizz. notes on adjacent strings. Intervals of 3rds, 4ths or 5ths are common double stops, but fingering should be considered. Triple and quadruple stops are possible but impractical to bow (see page 322).

MUTE Fits onto bridge; absorbs some of the vibrations.
Soft sound, lacking overtones. Allow a few seconds or beats to attach mute (*con sordino*) and remove (*senza sordino*).

RANGES: See page 266.

A WORLD OF INSTRUMENTS

Non-orchestral musical instruments—ethnic, exotic, experimental—abound. Film score source music (cultural, regional, era) requires research for authentic instruments and their players. Check your local library for sound recordings. Unusual instruments, from Alpen Horn to Zampona and ethnic percussion instruments of the world are listed in the directory of Professional Musicians, Local 47, Hollywood (www.promusic47.org). If you are writing for an unfamiliar instrument, interview the player to learn the range, transposition, available scales, and—most important—the temperament, or actual pitch of each note. More on page 393.

COMPUTER GENERATED NOTATION

Music is a fluid medium. As artists, we must be aware of the limitations of the digital domain and not compromise creativity. If we are to create beautiful curves and infinite shades of color with blocks, we need many tiny blocks. We necessarily dissect the elements of music—pitch, rhythm, amplitude and timbre into standard measurable units so we can organize, manipulate and reproduce music. Slicing music up into digital segments is akin to equal temperament; it serves as a convenience and allows a greater degree of organization and control.

Music notation software is a tool of expression; not a substitute for creativity. It is another instrument to be mastered. There are advantages and disadvantages to using computer assisted notation. On the plus side: speed; duplication of layout; duplication of common elements; duplication of phrases and unison doubling; automatic proportional spacing; alignment of beats—especially in keyboard notation and scores; ease of creating transposed and alternate versions; ease of correcting and reformatting; updating parts from a previous performance and printing a clean copy; MIDI playback (audio proofing); uniform music symbols; variable printing formats; publishing quality output; and digital storage. Finally, computer copyists have reported less physical strain, as the body is used symmetrically, rather than the torqued posture of hand copying.

On the minus side: the expense of a computer, printer and software; limitations of music notation software; paper consumption—pages are usually reprinted several times before the notation is acceptable; potential eye strain and exposure to radiation; an impersonal look—some musicians prefer the personal touch of hand-copied manuscript and the implication that the part was created for a particular musician on a particular occasion.

There is a considerable investment in time and money necessary in order to successfully produce music notation with computer—researching the best software, computer and printer for your needs, training yourself, as well as configuring the application's variables, or preferences, and coordinating hardware and software to produce a respectable page of music.

Professional hand copyists who have made the transition to computer copying claim that their production has increased by at least two times. This is due, in part, to the automation of repeatable music elements. Of course, the learning period for computer copying may be weeks or months.

The process itself makes computer copyists prone to more errors, as more of the copyist's attention is focused on the procedure rather than the music. The immediacy of looking at each note as your hand draws it is replaced by the faster manipulations of keyboard input. Whether entering notes with a computer keyboard or MIDI keyboard, multiple passes are required to add articulation, phrasing, dynamics, verbiage, etc. While the hand copyist normally draws everything in one pass, the computer copyist may lose sight of peripheral information.

A major problem is the duplication of errors. When copying phrases, accompanying symbols such as ties, slurs, dynamics and articulations could be omitted or misaligned when pasted to other staff lines. Inappropriate symbols may be carelessly transferred to other instruments, such as a crescendo attached to a sustained piano or harp note. Transpositions may extend instruments out of range. One frequent problem is that scores are often generated with vertical, or even haphazard, note spelling. Part extraction usually maintains that spelling, when in fact, each part should reflect linear spelling. The sequencer or notation software may be able to spell notes based on some considerations such as key centers, but the final notation needs the enharmonic tweaking of a human eye. For every labor saving shortcut there are time consuming corrections, adjustments and reformatting.

It is strongly recommended that musicians copy by hand to learn notation skills before learning to copy with computer software. Hand copying is slower paced, allowing more concentration and direct control over the placement of symbols, enharmonic choices, spacing of characters on the staff line, layout of the page, and the opportunity to develop an eye for clarity. When you are able to produce performance-friendly pages of manuscript, you will have a basis with which to train yourself and your notation software.

SOFTWARE EVALUATION

The music engraving tradition has set the standard for printed music and has been rigorously maintained by astute music editors through published music. When the personal computer and laser printer enabled "the rest of us" to print and publish music, the standards of music notation became our responsibility, as well as that of industry publishers.

The engravers' rules of standard notational practices have been incorporated in music notation programs, although not always faithfully. Music copyists, composers, orchestrators and performers have contributed suggestions and refinements, bringing music notation applications to a level of quality acceptable by music preparation offices as well as print publishers.

Notation from sequencers invariably needs adjustment to conform to the format, rules and conventions of standard notation. Following are suggestions to test your software, whether your notation is transcribed from MIDI files, step entered or played in real time. (See also TRANSCRIBING MIDI, page 202.)

▶ Quantize rhythms in "raw" MIDI files, that is, those that have been entered in real time. You may have to experiment with different quantization settings to find a balance between accuracy and simplicity. The style of music will influence the degree of quantization.

▶ Set page layout requirements and print out a few pages.

▶ Check for horizontal and vertical spacing alignment and collisions. Bar numbers often need to be moved individually to avoid obscuring a note or tie. Check notes with leger lines, as they require slightly more horizontal space than notes in the staff. Leger lines of adjacent notes should never touch.

▶ Check the note spacing—it should be proportional (approximately 3:2) so that a half note receives slightly less space than two quarter notes. Engravers and hand copyists measure proportional spacing by eye but a computer program must calculate the placement of each character on each line or system. Some notation programs provide several proportion algorithms, perhaps labeled "engravers spacing." In situations with many subdivisions of the beat or complex rhythms, a proportion such as 4:3 allows smaller rhythmic values to receive more relative space. The computer must calculate the proportional spacing of each line or system while allowing for fixed spaces, such as those required by accidentals. (More about proportional spacing on page 309.) The distance from the bar line to the first note should be one staff-space. Whole notes are placed on the first beat of the measure while whole rests are centered between bar lines. Accidentals should be close to note heads but not touching. Note clusters and their accidentals should be configured properly, not overlapping (see page 308).

♦ When an individual part is extracted from a score, the spacing must necessarily be reapportioned to provide a page layout such as a hand copyist would produce. Often, individual notes or accidentals need to be nudged left or right. Your software should allow manual movement of all symbols.

♦ Stems should extend from notes in leger line areas to the center staff line. Stems should be shortened or lengthened automatically when beamed. Beams should gently slant in the direction of the melodic contour.

♦ Your notation program should allow for the unrestricted placement of peripheral symbols, performance indications, text instructions, properly spaced lyrics and chord symbols. You should be able to move (nudge) any object, overriding the program's automatic placement.

♦ Mentally play through your printed notation. If it is not a smooth read, circle the problems and set about correcting them.

♦ Are you able to perform all necessary editing functions to produce satisfactory notation? Are you comfortable with the method(s) of note input and will you be able to develop a fast and accurate technique with this software? Do you like the look of the music font and does it include any unconventional symbols that you may need? Can other music fonts be substituted? Can you change the default parameters to customize the notation? Is the software developer accessible for questions or suggestions and willing to accommodate specific requests? Does the software developer have a history of periodic upgrades?

Computer notation programs have come a long way but even the most sophisticated software cannot anticipate every musical situation; there are too many instances where a human decision is needed. If you are generating notation for live performance, your orchestration skills must be employed to assure a playable part for each instrumentalist. A successful performance depends on your editorial choices regarding every detail of notation.

BEYOND STANDARD NOTATION

The common ground of standard notation enables music to be performed by anyone, anywhere. The elegance and familiarity of conventional notation transcends language barriers and allows musicians of diverse cultures to perform together.

Standard music symbols, however, should not limit the conception and performance of new music. There are many nonstandard effects, such as blowing air through a wind instrument, strumming strings inside a piano, and generally, creating unusual sounds with conventional instruments. When standard notation will not serve the requirements of a contemporary composition, the composer finds a genuine need to invent variations or new notations. Of course any new system of symbols must be defined by the composer and studied by the performer. Unfamiliar symbols must be described on the score and parts with words and symbols. When a new symbol proves to be particularly useful or innovative, it is adapted locally and eventually finds its way into the language.

As the need arises, music notation could be amended to include information such as specific pitch, microtonal intervals or fractional portions of the octave. Notation for electronic instruments, primarily verbal descriptions of acoustic instruments and effects, may need to be more specific in the description of timbre. Software will continue to be developed with the goal of translating audio as well as MIDI data to the human performance language of music notation.

See section 12 for NEW MUSIC NOTATION resources.

11

PREPARATION FOR PERFORMANCE AND PUBLISHING

11

PREPARATION FOR PERFORMANCE AND PUBLISHING

The production of music, whether for recording, live performance or publication, requires an overview of the whole process as well as knowledge of each phase.

The flow of music from conception to publication usually includes the following job categories: composer or arranger, orchestrator, copyist and proofreader. Live performance requires the additional jobs of music librarian, contractor, conductor and performer. Studio recording adds related jobs such as score consultant, music editor, recording engineer, mixer and producer. There are organizations—unions, guilds, societies—dedicated to the interest of those working in most music jobs. (See MUSIC TRADE ORGANIZATIONS, page 381.)

If you produce your own music from start to finish, you may feel overwhelmed at the scope of work to be done, not knowing what to do first or how to allocate your time. It is helpful to divide the job into specific tasks so you are able to focus on details.

At all levels of music production, careful organization is essential. Information such as schedules, instruments, musicians and other personnel must be available and current, as these details affect your musical choices. Keep track of each piece of music, including revisions or alternate versions, as it progresses through each phase of the project. When the music arrives (on time) at the rehearsal or recording session, if a part is missing, it will become very clear how important it is to be organized!

Plot out your schedule so that you allow ample time to complete your project. We all tend to underestimate the time a job will take and consequently the cost. Until you have plenty of experience, you can start by allowing twice the amount of time of your initial estimate.

There are key questions that must be asked in order to perform your job well. Ask the right questions, especially if you are working with someone—a director, composer or orchestrator—for the first time. Since everyone at the creative level is always busy, it is worth taking the time to write your questions as they occur to you. Arrange the questions in order of importance, then ask at a convenient time. You will then have had time to think about how to phrase each question, perhaps answering some of them yourself. Then the use of your limited time with your busy colleague will be efficient and appreciated.

MUSIC PREP

Music preparation is the path between the composer and the performer. Everyone in the chain should understand the nature of the project—the musical objective, its scope and style. The success of a project depends on communication through words and music notation.

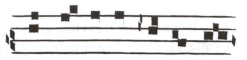

MANUSCRIPT COPYING   15TH CENTURY MANUSCRIPT

Music copying by hand, a grand art and tradition, has become virtually obsolete in the mainstream recording and publishing industries. However, sketching, arranging and orchestrating with pencil is still an essential part of the music making process. As stated previously, it is strongly recommended that you copy by hand before learning computer copying so that your concentration is focused on music notation, rather than the manipulation of hardware and software. (See pages 334-335, COMPUTER GENERATED MUSIC NOTATION.)

Basic copying tools are pencil, pen, eraser, triangle, broad felt tip pen for titles and manuscript paper. (See also page 155, RECOMMENDED TOOLS FOR SKETCHING.) Keep your copying equipment and supplies in one place, ready for work. You don't want to spend your initial energy searching for tools.

A good copyist produces legible and consistent symbols, spaced proportionally within each bar and across each line or system, as well as uniform lettering. Composers, orchestrators and copyists sometimes make eighth rests that look like quarter rests; half rests that look like whole rests; sharps, flats and naturals, even clefs, that are indistinguishable. Make an effort to produce symbols that cannot be mistaken for other symbols. A straight edge (triangle) is used by professional copyists for stems, beams, leger lines, and as a guide for lettering. Good copying, like the mastery of any instrument, is achieved through dedicated practice and working experience.

Keep in mind that the part is for the performer—not the composer, orchestrator, conductor or anyone else. Phrases should be spelled diatonically whenever possible, emphasizing the single-staff performer's linear role or the double-staff performer's vertical perception.

A professional copyist produces easy to read, flowing phrases. After copying a part, read it through, mentally performing the music. Is all the necessary information on the page? Are there rests preceding page turns?

While copyists are obligated to maintain a uniformity of conventional music notation, the personal style of each copyist emerges, especially in lettering and the drawing of clefs.

MEG MARYATT

LLOYD LUHMAN

STUDIO STAFF COPYIST (The Hollywood film studios employed staff orchestras, composers, orchestrators and copyists from the mid 1930s until 1958.)

CONTEMPORARY MUSIC NOTATION

Contemporary music may require new music symbols and performance direction. Musicians can easily adapt to innovative performance techniques if symbols and instructions are based on the logic and conventions of traditional music notation. (Also see pages 301 and 338.)

Many contemporary symbols appear in Gardner Read's *Music Notation* and Kurt Stone's *Music Notation in the Twentieth Century* (currently out of print but you may be able to find it).

Today, much contemporary symphonic music has evolved to be more complex, difficult and time consuming to prepare than ever before in the history of Western music. Preparing scores and extracting parts requires careful planning and more stringent adherence to internationally accepted notation practices. The music is usually more dense, with rhythmic complexities and numerous meter and key changes; contains much additional information, and is laid out with more care, utilizing extensive cueing and often special notation.

From the *American Society of Music Copyists*

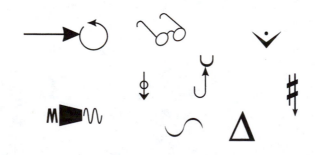

STANDARD MUSIC FORMATS

There are many types and sizes of preprinted score paper. The score format should be carefully chosen to accommodate the music it will contain. If you print your own score paper, use the same considerations in designing your layout. (See SCORE LAYOUT, page 346.)

♦ **FULL SCORE** Orchestra, band or smaller ensemble. A common score page is 11 x 17" or A3, which is convenient for reproduction. Preprinted score papers can be found as small as 11 x 7" (9 line, wide) or as large as 19 x 31" (60 line, tall). Notice that scores are measured width x length, regardless of orientation. Score paper is generally printed with 4 or 8 bars per line or no bar lines; with or without instrument names. If you buy preprinted score paper, choose the format that best suits your needs for each project. Allow extra staff lines for string divisi, added instruments, bar numbers, etc. (Review pages 281-282 before choosing score paper.)

♦ **CONDENSED SCORE or CONDUCTOR'S SCORE** is often used for live performance, such as theater productions. The smaller score page and fewer page turns is more manageable for the conductor. Once a piece is scored, copied, proofed and rehearsed, a condensed score may be substituted for a full score. Condensed scores range from a single staff lead line with chord symbols to a more detailed orchestral reduction showing all entrances, important lines and cues. Use as many lines as necessary to show clearly the amount of detail required. While full scores may be in concert or transposed, a condensed score is necessarily in the concert key. Extreme range instruments such as piccolo and bass may be notated as sounding or as written, and should be labeled as such on the score.

♦ **SKETCH** The blueprint for a score, the bare bone composition with indications of orchestration. Systems may be grouped in compositional elements (melody, bass, counter-lines, arpeggiated or rhythmic figures) or orchestral choirs (woodwinds, brass, percussion, harp, keyboards, strings, or combination thereof). A sketch represents all instruments in concert pitch with extreme range instruments notated at actual pitch or at the octave. See orchestral sketch and compositional sketch examples, pages 278 and 279.

FILM SCORE CHECK LIST

FIRST PAGE:
> Name of Film
> Number of cue (5M2) Cue title optional (The Chase)
> Composer's name and licensing organization (ASCAP or BMI)
> Orchestrator's name
> Concert Score or Transposed Score (Don't make the copyist guess)
> A Orchestra or B Orchestra or C Orchestra, if applicable
> Click setting, if applicable (16-0)
> Metronome marking, if applicable ($\quarternote = 90$)

EVERY PAGE:
> Cue number
> Page number
> Bar numbers (large, away from the music, preferably on a separate staff)
> Beat numbers (small, aligned with the 1st beat of each measure,
>   preferably at the top of the page)
> Important timings (04:19) and visual cues *Jake slams door.*
> Any other information from the composer's sketch, however
>   insignificant it may seem.

SCORE LAYOUT:

1. Choose score paper (if not provided) by determining how the orchestra will fit on the score with regard to doubling and divisi. Provide enough staves for any splits that may occur from independent parts. If you have spare staves, leave a blank one above Vln. 1 and below Tuba to allow for leger lines. You may also need extra staves for bar numbers, visual or dialog cues, chord symbols, etc.

2. Lay out all score pages by BEATS, putting in meter signature changes as required. Meter numbers should be large and bold—they are the most important score element for the conductor.

3. Label the instruments on the first page, listing each player (by chair) with all doublings, such as FLUTE 1 (FL., PICC., ALTO FL.); FLUTE 2 (FL., ALTO FL.); TRUMPET 1 (TRPT., FLUGEL), PERC. 1 (MARIMBA, SUSP. CYM., PIATTI); KEYBOARD 1 (ACOUSTIC PIANO, CELESTA) etc. Be specific, as this is often an area of confusion. If the woodwinds are mixed doubles, label WOODWIND 1 (FL., ALTO SAX., CLAR.), WOODWIND 2 (ALTO FL., TENOR SAX., BASS CLAR.), etc. Indicate the number of violins, violas, celli and basses; and how they are normally divided. No need to indicate studio-standard instrument keys such as Horn in F, Trumpet in B♭, etc. However, be very specific with instruments such as E♭ contrabass clarinet or B♭ contrabass clarinet.

4. Complete the layout by numbering pages, labeling the cue number *on each page* and indicating instruments clearly. (Put yourself in the copyist's and the composer's place; you don't want to search the score for information that should be on each page.)

5. Go through the score and add important timing information or visual cues provided by the composer.

6. *Now* you are ready to put music on the score.

ORCHESTRATION TIPS:
Place dynamic marks at every entrance.

Leave no doubt as to which player is playing which line in which octave; use *a2, div., tutti*, etc.

These conventions always apply, whether the score is transposed or concert:
        Picc. and Xylophone sound *8va*
        Orch. Bells (glock.)sound *15ma*
        Contrabassoon, Guitar and Bass sound *8vb*

When you have completed a score:
Place consecutive score pages side by side to check the continuity of each line: register, mutes, articulation, ties, etc.

Every detail is critical to a successful recording session. The composer needs all the information in one place—on the scorepage; not on cue sheets or loose pages of sketches or notes. If any timing problems arise at the recording session, all the relevant information will be at the composer's fingertips so an adjustment may be made quickly.

Studio time is very expensive. A minimum of orchestration/copying errors and questions from the players about their parts will leave the maximum time to concentrate on the quality of the recording.

♦ **FILM SCORE**   A typical film score has hundreds of score pages. Every symbol and word must be placed with clarity, accuracy and speed. This example illustrates all of those traits. Now that you are hearing with confidence, you can train your pencil hand to make swift, accurate strokes without hesitation, coordinating your hearing and writing.

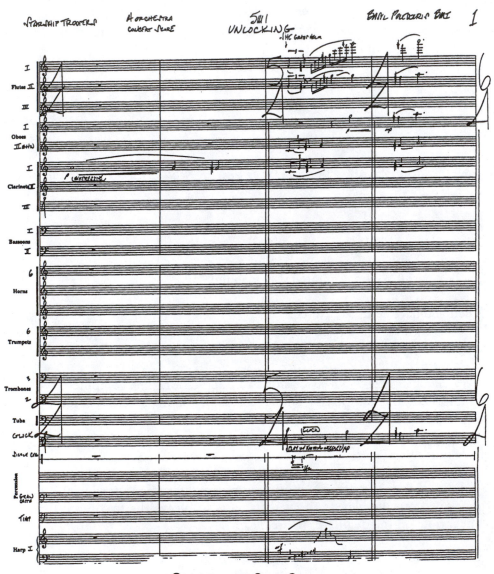

ORCHESTRATION: SCOTT SMALLEY
Used by permission of the composer

◆ CONDENSED SCORE or CONDUCTOR SCORE

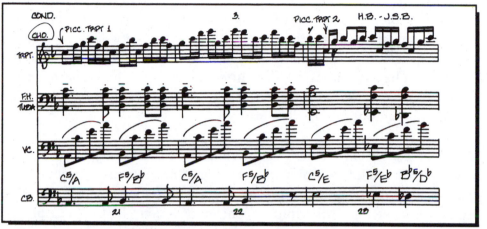

◆ **INSTRUMENTAL PART** Standard size parts (9½ x 12½") for orchestra, concert band and other ensembles; studio recording as well as live performance. Letter-size (8½ x 11") or A4 parts should be enlarged to at least 9 x 12".

‣ **MASTER RHYTHM CHART**   Sometimes referred to as a road map, a master rhythm chart is a multi-instrument part which allows musicians to see the complete rhythm section ensemble from beginning to end, often using repeats with multiple endings. (See CONVENTIONS OF FORM, page 326.) It may take the form of a simple, single line chord chart or an elaborate multi-staff part. The amount of detail required depends on the scope and style of the arrangement. (Rhythm section musicians generally play better with a minimum amount of detail to read.)

Rhythm section players (keyboards, guitars, bass, drums, percussion) are usually required to improvise a certain amount. A master rhythm part enables each player to see the total rhythm section arrangement—bass line, figures, fills, etc. and therefore to contribute effectively. Often, a one or two-bar pattern is notated to establish the style, followed by "simile" and chord symbols, perhaps indicating figures or fills along the way.

A master rhythm part should include enough staves to represent the required information, yet similar parts may be combined on one staff if clarity is maintained. The decision of simplicity vs. complexity requires careful consideration of the style of the music and the performers' level of experience.

▶ **LEAD SHEET** A lead sheet contains a single line melody with chord symbols above and lyrics below. A lead sheet represents a song—the composition, as opposed to a specific arrangement. Introductions, instrumental solo sections and endings are generally omitted. (See LEAD SHEETS, pages 254-259)

Many people confuse lead sheets with sheet music. While sheet music is typically a published and printed vocal/piano arrangement for sale commercially, lead sheets are for industry use only. A lead sheet may be used for copyright registration, song promotion, as a guide for an arranger, or as a resource for song comparison. If you are asked to prepare a lead sheet or a sheet music arrangement, it is important to clarify with your client the exact nature of the request, the intended use and format.

PIANO/VOCAL ARRANGEMENT   Commercial songs with piano accompaniment usually simulate the recording, including the original key, tempo, rhythmic feel, introduction, solos and the complete form.

© 1997, REBUS MUSIC Used by permission

CHORAL PARTS (choir parts) are usually 8½ x 11" or A4, as they are often held, rather than placed on a music stand. Choral parts are normally notated on four staves (SATB), but more or less staves may be used as necessary. The lyrics are written under the staff while the dynamics are written above the staff for each part.

© 1998, MORGAN AMES MUSIC (ASCAP) Used by permission

PRINTING MUSIC

In 1984, the combination of Apple Macintosh computers and laser printers revolutionized printing. While this was good news for musicians, it necessitated printing a reduced page of music to U.S. letter-size (8½ x 11") paper. This reduction is not suitable for the professional musician, who usually reads music at arm's length. Music preparation offices print manuscript size parts (9½ x 12½") with 11 x 17" laser printers and specially cut paper. The individual should make an effort to enlarge music pages whenever possible. Letter size to manuscript size requires an enlargement of approximately 115%.

Music should always be printed on heavy (at least 80 lb.) paper, even if used only once. Heavy paper will lay flat on a music stand and lends itself to quick and easy page turns.

Studio parts are normally printed on one side and taped accordion style (folded alternately). Concert parts are normally printed on both sides and bound (taped or stapled) in book form. Cover pages or blank insertion pages may be required to facilitate page turns.

Printing, the final step in music preparation, should be overseen and checked so that every page of every part is printed and bound in proper order. The original master pages or digital media should be available for emergency replacement.

While music is international and copyright laws are moving toward universality, the U.S. continues to resist the metric system of measurement. Metric measurement is used virtually everywhere but the U.S. If your music is to be played or published internationally, you may find the following table useful.

A4 = 21 x 29.7CM (8.27 x 11.69")	U.S. LETTER = 8½ x 11" (21.59 x 27.94CM)
A3 = 29.7 x 42CM (11.69 x 16.54")	U.S. TABLOID = 11 x 17" (27.94 x 43.18CM)

Conversion from one format to another requires a 3% to 6% reduction or enlargement.

COPYRIGHT LAW AND YOU

As a composer, you must be sure your original music is protected. If you work in the music business in any capacity, you probably handle music created by others. On either side of the fence, you need to be aware of the basic laws of copyright for your protection both as a creator and as a user of music.

The following terms summarize the basics of copyright law. With a little research, you can find out your status as a creator and user of music by investigating current international copyright laws, as well as those of your nation. Following is an overview of copyright terms and resources.

COPYRIGHT PROTECTION

Original works are protected from the moment they are first fixed in a tangible medium of expression, such as a score, a lead sheet, printed sheet music or a recording on disc or tape. Anything you create: music, words, e-mail, drawings, photos, software—virtually everything that is original—is copyright protected. This protection of intellectual property is automatic and lasts for the duration of the author's life plus 70 years in the U.S. in most European countries. Titles, names and other short phrases are not copyrightable. (BMI lists 13 songs titled "Happy Birthday To You"!)

The copyright notice is not required in most countries. However, it is to your advantage to include the information on your creations so people can contact you to obtain permission to use or license your work. The copyright symbol © is typed with the keystroke *option G* in Mac computer text fonts. Windows applications: try *alt 169* or *alt 0169* or copy from the character map. The © symbol is followed by the year of creation or publication and the author or publisher's name and often the address. The phrases "all rights reserved" and/or "int'l copyright secured" are sometimes added, although there is no global copyright as of this writing. (See INTERNATIONAL COPYRIGHT LAW, page 358.)

The symbol ℗ appears on sound recordings and protects the "production" rather than the composition.

BUNDLE OF RIGHTS

The owner of a copyright actually owns a "bundle of rights"—the exclusive rights to reproduce, distribute, display or perform the protected work. The bundle includes the right to sell, rent, lease or lend the work; the right to make copies or authorize others to make copies; the right to prepare derivative works from the original or license different rights of the same work to different people; and the right to bring a lawsuit if your rights are violated. A copyright is property, and as such can be transferred, sold or left to heirs.

PUBLICATION

A work is published when it is "issued and made available in sufficient quantities to the public" by means of sale, rental, lease or lending. Performances, exhibitions, recitations and broadcasting do not constitute publication. You may decide to relinquish ownership of your work to a publisher who is in a better position to license your music for various media (recordings, video, film, tv, CD-ROM, commercials, industrial soundtracks). Or you can be your own publisher. Either way, you are always the composer; your name appears as "author" on the registration. A work receives automatic copyright whether published or unpublished.

FIRST SALE DOCTRINE

Although the "bundle of rights" includes the right to control distribution of your work, once the work is sold or transferred to a new owner, you cannot prevent the new owner from reselling the work to someone else.

INFRINGEMENT

A violation of rights protected under copyright constitutes an infringement, which is subject to both criminal and civil penalties. In determining if one music work infringes upon another, two occurrences must have taken place: access to the copyrighted work and substantial use of similar material. You may have heard that a certain number of bars constitutes infringement— that is a myth. Each case has its own circumstances. In a court trial, the works are compared both aurally and visually, using charts of music notation.

FAIR USE

You may make limited use of copyrighted material without the owner's consent if the use is reasonable and not harmful to the owner's rights. Generally, fair use is intended for education, research or review. A portion of a copyrighted work may be used "for purposes such as criticism, comment, news reporting, teaching, scholarship or research."

Guidelines have been submitted by various music associations which permit "emergency copying for a performance, making a single copy of a sound recording for aural exercises or examinations, editing or simplification of printed copies and making multiple copies (not more than one per student) of partial excerpts not comprising a performable unit and not exceeding 10% of a whole work." An entire work may not be copied without permission under any circumstances.

Parody of an original work as a form of entertainment is recognized as fair use. Parody may have "social or political merit which exceeds any economic loss to the copyright holder."

What actually constitutes fair use must be determined on a case by case basis. The court has considered such things as the general purpose and character of the use; whether for commercial or nonprofit educational purposes; the amount and substantiality of the portion used; and the effect of the use upon the potential market value of the copyrighted work. When in doubt, seek permission of the copyright owner or consult an attorney.

A copyright search to obtain rights should start with the © notice. If you cannot locate the owner or publisher, try the "Catalog of Copyright Entries" at a public library or song search services on-line. The U.S. Copyright Office (page 362) can perform a search which could take weeks at a nominal hourly rate. A faster but more expensive approach is to contact a copyright attorney.

MORAL RIGHTS

Many countries recognize the author's intent to protect a work after publication. Moral rights may include the right to: control publication of a work; attach or display the author's name on a work; prevent the distortion of a work through alteration; withdraw, alter, or disavow a work after publication. A contract between author (composer) and publisher should specify conditions of control of the work.

WORK MADE FOR HIRE

If you create an original work as an employee and that work was within the scope of your employment, your employer owns the work as a "work made for hire." However, if you are considered an independent contractor, your creation may be copyrighted by you. Even so, if the party paying for the work has made creative contributions, the copyright could be shared jointly. The ownership of music composed for a film is a point of contract negotiation. When in doubt, it is best to agree in writing before starting a project who will own the copyright. The duration of a work made for hire is currently 75 years from the date of publication or 100 years from the date of creation, whichever comes first.

PUBLIC DOMAIN

A work that is in the public domain is "free for use by all." That is, it belongs to the public and may be used by anyone without paying the creator. You may obtain a copyright for your unique arrangement of a composition that is in the public domain. Generally, a work published in the U.S. more than 75 years ago is in the public domain. Be aware, however, that even if a work was created long ago, every published edition or arrangement of that work probably carries a copyright, which may be active. Look for the © information on the first page. If the term of copyright is still in effect, you must obtain permission from the copyright owner to avoid infringement. You should assume that any music, literary or art work is protected by copyright unless you can prove it is in the public domain.

The Public Domain Report (monthly subscription) lists works of music, art and literature that are in the public domain. They also publish the Public Domain Music Bible and Sheet Music Library (available on CD-ROM). www.pubdomain.com

INTERNATIONAL COPYRIGHT LAW
Your creations are protected under your nation's copyright laws and any of the international treaties that your nation has signed.

TOWARD A UNIVERSAL COPYRIGHT PROTECTION
There are treaties among various nations giving reciprocal protection to works copyrighted in each member country; however, there is still no world-wide copyright law. Many countries have signed the Berne treaty and/or the Universal Copyright Convention, both of which encourage international trade through the mutual protection of music, literary works, recordings, films and computer software.

BERNE CONVENTION
Most major countries of the world (approximately 80) are members of the Berne Convention treaty, which maintains a high standard of copyright protection on an international scale. A country that has signed the Berne treaty gives its citizens the same copyright protection as the other participating countries. Copyright duration under this treaty is the life of the author plus 50 years.*

UNIVERSAL COPYRIGHT CONVENTION
Over 100 countries are signatories to the UCC, which affords the same copyright protection in any signatory country as the author's country. The UCC requires the © symbol, year of creation and author's name to appear on all copies of the work. Copyright duration under this treaty is the life of the author plus 25 years or 25 years from the date of publication. However, a country that is also a Berne signatory receives the life plus 50 year copyright duration.*

> * The current copyright duration as of this writing is the life of the author plus 70 years in the U.S. and most European countries.

As a composer or a user of copyrighted material, you are obligated to know your rights as well as those of others. Copyright law affects you as a citizen, depending on your nation's laws and whether your nation is a member of the Berne Convention, Universal Copyright Convention, International Copyright Union or a number of other conventions. A list of countries signed to the Berne Convention and the Universal Copyright Convention may be found on the U.S. Copyright Office web site (see page 362).

COPYRIGHT IN THE DIGITAL DOMAIN

The "rights" of copyright are constantly challenged with the digital transmission of music, art and words over the internet. Established publishers and distributors are not the only ones threatened, since anyone with a web site is a publisher and susceptible to commercial piracy, as well as "harmless" copying of protected materials. Audio, video, graphic images and words fall under the same copyright protection on the net as they do in any other media.

The storage and transmission of music in digital form is relatively safe. Yet your music on a web site is vulnerable to unauthorized copying and distribution. You can inhibit commercial stealing of your music by posting a copyright notice; then you have a right to sue anyone that copies your work without your permission. Lawsuits concerning digital copying have been effective in discouraging piracy and establishing guidelines for future cases. Digital watermarking (fingerprinting) technology is available to embed copyright information in your music.

The symbol © does not always display properly on web sites, therefore it is advisable to use the word "copyright" instead or in conjunction with the symbol. Remember to always follow "copyright" with the year and name of the author or publisher.

If you offer your music in the public domain, display a notice so that people can download it with gratitude, not guilt. Whenever you send your creation into cyberspace, always state the conditions for its use and reproduction.

If you have questions as to a particular copyright issue, there is further information available in published periodicals, in books, at various web sites, or from the U.S. Copyright Office. When in doubt, consult an attorney who specializes in copyright law.

Internet-related issues are changing so fast and profoundly, it is imperitive to obtain up-to-date information.

COPYRIGHT LAWS OF THE U.S.

The history of U. S. copyright law is a series of overlapping copyright stipulations, a source of ongoing confusion in the courts. Following is a summary of the major changes in U.S. copyright law. Always check the U.S. Copyright Office website, page 362, for the latest information.

Oct. 27, 1998 (Copyright Extension):
 Duration: author's lifetime plus 70 years. This aligns U.S. copyright duration with most European countries.

Mar. 1, 1989: The U.S. signed the **Berne Convention for Protection of Literary and Artistic Works.**
 © notice not required; registration not required. However, registration is necessary within three months of publication in order to collect statutory damages and attorney's fees in a lawsuit.
 Duration: author's lifetime plus 50 years. If more than one author, 50 years after the death of the last surviving author. If work for hire, 75 years from the date of publication or 100 years from date of creation, whichever comes first.

Jan. 1, 1978 to Mar. 1, 1989 (The 1976 Copyright Act):
 © notice not required; registration required.
 Duration: author's lifetime plus 50 years.

pre-1978 (Copyright Act of 1909):
 © notice, year, author or publisher's name required on each copy; registration required.
 Duration: 75 years from date of registration (28 years plus a 28 year renewal plus a 19 year extension.)

Since the U.S. signed the Berne Convention treaty on March 1, 1989, any work created after that date does not require a copyright notice. However, it is still advisable to include the © symbol, the year, and the author's (composer's) name so that there is no doubt as to the originator of the work.

HOW TO REGISTER A U.S. COPYRIGHT

If you are a U.S. citizen, your work is automatically protected by copyright immediately upon creation. It is advisable, however, to register your score, lead sheet or sound recording with the Copyright Office. Your copyrights will be kept as public record.

There are alternate means of copyright registration with various songwriting organizations but your work will not be protected to the extent that formal registration with the Copyright Office provides.

To register notated music, use form PA (performing arts) and to register sound recordings use form SR. You may register music that is on tape or CD; however, MIDI files are not accepted. If you wish to copyright a MIDI sequence, print out a score or dub to tape or disc. You must submit a form with an original signature (not a photocopy), the current registration fee and one or two copies of your work, depending on publication status and media. Get specific and up-to-date information from the sources listed below.

FORMS

The U.S. Copyright Office provides free copyright registration forms.

Web:
Download copyright forms from The U.S. Copyright Office web site:
www.lcweb.loc.gov/copyright/forms

Phone:
U. S. Copyright Office forms hotline: (202) 707-9100 to order registration forms and circulars describing copyright information.

Mail:
Copyright Office, Publications Section, LM-455, Library of Congress, Washington, DC 20559

COPYRIGHT INFORMATION SOURCES

The U.S. Copyright Office will answer questions regarding registration, but cannot offer legal advice.

Web:
The U.S. Copyright Office web site:
www.lcweb.loc.gov/copyright
You will find answers to questions regarding copyright, as well as a list of every country and its copyright relationships with the U.S.

Phone:
U. S. Copyright Office information line: (202) 707-3000.

Mail:
Information section, U. S. Copyright Office, Library of Congress, Washington, DC 20559

OTHER WEB SITES:
The Copyright Web site:
www.benedict.com

American Society of Composers, Authors and Publishers (ASCAP):
www.ascap.com

Broadcast Music Inc. (BMI):
www.bmi.com

SESAC: www.sesac.com

National Music Publishers Association:
www.nmpa.org
Links to many related sites.

12

REFERENCE AND RESOURCES

12

REFERENCE AND RESOURCES

REVIEW QUESTIONS

The reviews may be used as quizzes, as forums for discussion, or as impetus for research projects. Answers on pages 368-373.

SOLUTIONS TO NOTATION PROBLEMS

Pages 374-379.

EXERCISES

The student chooses music for many of the exercises, as this training emphasizes personal involvement, particular interest and taste with regard to musical genre and style. Section 9 contains many hours of exercises, which may be extended to a one or two year course. These exercises are models for lifetime study.

RESOURCES

Where to find supplies, organizations, information, inspiration. We've tried to list only books, businesses, phone numbers and web sites that are current.

SUPPLEMENTARY INFORMATION

Augments various sections of the text. Reference and resources for transcribing, orchestrating, composing, film scoring.

This book is divided conceptually into four parts. You may emphasize various sections according to personal or class experience and goals.

I. YOU AND MUSIC

1. THE COMPLETE MUSICIAN: What may be accomplished with this book; principal jobs in the music business; your personal training.

2. DEVELOPING YOUR EAR: Your perception; tools to develop your ear for music; increasing your awareness while listening.

3. FROM SOUND TO MUSIC: The nature of sound as the medium of music; how nature has provided the resources for music; how music evolved and redefined itself through history; the elements of music as raw material for today's music.

II. PERCEPTION

4. THE MATERIAL OF MUSIC: Various aspects of intervals; tools to help you identify intervals.

5. HEARING INTERVALS: Extensive discussion and exercises to help you distinguish each interval and develop instant recognition.

6. HEARING PHRASES: How intervals are combined to create phrases; tools and exercises to sharpen your perception.

III. TRANSCRIPTION

7. TRANSCRIBING MUSIC: Preparation to develop this essential skill for composing, orchestrating, improvising, etc.

8. TRANSCRIPTION TECHNIQUE: Development of the procedure from all aspects that you may encounter in the art and business of music.

9. PERCEPTION TO NOTATION: Applying your skills developed thus far to specific elements of music: rhythm, melodic lines, counterpoint, chords, chord progressions, orchestration and full scores.

IV. NOTATION

10. COMMUNICATION WITH MUSIC NOTATION: The language, elements and general practice, with emphasis on common discrepancies and how to make good choices in your notation; computer generated notation.

11. PREPARATION FOR PRODUCTION AND PUBLICATION: The final step in finishing your music; scores, parts and various formats; copyright law.

12. REFERENCE AND RESOURCES: Study plans; answers to review questions; music notation solutions; music professions; books; websites; locations.

STUDY PLANS

The following time table will help you plan your course, whether for a class or personal study. Reading exercise times very greatly according to the individual. Times listed here are an average. Extra time may be devoted to further research, exercises and transcriptions.

	READING TIME	EXERCISES	TOTAL TIME
SECTION 1	¼ HR.	NONE	¼ HR.
SECTION 2	¾ HR.	¾ HR.	1½ HR.
SECTION 3	1 HR.	½ HR.	1½ HR.
SECTION 4	½ HR.	NONE	½ HR.
SECTION 5	1½ HR.	1 HR.	2½ HR.
SECTION 6	1½ HR.	¾ HR.	2¼ HR.
SECTION 7	¾ HR.	½ HR.	1¼ HR.
SECTION 8	1 HR.	1 HR.	2 HR.
SECTION 9	2½ HR.	20+ HR.	22½+HR.
SECTION 10	1 HR.	½ HR.	1½ HR.
SECTION 11	½ HR.	NONE	½ HR.
TOTAL TIME:	**11 HOURS**	**25 HOURS**	**36 HOURS**

COURSE PLANS

The following outlines are minimal and intense. The material is easier to assimilate if spread over longer periods. Transcription exercises in section 9 may be continued in following terms or at the student's discretion.

10-WEEK QUARTER COURSE:

Wk.	Sec.	Pgs.	Hrs.
1	1,2,3	48	3¼ HR.
2	4,5	34	3 HR.
3	6	37	2¼ HR.
4	7,8	56	3¼ HR.
5	9A	14 (206-221)	3½ HR MIN.
6	9B	32 (222-253)	3½ HR MIN.
7	9C	10 (254-273)	3½ HR MIN.
8	9D	11 (274-284)	3½ HR MIN.
9	10,11	75	2 HR.
10	Individual final project (transcription, orchestration or score preparation)		

15-WEEK SEMESTER COURSE:

Wk.	Sec.	Pgs.	Hrs.
1	1,2	20	1¾ HR.
2	3,4	45	2 HR.
3	5	26	2½ HR.
4	6	37	2¼ HR.
5	7	19	1¼ HR MIN.
6	8	39	2 HR
7	9A	14 (206-221)	3½ HR MIN.
8	9B	32 (222-253)	3½ HR MIN.
9	9C	10 (254-273)	3½ HR MIN.
10	9D	11 (274-284)	3½ HR MIN.
11	10,11	75	2 HR.
12-15	Continue transcriptions, orchestrations and score preparation for individualized final projects		

FOLLOWING QUARTERS OR SEMESTERS:
Continue exercises and projects in section 9;
Individual transcription, orchestration and score projects

1 or 2 YEAR COURSE:
Augment the schedule above with personal projects, such as transcriptions, orchestrations and preparation of score and parts, as suggested throughout the text.

ANSWERS TO REVIEW QUESTIONS

Answers are somewhat subjective; several answers are provided.

SECTION 2 REVIEW, PAGE 24

1   Describe the difference between a tone and a note.
    Tone: sound / hear / in the air
    Note: symbol / see / on the page
    [page 15]

2   Describe the phenomenon of resonance.
    All objects vibrate at a particular frequency, depending on size, shape density and material. A vibrating object can cause another nearby object to vibrate if they share the same frequency. This is called sympathetic vibration, or resonance. [pages 18, 19]

3   Describe each tool and how you may use it to hear music.

    Matching
    Sing or hum, unison or octave, with an audible pitch creating resonance. [page 20]

    Your voice
    Your portable instrument, accessible at all times, used to produce intervals and verify tones with resonance. [page 21]

    Internalizing
    Listening to your inner voice. Use as a playback device to recreate melodic lines stored in your memory. [page 22]

    Tonal Memory
    Verify the pitch of a tone through the memory of a recent tone of the same pitch. [page 23]

    Physical Connection
    Use of the memory of playing your instrument to help recreate a phrase. Fingers recreate interval patterns. [page 23]

SECTION 3 REVIEW, PAGE 59

1 What is sound?
   Vibrations moving through the air in waves, perceived through our sense of hearing. [page 27]

2 What is the basic building block of music and how is it defined?
   A tone: a sound of constant, discernible pitch (frequency). [page 27]

3 Why is a melody recognizable at any pitch, in any key?
   A melody is composed of a series of intervals and their rhythms, which are transposable to any pitch or key and playable at any tempo. The melodic shape is retained and therefore recognizable. [page 52]

4 Are all sounds material for music?
   Yes. They may be classified as tones or percussive events or effects. [page 27]

5 What are the attributes of a tone?
   Frequency. or period = pitch
   Amplitude = loudness level
   Waveshape = timbre
   [page 31]

6 How has nature contributed to the shape of music?
   Nature has provided a collection of intervals that resonant together, known as the harmonic series. Their sonic and mathematical relationship, that of the golden mean, is the model for the development of western harmony and the basis for the construction of musical instruments. [pages 32-37]

7 Which of the elements of music are natural and which are artificial?
Natural elements are the octave [pages 32, 35, 41], the natural (or just) intervals of the harmonic series [page 36] and the concept of rhythmic events [page 30]. Artificial elements are tempered intervals [page 45], designated pitch, or note names and keys [pages 51, 52].

8 Which intervals are common to all tunable music systems?
The octave and fifth [page 42].

9 What are the advantages and disadvantages of equal temperament?
Advantages: a system of equal keys, modulation without retuning; near-perfect fifths and ninths. Symmetrical structures of 2, 3, 4, 6 and 8 tones are possible.

Disadvantages: Imperfect intervals and harmonies do not correspond with the natural intervals of the harmonic series.
[pages 45-47]

10 Describe the TONAL STRUCTURE.
The tonal structure is the octave and its primary division (3:2) by the 3rd harmonic, corresponding to the fifth scale degree. The tonal structure is a reference for all other tones. [pages 42-44]

SECTION 4 REVIEW, PAGE 71

1 Name three methods of identifying intervals.
    Scale degrees, numbered diatonic scale-tones
    Solfege (fixed or movable Do)
    Pitch class
    Association (optional)
    [pages 67, 68]

2 What is an idealized interval and why is it practical?
    An idealized interval is one which is agreed upon as an average or
    accepted norm. Practical because it is easily represented with music
    notation, yet encompasses infinite shadings or variations of the interval.
    [pages 63, 64]

3 What attribute does a vertical interval possess that is missing in a
    melodic interval?
    Resonance. [page 65]

4 Describe how these tools help us distinguish each interval:
    TONALITY:
    Each interval has its source in the harmonic series. Its place in the series
    reflects its relationship to the root, or its inherent tonality. [page 68]

    SPAN:
    The size of an interval in relation to the octave. The amount of en-
    ergy required to produce a melodic interval. [page 69]

    RESONANCE:
    Each vertical interval produces a different amount of vibrancy which
    helps us to discern one interval from another. [page 69]

SECTION 6 REVIEW, PAGE 139

1 Name the four diatonic tetrachords and describe in terms of scale degrees,
that is, 3 or ♭3, etc.
    Lydian: 1, 2, 3, ♯4
    Major: 1, 2, 3, 4
    Minor: 1, 2, ♭3, 4
    Phrygian: 1, ♭2, ♭3, 4
    [page 105]

2 What is the characteristic interval of an exotic tetrachord?
    Augmented second
    [page 106]

3 Name the seven diatonic modes in descending or ascending order of
key signatures.
    Lydian
    Major (Ionian)
    Mixolydian
    Dorian
    Minor (Aeolian)
    Phrygian
    Locrian
    [pages 108, 109]

4 Describe the characteristics of the four modal effects.
    Lydian: augmented 4th (♯4)
    Mixolydian: major 3rd, minor 7th (3, ♭7)
    Dorian: minor 3rd, major 6th (♭3, 6)
    Phrygian: minor 2nd (♭2)
    [page 113]

5 Which intervals are not contained in the pentatonic modes?
    Half-tone (minor 2nd) and tritone [page 116]

6 Name and describe the interval content of each of the symmetrical structures.

    Augmented chord - 3 major 3rds
    Diminished chord - 4 minor 3rds
    Whole-tone scale - 6 major 2nds
    Double-diminished scale / 8-tone scale / whole-tone, half-tone scale -
        alternating whole- and half-tones / 4 whole-tones and 4 half-tones
    Chromatic scale - 12 Half-tones
    Tritone structure - 2 tritones (optional)
    [page 117]

7 How does tonality enable us to perceive melodic lines?

    Tonality provides a point of reference; a sense of orientation; a basis of organization of all tones; a template which may be utilized in the perception of a phrase. [pages 118, 119]

8 Describe different types of tonal organization in terms of tonality.

    Monotonal - Sustained, non-shifting tonality; drone
    Modulatory - Changing tonalities; chord progressions
    Abstract - No apparent sense of tonal center
    Random - Collection of tones, unordered (like wind chimes)
    [page 130]

9 Describe four types of tonal movement.

    Monophonic - single line, unaccompanied
    Polyphonic - multiple independent voices; counterpoint
    Homophonic - parallel voices; block harmony
    Chordal - single line melody accompanied by chord progression
    [page 132]

10 Group the diatonic modes that are closely related to the major mode and those that are closely related to the minor mode.

    Lydian-Major-Mixolydian
    Dorian-Minor-Phrygian
    [pages 108, 112]

SOLUTIONS TO NOTATION PROBLEMS

EXERCISE 55 (SECTION 6, PAGE 107)

Sing and identify the mode of the following phrases.

1—4—3—♭2—1.

1—2—♭3—♯4—♭3—2—1.

1—♯4—♭3—♭2—1.

1—♭2—3—♯4—3—♭2—1.

EXERCISE 58 (SECTION 6, PAGE 111)

Indicate the corresponding key signature (number of sharps or flats) to designate the following modes:

F MINOR	4♭
G LYDIAN	2♯
E♭ DORIAN	5♭
D♭ MIXOLYDIAN	6♭
F♯ MAJOR	6♯
A♭ MINOR	7♭
E LYDIAN	5♯
A PHRYGIAN	1♭
B DORIAN	3♯
C LOCRIAN	5♭
D MIXOLYDIAN	1♯
B♭ PHRYGIAN	6♭

EXERCISE 89 (SECTION 9, PAGE 226)

Write a chord symbol that describes the "crunch" chord from Stravinsky's *The Rite of Spring*, as notated below. (Spell enharmonically if desired.)

$$\frac{E\flat 7}{F\flat} \quad or \quad \frac{E\flat 7}{E}$$

EXERCISE 91 (SECTION 9, PAGE 240)

Circle the chord tones:

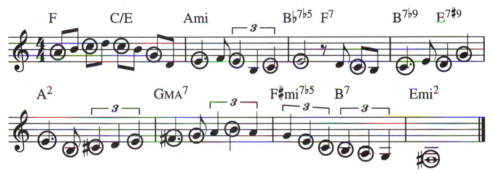

EXERCISE 92 (SECTION 9, PAGE 240)

Place a chord symbol above each chord type:

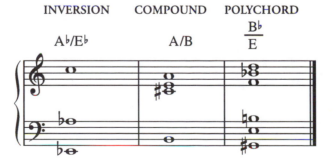

EXERCISE 93 (SECTION 9, PAGE 241)

Designate a chord symbol for the following common chords. If the symbol is not immediately apparent, collapse the chord to a stack of thirds. Use enharmonic spelling if necessary. There are often two or more chord symbols to describe a chord. Try to use the simplest chord symbol here.

EXERCISE 102 (SECTION 9, PAGE 252)

There are several solutions, depending on the voicing of the first chord. Remember that third-related major triads have one common tone; also third related minor triads. Mixed (major/minor) triads have two common tones if diatonically related; no common tones if the relationship is chromatic.

EXERCISE 103 (SECTION 9, PAGE 253)

The following pop tunes contain "hook" chord progressions. All have been transposed to the same tonality for comparison. Identify the unique quality in the sound of each progression. Find two characteristics these progressions have in common.

Sittin' On The Dock Of The Bay	C	E	F	D
Lay, Lady, Lay	C	Emi	B♭	Dmi
Since I Don't Have You	C	Ami7	Fmi	G7♭9
Sunny	Cmi	E♭7	A♭7	G7

Two characteristics these progressions have in common:

1) Third-related chords: those whose roots are either a minor third or major third apart.

2) Non-diatonic chords: those that extend outside the diatonic key center, i.e. introduce chromatically altered tones. The chromatic tones are:

Sittin' On The Dock Of The Bay	G♯ and F♯
Lay, Lady, Lay	B♭
Since I Don't Have You	A♭
Sunny (C minor)	D♭, G♭ and B♮

EXERCISE 119 (SECTION 9, PAGE 271)

Write the following phrase in prime unison (no octaves) for the instruments listed. Find the tonality of the phrase; internalize; sing as you write the phrase in the appropriate clef and key.

EXERCISE 138 (SECTION 10, PAGE 294)

Quickly identify these major or minor triads.

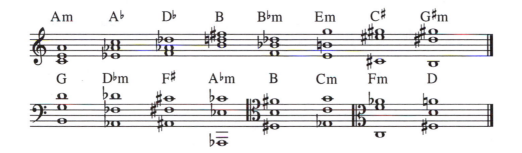

EXERCISE 139 (SECTION 10, PAGE 294)

Label the following diminished or whole-tone chords, disregarding roots.
Use only the symbol ° (for diminished) or * (for whole-tone).

PROFESSIONAL MUSIC JOBS

General job descriptions follow. Composers, orchestrators and music librarians sometimes use assistants. Typically, a musician's career will have included several of these jobs.

COMPOSER conceives original music. A composer may collaborate with a director, producer, choreographer, lyricist, music editor or print editor.

ARRANGER tailors a piece of music for a specific artist or occasion, setting the style, form and key centers.

ORCHESTRATOR sets music in score form, assigning lines and verticals to designated instruments, finalizing the nuances of performance in notation.

TRANSCRIBER sets sound in music notation, from audio or MIDI. A transcription may consist of a single melodic line, a master rhythm chart or a complete score.

COPYIST extracts individual parts from a score or sketch in notation suitable for performance. Copyists use pen and ink, pencil or computer.

PROOFREADER checks parts and scores for accuracy, completeness, conventions of notation.

MUSIC LIBRARIAN duplicates scores and parts, collates parts into books for individual musicians. A music librarian may deliver music to a performance venue, assist in a rehearsal, recording or performance, make notational changes in the score or parts, catalog and store music for later use.

SCORE CONSULTANT reads the score during a recording sessions; listens for mistakes, balance, and checks timings.

MUSICOLOGIST In the commercial world, a musicologist may prepare comparative music examples and be called upon as an "expert witness" in music infringement cases. There are many other branches of musicology—related to acoustics, aesthetics, ethnic or folk music, history, music theory, music therapy, physiology, psychology and sociology.

Also: PERFORMER, LEADER, CONDUCTOR, CONTRACTOR, PRODUCER, MUSIC EDITOR, MIDI or ELECTRONIC CONSULTANT.

Tips: Always be on time (early is better)! Be prepared for anything! Anyone you know now could be important to your career in the future!

PROFESSIONAL MUSIC ORGANIZATIONS

Organizations—unions, guilds, societies—dedicated to the interest of those working in music jobs.

Composition and arranging are not covered by the musicians union (AFM) wage scales. Those jobs are negotiated directly with the employer or through an agent. The musicians union maintains contracts for all media covering wages for orchestrator, copyist, proofreader and librarian, as well as performer, conductor (leader) and contractor.

American Federation of Musicians (AFM) New York (800) 762-3444 (212) 869-1330
    www.afm.org Job categories defined, information, links to other organizations

Professional Musicians, local 47 (AFM) (323) 462-2161 (800) 834-4789
    www.promusic47.org Current wage scales, information

Recording Musicians Association (RMA) (323) 462-4762
    www.rmaweb.org Wage scales, links

Society of Composers and Lyricists (SCL)
    www.filmscore.org   (310) 281-2812

American Society of Music Arrangers and Composers (ASMAC)
    (818) 994-4661   P.O. Box 11, Hollywood, CA 90078

Recording Industry Association of America (RIAA) 1020 19th St. NW #200,
    Washington, DC 20036 (202) 772-0101 www.raii.org

Professional Composers of America, 52 Main St., Port Washington, NY 11050.

American Society of Music Copyists, P.O. Box 2557, Times Square Station,
    New York, NY 10108

The Los Angeles Music Industry Directory (805) 299-2405
    musiciansphonebook.com

Recording Industry Sourcebook (800) 543-7771 (913) 967-1719
    Available in book form or CD-ROM.

Film Music Magazine Film and Television Salary and Rate Survey at
    The Film Music Network web site: www.filmmusic.net
    Information on composers and related film music jobs

BOOKS AND SUPPLIES

Books, especially music books, seem to go out of print frequently. We have tried to recommend books that are currently in print. It is not necessary to list ISBN numbers, or even publishers, as it is easy to find any book using internet bookstore search engines. Search by title, author or category. Most titles are available at musicbooksplus.com.

FILM SCORING
Advanced Techniques for Film Scoring by Earle Hagen
On The Track by Fred Karlin and Rayburn Wright

ORCHESTRATION
There are over a dozen orchestration books currently in print with essentially the same information, but each with a different approach to organization and detail. We suggest you browse through available orchestration books and choose three that appeal to you. Same with music dictionaries.

RANGE AND TRANSPOSITION
Always carry one of these references with you, as you will not remember the range and transposition of every instrument.
Essential Dictionary of Orchestration by Dave Black and Tom Gerou
Range and Transposition Guide to 250 Musical Instruments by Robert Bornstein

WHERE TO FIND SCORES
Brand Library, 1601 West Mountain St., Glendale, CA 91201-1209 (818) 548-2051
    A public library devoted exclusively to music and art.Books, scores, recordings.
Theodore Front Musical Literature, 16122 Cohasset, Van Nuys, CA 91406
    (818) 994-1902
Baxter Northup Music 14534 Ventura Blvd., Sherman Oaks, CA 91403
    (323) 872-0756
Alfred Publishing Company, P.O. Box 10003, Van Nuys, CA 91410-0003
    www.alfredpub.com
Luck's Music Library, P.O. Box 71397, Madison Heights, MI 48071
    (800) 348-8749
Patelson's Music (conductor's scores) 160 W. 56th St., New York, NY 10019
    (212) 582-5840
Dover Publications, 31 East 2nd St., Mineola, NY 11501 (write for catalog)
Music Publishers Association, www.mpa.org (many links)

MUSIC NOTATION, ENGRAVING, MANUSCRIPT COPYING

Essential Dictionary of Music Notation by Tom Gerou and Linda Lusk
Music Notation by Gardner Read
The Norton Manual of Music Notation by George Heussenstamm
The Art of Music Engraving and Processing by Ted Ross

MUSIC WRITING SUPPLIES

Judy Green Music, 1616 Cahuenga Ave., Hollywood, CA 90028
      (323) 466-2491.
Valle Music, 12443½ Riverside Dr., North Hollywood, CA 91607
      (818) 762-0615.
ABC Reproduction Service, 1633 Broadway, New York, NY 10019
      (212) 582-9334
Associated Music Service, 333 W. 52nd St., New York, NY 10019
      (212) 265-2400

VOICE, BODY, MIND

You Are Your Instrument by Julie Lyonn Lieberman
Music, the Brain, and Ecstasy by Robert Jourdain
Keep Your Voice Healthy by Friedrich Brodnitz
The Artist's Way by Julia Cameron
Rhythms of Vision by Lawrence Blair
Biographies of composers, artists

EAR CARE

Refer to pages 149-151.
Sound Health by Steven Halpern
Musicians and the Prevention of Hearing Loss by Marshall Chasin
House Ear Institute: 2100 W. Third St., Los Angeles, CA 90057 (213) 483-4431
      www.hei.org

TONING, HARMONIC SINGING, OVERTONE SINGING

Refer to page 40.
www.harmonicworld.com
www.compsol.net/users/jimcole
www.feynman.com/tuva/
Search the web for "harmonic singing" or "overtone singing"

ACOUSTICS

On the Sensations of Tone by Hermann Helmholtz, Trans. by Alexander Ellis
Fundamentals of Musical Acoustics by Arthur H. Benade

TRANSCRIBING MUSIC

> Mozart, walking in the country:
> "If I but had the theme on paper."

TRANSCRIBING EQUIPMENT

Currently, the only analog tape cassette player/recorder on the market that is built for transcribing music, i.e. starting, stopping and "sliding" the tape:

> Marantz PMD430 stereo portable cassette recorder: 3 head, *cue* and *review* type transport, ±6% pitch control, volume control, headphone jack/ external speaker, built-in monitor speaker, index numbers/memory rewind, AC/batteries.
> Available at Musician's Workshop (800) 543-6125. Ask for catalog.

There are similar models that play at half-speed (one octave lower) but they are monaural. I believe the stereo "space" is valuable for separation, an aid to hearing lines. When you have developed your transcribing technique, you won't need the half-speed feature.

TUNING FORKS

> Baxter Northup Music, 14534 Ventura Blvd., Sherman Oaks, CA 91403
> (323) 872-0756

A TRANSCRIBING TALE

> Three in the morning the doorbell rang. There was Bird, horn in hand, and he says, "Let me in, Diz, I've got it; you must hear this thing I've worked out." I had been putting down Bird's solos on paper, which is something Bird never had the patience for himself. "Not now," I said. "Later, man, tomorrow." "No," Bird cried. "I won't remember it tomorrow; it's in my head now; let me in please." From the other room, my wife yelled, "Throw him out," and I obediently slammed the door in Bird's face. Parker than took his horn to his mouth and played the tune in the hallway. I grabbed pencil and paper and took it down from the other side of the door. *Dizzy Gillespie*

TRANSCRIBING: SUGGESTED MUSIC

HEARING AND WRITING: LINES AND COUNTERPOINT
Paul Hindemith: *Concert Music for Brass and Strings:* String unison @ c.5:06
William Schumann: *Symphony #3:IV Toccata:* Bass clarinet solo @ c.0:28
Sibelius: *Symphony #4:I*: Abstract unison @ c.5:00
Mozart: *Symphony #40:III Menuetto*
Mendelssohn: *Symphony for Strings #12: III Allegro molto:* Fugue @ c.0:47

SKETCHING
Refer to pages 153-155

> Art is not about thinking something up. It is about getting something down.
>   Julia Cameron: *The Artist's Way*

> Repeatedly, [Michaelangelo] dipped the quill in the ink, impatient to have to interrupt the continuity of his linear passage.
>   Irving Stone: *The Agony and the Ecstasy*

> During my years with the Carpenters, I transcribed "live" while Richard Carpenter played the arrangements on the piano. We both preferred the Yamaha Electric Grand—he for the sound and I because it made a great desk, the perfect height. I sat at the opposite end of the piano, sketching as fast as possible, while he played each orchestral part. It was a point of pride that I never looked at the keyboard.
>   *The author* (See TRANSCRIBING "LIVE," page 200)

COMPOSITION

SYSTEMS OF INTERVALS, CHORDS AND COMPOSITION

University Music Departments around the world:
www.sun.rhbnc.ac.uk/Music/Links/musdepts

Angel, David:
> The study of orchestral sound. Tonality based on the fifth structure, the common ground throughout music history. Publication pending. For information: www.rongorow.com

Hanson, Howard: *Harmonic Materials of Modern Music*
> Symbols (PMNSDT) represent intervals. An elegant system of notating according to interval content so that you have an immediate sense of the sound of any sonority. Projection of each interval.

Hindemith, Paul: *The Craft of Musical Composition*
> Composition based on the harmonic series.

Murphy, Lyle "Spud": *Horizontal Composition based on Equal Intervals*
> A 12 volume music composition course of horizontal line writing based on equal intervals. www.equalintervalsystem.com

Persichetti, Vincent: *Twentieth Century Harmony*
> Survey of 20th century methods and techniques with exercises.

Schillinger, Joseph: *The Schillinger System of Musical Composition*
> Measure both scales and chords with intervallic units of half-tones. Emphasis on expanding traditional parameters.

Tremblay, George: *The Definitive Cycle of the Twelve Tone Row*
> Permutations and examples of twelve tone writing.
> Out of print, but you may be able to find it.

Writer's block? Try *The Artist's Way* by Julia Cameron

WHERE TO GET YOUR COMPOSITIONS PERFORMED

▶ Form a composers co-op group, find a venue and some musicians.
▶ Local schools, universities.
▶ Community orchestras.
▶ Gather musician friends for a rehearsal/performance of your music.
▶ Write a piece for a specific soloist who has orchestra connections.

THOUGHTS ON COMPOSING

You should draw not a line, but an inspired line.

Robert Henri: *The Art Spirit*

Berlioz, who did not play the piano, or any other instrument: "I feel grateful to the happy chance that forced me to compose freely and in silence...this has delivered me from the tyranny of the fingers, so dangerous to thought." Somehow, this relatively untrained composer, this ex-medical student who could not play a respectable musical instrument, had the ear to conceive tonal combinations undreamed of until then.

Harold Schonberg: *The Lives of the Great Composers*

Composition is using the elements of music in the abstract—relative to each other.

Orchestration is concerned with actual pitch and real time.

Orchestration is designating specific instruments to produce specific sounds.

Orchestration transforms all the elements of composition from relative to specific.

ORCHESTRATION: MORE TRANSCRIBING MATERIAL

Woodwinds: Schubert or Mozart symphonies. Trios, quartets, quintets by many composers.
Brass: Various ensembles by Corelli, Purcell. Aaron Copland: *Fanfare for the Common Man*
Strings: Quartets. William Walton: *Sonata for String Orchestra: I* (fugue @ c. 3:56)
Also, transcribe works for voice, piano, harp, percussion.

When you see a beautiful sunrise, sunset or cloud formation, think about orchestration.

YOUR FIRST FILM SCORE

Your first film score will entail the same craft, techniques and problems as the biggest budget Hollywood film. The only difference is the scale— you'll probably hire your friends to play for nothing, scrimp on supplies and studio, and you'll be paid in experience, rather than money. But you'll learn how to put music to film. There is no other way to learn the craft.

While film scoring may not be the ultimate forum for some composers, it does present a way to survive while writing music. The paradox of film music is that it is the most restrictive form of composition due to the mechanics of timing and synchronization to picture, yet the composer is free to use any technique or style to fulfill the dramatic requirements of the film.

You may be able to gain experience as an assistant to a composer, orchestrator or music editor. Be prepared to orchestrate or compose a film score; the opportunity could come at any time.

You can listen to sound tracks, go to movies, subscribe to:
> Film Score Monthly: www.filmscoremonthly.com
> Film Music Magazine: www.filmmusicmag.com

Locate film score sound tracks at:
> www.soundtrak.com
> www.hollywood.com/movietunes

If you are in Los Angeles, you can look at film scores at:
> The Academy of Motion Pictures Arts & Sciences,
> 333 S. La Cienega Blvd., Beverly Hills, CA 90211 (310) 247-3020.

Join organizations to meet people in the music business:
> The Society of Composers and Lyricists: www.filmscore.org
> The Film Music Network: www.filmmusic.net
> Pacific Composers Forum: www.composersforum.com

Accumulate industry resources: (also see pages 381, 382)
> Film and Television Music Guide, available in book form or on disk.
> (800) 377-7411 (818)769-2722
> Film Composers Guide (800) FILMBKS (310) 471-8066 loneeagle.com
> Film and Television Composer's Resource Guide www.filmmusicmag.com

The best place to find your first film to score is a film school. Many universities have film schools or drama departments where you can locate student filmmakers or place your resume on file. Some dedicated film schools are:

American Film Institute (AFI), 2021 N. Western Ave.,
    Los Angeles CA 90027 (213) 856-7600
    www.afionline.org

University of California Los Angeles (UCLA), 405 Hilgard Ave.
    Los Angeles, CA 90024 Film and TV dept. (310) 825-5761
    www.ucla.edu

University of Southern California (USC), University Park,
    Los Angeles, CA 90089 Film school: (213) 740-2804
    www.usc.edu

California State College, Long Beach (CSLB), 1250 Bellflower Blvd.,
    Long Beach, CA 90840 (562) 985-4111
    csulb.edu/depts/fea

California Institute of the Arts (CALARTS) 24700 McBean Pkwy.,
    Valencia, CA 91355 (805) 255-1050
    www.calarts.edu

Hollywood Film Institute, (323) 933-3456 fax (323) 933-1464
    www.hollywoodu.com

The Los Angeles Film School, 6363 Sunset Blvd., Hollywood, CA 90028
    www.lafilm.com (877) 952-3456.

New York Film Academy, 100 E. 17th St., New York, NY 10003 (212) 674-4300
    www.nyfa.com

Columbia University School of the Arts, Film Division,
    2960 Broadway, 513C Dodge Hall, New York, NY 10027 (212) 854-2815
    www.columbia.edu/cu/arts/film

New York University Film School, 70 Washington Square South,
    New York, NY 10012 (212) 998-1212
    www.nyu.edu/tisch/filmtv

Emerson College, 100 Beacon St., Boston, MA 02116 (617) 824-8500
    www.emerson.edu/visual/media/arts Also: Los Angeles, Netherlands

TONAL ROWS

> The best proof of Schoenberg's harmonic dilemma, and that
> of the composers who have followed in his path, is that they
> all deliberately attempted to avoid the strong natural intervals
> of the fourth, fifth and octave. Instead they stress the minor
> second and major second, intervals which are furthest from
> those we call perfect. These abrasive sounds help to prevent
> twelve-tone music from displaying any sense of harmonic center.
> Yet I wonder if we can really totally escape from our center of
> gravity except by leaving the earth altogether. What remains
> forever fascinating to me is that touch of genius in man which
> finally allows him to express himself, to break through any
> self-imposed bonds, however tight.
> Yehudi Menuhin and Curtis Davis: *The Music of Man*

Since tonality is a natural phenomenon and a human response, it is difficult
to avoid in composition. There is not a tone row that does not contain an
implication of tonality.

The restrictions imposed in "pure" 12-tone composition present a great
intellectual challenge—to create music that has emotional or sonic appeal.
Some would argue that composing with 12 tones amounts to writing poetry
with sets of 26 letters, that retrograde music is like talking backwards, that
inversion makes as much sense as hanging a picture upside down. However,
without being a strict serialist, you can use tone rows as a source of ideas or
inspiration, as you would use text or film or a painting as inspiration.

> When I compose I try to forget all theories and I continue
> composing only after having freed my mind of them.
> Arnold Schoenberg

Hollywood composers have used tone rows for decades, to avoid melody in
underscore, to generate new ideas, or for their own amusement. Design
your own set of "rules" or limitations for each work.

TONE ROWS PLUS

The Go-Rows are tone row generators with internal organization, designed to maintain note relationships within row permutations. Segments of 2, 3, or 4 tones stay intact throughout the permutations, hinting at tonality. Each 2, 3, or 4-tone segment is a potential phrase which cycles internally. The *a6* modulates, integrating each trope.

Use grid paper. Start with any tone row. Write the first note in each square numbered 1, the second note in squares numbered 2, etc. Continue until the squares are filled with the 12 notes.

See if you can recognize segments as you sing or play through the rows. Great ear training. Experiment with voicing configurations of the verticals. My students have enjoyed working with "the squares" as resources for composition or just investigative fun.

Go-Row *a2*

1	2	3	4	5	6	7	8	9	10	11	12
4	3	5	6	8	7	9	10	12	11	1	2
6	5	8	7	10	9	12	11	2	1	4	3
7	8	10	9	11	12	2	1	3	4	6	5
9	10	11	12	1	2	3	4	5	6	7	8
12	11	1	2	4	3	5	6	8	7	9	10
2	1	4	3	6	5	8	7	10	9	12	11
3	4	6	5	7	8	10	9	11	12	2	1
5	6	7	8	9	10	11	12	1	2	3	4
8	7	9	10	12	11	1	2	4	3	5	6
10	9	12	11	2	1	4	3	6	5	8	7
11	12	2	1	3	4	6	5	7	8	10	9

Go-Row *a4*

1	2	3	4	5	6	7	8	9	10	11	12
6	8	5	7	11	10	12	9	4	3	2	1
10	9	11	12	2	3	1	4	7	5	8	6
3	4	2	1	8	5	6	7	12	11	9	10
5	7	8	6	9	11	10	12	1	2	4	3
11	12	9	10	4	2	3	1	6	8	7	5
2	1	4	3	7	8	5	6	10	9	12	11
8	6	7	5	12	9	11	10	3	4	1	2
9	10	12	11	1	4	2	3	5	7	6	8
4	3	1	2	6	7	8	5	11	12	10	9
7	5	6	8	10	12	9	11	2	1	3	4
12	11	10	9	3	1	4	2	8	6	5	7

Go-Row *a3*

1	2	3	4	5	6	7	8	9	10	11	12
6	5	4	8	9	7	12	11	10	3	1	2
7	9	8	11	10	12	2	1	3	4	6	5
12	10	11	1	3	2	5	6	4	8	7	9
2	3	1	6	4	5	9	7	8	11	12	10
5	4	6	7	8	9	10	12	11	1	2	3
9	8	7	12	11	10	3	2	1	6	5	4
10	11	12	2	1	3	4	5	6	7	9	8
3	1	2	5	6	4	8	9	7	12	10	11
4	6	5	9	7	8	11	10	12	2	3	1
8	7	9	10	12	11	1	3	2	5	4	6
11	12	10	3	2	1	6	4	5	9	8	7

Go-Row *a6*

1	2	3	4	5	6	7	8	9	10	11	12
7	1	2	3	4	5	8	9	10	11	12	6
8	7	1	2	3	4	9	10	11	12	6	5
9	8	7	1	2	3	10	11	12	6	5	4
10	9	8	7	1	2	11	12	6	5	4	3
11	10	9	8	7	1	12	6	5	4	3	2
12	11	10	9	8	7	6	5	4	3	2	1
6	12	11	10	9	8	5	4	3	2	1	7
5	6	12	11	10	9	4	3	2	1	7	8
4	5	6	12	11	10	3	2	1	7	8	9
3	4	5	6	12	11	2	1	7	8	9	10
2	3	4	5	6	12	1	7	8	9	10	11

MICROTONAL MUSIC, ALTERNATE TUNING

> The world's scales differ in only two ways: the number
> of tones they use and the distances between those tones.
> Robert Jourdain: *Music, the Brain and Ecstasy*

Ratios, such as 5:3, describe the natural harmonic intervals accurately. While tempered intervals maintain their position in the equal tempered grid, true natural harmonics form relationships that transcend temperament, spinning off into the free space of the tonal spectrum. Although impractical for conventional instruments, the combination of synthesizers and computers has provided a solution to the problem of tuning natural intervals on the fly and has generated a renewed interest in Just Intonation systems.

A benefit of the digital revolution is the ability to produce microtonal scales—new temperaments, as well as new timbres.

There is an active community of individuals and organizations that promote microtonal music and instruments:

RESOURCES

Just Intonation Network: www.dnai.com/~jinetwk
   Interval magazine: 1/1; *The Just Intonation Primer* by David Doty; links to alternate tuning resources
Xenharmonikon—Journal of experimental music
   www.tiac.net/users/xen/xh
The American Festival of Microtonal Music (AFMM)
   www.echonyc.com/~jhhl/afmm
Frog Peak Music: www.sover.net/~frogpeak
   Books, periodicals, recordings, scores, software of many innovators.
Computer Music Journal (many links)
   mitpress.mit.edu/e-journals/computer-music-journal/cmj
The World Music Menu tuning software: www.freeplay.com
   just intonation and world scales

A WORLD OF INSTRUMENTS

THE EXTENDED ORCHESTRAL PALETTE
Some non-orchestral but frequently used instruments are: accordion, African drums, bagpipe, balalaika, banjo, classical guitar, steel guitar, harmonica, lute, sitar, tabla. (Also see page 333.)

> *Musical Instruments of the World*
> by the Diagram Group
> An encyclopedia of virtually every instrument known, organized according to genre, as well as geographical distribution and historical period. Descriptions, illustrations, but no ranges or transpositions.
> *Planet Musician: The World Sourcebook for Musicians*
> by Julie Lyonn Lieberman
> *Range and Transposition Guide to 250 Musical Instruments*
> by Robert Bornstein
> *Essential Dictionary of Orchestration*
> by Dave Black and Tom Gerou

ALTERNATIVE INSTRUMENTS
> *Gravikords, Whirlies & Pyrophones: Experimental Musical Instruments*
> by Bart Hopkin. Book and CD.
> Unusual and innovative instruments and their designers.
> (800) 788-6670 e-mail: elliarts@aol.com
> Theremin. www.nashville.net/~theremin
> Information and manufacturers.
> Experimental Musical Instruments: www.windworld.com/emi
> 21st Century Instruments: www.c21-orch-instrs.demon.co.uk

MUSIC OF HARRY PARTCH
> BOOK: Genesis of a Music by Harry Partch, Da Capo Press, 1974
> RECORDINGS: Composers Recordings, Inc., 73 Spring St., Suite 506, New York, NY 10012-5800 (212) 941-9674
> Also: Tomatoe Records and New World Records
> INSTRUMENTS: The Harry Partch Foundation in San Diego, Danlee Mitchell.
> On indefinite loan to Dean Drummond, New York.
> www.spyral.net/newband

BRIDGING THE PAST TO THE FUTURE

Spherecles wakes at 3:30 am. He can't wait to sing with his brothers. The music fills his soul but also stirs something deep within his bowels. The stone floor and walls reverberate with the rich sound of their voices, as the unison seems to compound and feed on itself. His voice is changing and he is uncomfortable trying to sing in the higher register, yet he cannot reach the lower octave. He manages to sing a parallel melody in between the octave that sounds okay and soon others gravitate to his line. The fifths and fourths that result solidify and blend into one huge voice. The sound is emotionally overwhelming—thirds would be almost too much!

Such is the probable evolution of harmony, propelled by the physical sensation of resonance.

A MUSIC TIME LINE

Unison/octave singing; chant - ancient world to the middle ages
Organum (parallel 4ths & 5ths) - late 9th century
Triadic music - early 15th century
Music printing - late 15th century
7th Chord - early 17th century
9th Chord - mid 18th century
Woodwind keys - late 18th century
Valved brass instruments - early 19th century
Whole-tone scale - late 19th century
12 tone composition - early 20th century
Microtonal music - early 20th century
Electronically generated sound - early 20th century
Digital media - mid 20th century
Amalgamation of all styles of the world's music - late 20th century

Over time, historical styles have become "averaged out," eventually fitting neatly into a particular century or culture. But if there is one characteristic of 20th century music, it is a *diversity* of styles. Schoenberg, Stravinsky and Bartok, as well as many forms of jazz, pop and rock, have led music in many directions and the divergence of styles has produced boundless concepts. Today, electronic media provides access to music of all cultures. It seems evident that the 21st century will foster international or global styles, new visions that draw from varied sources of the world's music.

HOW TO CONTACT THE AUTHOR

This book will be updated periodically to include current resources and information. Your comments and suggestions are welcome. Contact the author at:

www.rongorow.com

Visit our web site for information on classes and seminars.

HEARING AND WRITING MUSIC is available at bookstores and online bookstores.

INDEX